STARTING YOUR CAREER AS A

dancer

STARTING YOUR CAREER AS A

dancer

MANDE DAGENAIS

ALLWORTH PRESS
NEW YORK

Allworth Press books may be purchased in bulk at special discounts for sales promotion, corporate gifts, fund-raising, or educational purposes. Special editions can also be created to specifications. For details, contact the Special Sales Department, Allworth Press, 307 West 36th Street, 11th Floor, New York, NY 10018 or info@skyhorsepublishing.com.

15 14 13 12 11   5 4 3 2 1

Published by Allworth Press,
an imprint of Skyhorse Publishing, Inc.
307 West 36th Street, 11th Floor, New York, NY 10018.

Allworth Press® is a registered trademark of Skyhorse Publishing, Inc.®, a Delaware corporation.

www.allworth.com

Cover design by Mary Belibasakis

Library of Congress Cataloging-in-Publication Data is available on file.
ISBN: 978-1-58115-906-6

Printed in the United States of America

Because of the dynamic nature of the Internet, any web addresses or links contained in this book may have changed since publication and may no longer be valid.

The diet and exercise information in this book is not medical advice. Its intention is merely informational and educational. You should not undertake any diet/exercise regimen recommended in this book before consulting your personal physician. Neither the author nor the publisher shall be responsible or liable for any loss or damage allegedly arising as a consequence of your use or application of any information or suggestions contained in this book.

FOR *MY SWEETHEART,* MY HUSBAND, ALEX MARCHANT, WITHOUT WHOM THIS
BOOK WOULD NEVER HAVE BEEN POSSIBLE.

AND, IN LOVING MEMORY OF MY PARENTS: MY MOTHER, EMILY DAGENAIS,
A CONSTANT SOURCE OF INSPIRATION, AND MY FATHER, ELZEAR DAGENAIS,
WHO TAUGHT ME ABOUT FINE DETAIL AND PERFECTION.

"Break a Leg"
An idiom used in showbiz to wish someone luck before a performance.
You would say "break a leg" before going on stage,
but you would *never* say "good luck."

Contents

Foreword by Lou Paciocco

In the beginning of my career as a show producer, I did what was expected of me. I tried to hire the best team available to execute my creative concept. I gathered what I thought was necessary to meet my needs. I hired a director, a choreographer, a set designer, a costume designer, lighting and sound designers, and someone to coordinate it all.

Then luckily for me, I met Mande Dagenais, who in fact, *did it all*, and took my shows to an even higher level. Now, lucky for you, she has written this incredible guide for dancers and all performers alike. In her book, Mande teaches what it really takes to be in "the business." If you have ever aspired to dance, or to perform, or if you would simply like to know what *Show Business* is really all about, then this is the book for you. Mande covers it all: how to get in the business, where you can work—from Broadway to L.A. and everywhere in between, and what to expect when you get there!

Mande's talent is unique; she possesses a vast knowledge of show business and is an inspiration to all who have the opportunity to work with her. Her experience from both sides of the curtain, as a performer and as a producer, makes her an invaluable source of information to any aspiring artist. After reading her book, you will understand why I wish to all other producers a Mande Dagenais.

Lou Paciocco—creator of *La Cage Aux Folles* and *An Evening at La Cage*,
celebrity impersonation revues performed worldwide.

Acknowledgments

First I'd like to thank my husband, Alex Marchant. Without his constant love and never-ending support, none of this would be possible, from the first word to the last word and the many rewrites in between. He is my calm force and he keeps me sane through all the insanity—*or at least tries to*. And a huge thank you to my sister Lauraine Friskey for her endless hours and months of reading, advising, suggesting, and editing my early manuscript. To my niece Jody Tierney, for reading and rereading *every single word* I wrote, and for putting up with me through it all. And to Lou Paciocco for never tiring of my *one more question*, my *one more addition*, and my *one more proofread*!

A very special thank you to Tad Crawford for being the wonderful advocate for the arts that he is, and for believing in my book, agreeing to take it on board, and giving it a home with Allworth Press and Skyhorse Publishing. Thanks also to Delia Casa, editorial assistant, for her guidance and assistance throughout the publishing process, and to the rest of the editorial staff at Skyhorse Publishing for all their hard work and attention to detail. Thank you to all of you for making this possible.

A great big thank you to my family: my mother and father, Emily and Elzear Dagenais; my sisters, Beverly Cascanette, Joanne Sinclair, Lauraine Friskey, and Gail Dagenais; my brothers, Gary Dagenais and Ralph Dagenais; and my sisters- and brothers-in-law for their loving support always. From dance recitals as a kid to driving me to my first audition, and the many opening nights as a professional, they were always there for me! Thanks to all my friends and family who graciously read my first attempts at writing, made invaluable suggestions, and cheered me on every step of the way. Without those early enthusiasts, this might still be just conversation.

A very heartfelt thank you to my Aunt Cletis, I have never forgotten that it was she who suggested that Mom send me to dance class. For that, I am forever appreciative.

I believe that people come into our lives for specific reasons, and as fate would have, it I was sent to the Gauvreau School of Performing Arts. With a grateful heart I thank Gerry Gauvreau and his mother, Mrs. G. (as we lovingly referred to her), for their invaluable lessons both on the business of dance and on life!

To my mother- and father-in-law, Mum and Dad Marchant, a very warm thank you for their very early suggestions and words of encouragement that gave me the confidence to keep writing, and for always being available for yet another read-through. To Jay and Marilyn Jiggins, Diana Platts, John Ciotta, and Michael Gruber for the many checkpoints along the way and to Jane Bernard for her subliminal guidance through her book *Write-On: The Art of Re-Writing*. To Larry and Debbie Brown for "think tanks and writing escapes," and for all of their encouragement, and to Diana Weber for always being there no matter what, and cheering me on throughout my journey.

And to Arlene Uslander, my original editor, a very special thank you for her detailed work, for all of her fine-tuning and her teachings through her work; and for holding my hand and walking me through my first process and beyond. To Rusty Fisher for his clever contributions—the many subtitles and wonderful seg-ues—for making the book flow and giving it a sense of timing, and very important, for introducing me to Arlene. Special thanks to Dan Fickett, *artiste extraordinaire*, for all of his creative genius and for assisting me with my first publishing endeavor.

And last, but certainly not least, my assistant choreographers, the women who *danced by my side*, often through the wee hours of the night! For their round-the-clock devotion and stamina, I am forever grateful to Tracy (Kerr) Bianchi, Jemma (Sawyer) Mckeown, Helen (Chadwick) Timpano, and Tracy (Luce) Beetham. To Sandie Backus, Samantha (Wyles) Maxwell, Courtney (Newell) Sternick, Sta-cey Enyart, Alice Billman, and Angeliki (Piliouras) Pantelaras, warm and special thanks for their assistance and support on various ship and corporate projects. And to the many talented cast members who found their way into my rehearsal studio and made it through opening night—some, opening night after opening night. Thank you for sharing your talent. You are the gems that I have collected along the way.

And once again, a gracious thank you to all who so indulged me. My journey was so much richer for it!

Introduction

You may not know it, but your wish (or future wish) is my command! This book was written to fill what I believe to be a void; to answer the many questions that have been asked of me time and time again over the years by hundreds and hundreds of dancers, performers, aspiring performers, aspiring choreographers, teachers, and parents alike. *Starting Your Career as a Dancer* is intended to be the most comprehensive guide you will ever need—hence the multitude and variety of topics covered in these pages.

There has never been one single book that simply said it all and told it as it is! And so I have looked back over my years, my successes and my failures, and I have attempted to consider all the questions along the way; the identical questions that you might have on your own journey. There are so many things that we all wanted to know back when we were in your very position. I constantly hear the same thing from my peers and from the talent that has worked with me: "I wish there had been a book like this when I was first starting out."

My true desire is to give back to an industry that has given so much to me and has brought me so much pleasure over the years by giving to others who are as passionate about dance and show business as I am. I admire the complete courage and all that it takes to pursue your passion, and I commend you. Show business can be a complete mystery if you are sitting on the wrong side of the gateway. So go ahead, turn the page and take the first step through that gateway. Throughout the next sixteen chapters you will learn all there is to know about how to *get in* the business, *be in* the business, and *stay in* the business. I wish you much success on your journey and aspire to make it a little bit easier for you with my book. Happy reading!

My First Communion, age seven. I already had
stars in my eyes—and a swing in my hips!

Chapter One

Born to Dance—Turning Dreams into Goals into Commitments

"I don't want people who want to dance; I want people who have to dance."
~ **George Balanchine**

So, you want to be a dancer! Let me ask you something: *Why* do you want to dance? What is it about dance that attracts you? Its beauty, grace, and elegance? The excitement, the glamour, the stage, the lights, the music, the applause? Do you dream of being on stage, do you fantasize about being famous, or do you simply want to dance because you love how you feel when you're lost in the motion?

How about *all* of it?

Why not? Dancing is all that and so much more.

I ask these questions not merely for the sake of it, but because the teacher in me wants to make sure your eyes are squarely on the prize. I've seen so many dancers with big dreams and plans, with bright hopes and shiny fantasies, but it's the dancers who turn their dreams into goals—and their goals into commitments—who truly succeed.

Goals and dreams are the energy of life; commitment is the outlet through which that electricity turns into reality. It is tremendously important to have goals and dreams. They help fulfill us, they fuel us and drive us to great accomplishments, and they can relax and comfort us by providing our very own private sanctuary within—a sanctuary where all dreams are possible, limited only by our own imagination.

Throughout my career, people have asked me such questions as:

- How do I become a dancer, a performer, an entertainer?
- How do I get into the business?
- What should I expect?
- How can I ace that big audition?
- How do I know if I'm ready?

Now here's a question for all of you: What if I told you that within you lies the key to your own success? It does, you know. A simple road map that once you learn how to tap into will lead you to your own bright future. Fortunately, that's what this chapter—what this entire book—is all about.

Together, we are going to go through the entire process of becoming a dancer: from dream to goal to commitment, from audition to getting the part, from fantasy to reality. The first thing I want you to know, however, is that it all starts with *you*.

I firmly believe that when you want something badly enough, very little can stand in your way, and, even more importantly, when you know *why* you want it so badly, you will be truly empowered! Simply knowing why you want to dance is a huge secret to your success. And that's why this first chapter is so important. First we'll discover your "why"; then we'll find your "way."

ENCORE:
Goals and dreams are the energy of life; commitment is the outlet through which that electricity turns into reality.

FIND YOUR "WHY" AND YOU WILL FIND YOUR "WAY"

You may have heard this before (I've personally heard it repeated over the years by many great teachers), but it's so helpful—and central to our goals together—that I wanted to repeat it one more time: Find your why and you will find your way!

So many of us skip the why in favor of the how. We focus so much on how to get the part, how to be a star, that we lose sight of *why* we want to get the part or be a star in the first place. So do we really need to know the "why" in the first place?

Short answer? Yes, it really is that important.

Longer answer? Knowing why you want to dance can truly determine your outcome. When you know why, and that why is big enough, and when you know exactly what you want from the business, how you get there will be revealed. Your path will become undoubtedly clear.

So, take a moment and think about it: Why do you want to dance?

What are your goals and dreams? Be specific! What passion burns inside you? One thing is certain—dancers know about passion and burning desire, and if they don't, they shouldn't be in the business. If you don't have passion, then I ask you, what is the point? After all, there are certainly much easier ways to earn a living.

Dance is all about passion. Dance is art, art is passion, and all artists express their passion through their work. The musician plays an instrument, the fine artist uses paint and canvas, and a dancer tells a story through expression and movement.

A dancer is like a canvas that has come to life. The passion of dancers is witnessed and experienced by their every move; their body is their instrument. What an incredible way to be able to express oneself—and one's passion—through his or her entire body, with every gesture, no matter how subtle. A dance void of passion is like a life without purpose.

When you have passion, everything else falls into place. Everything that is required seamlessly comes together. They all go hand in hand: hard work, dedication, and commitment all come effortlessly when you know where you are going. Nothing is too difficult when you want something badly enough. When you know what you want and why you want it, there is only one thing left to do, and that is to *just go for it*!

ENCORE:
When you know why, and that why is big enough, and when you know exactly what you want from the business, how you get there will be revealed.

GETTING TO KNOW YOU

So you say that all you want to do is dance. Well then, let me tell you about what it takes to be in the business:

- Talent—of course!
- The right attitude—a must.
- Commitment—you won't get anywhere without it.
- Hard work—until your toes bleed!

- Dedication, desire, extreme passion, and vision—yes, they are all necessary.

Still interested? Of course you are; you love to dance, and it's all you ever wanted to do, but it doesn't stop there—the list goes on. How about tough skin and staying power? How many times can you take "no" before you get a "yes"? The answer had better be as many as it takes! Fall down seven times, get up eight. You love it, so enjoy the journey because the process can be amazing; this can be one of the most exciting rides of your life.

I'm sure you've heard the many proverbial sayings. Two of my favorites are "Where there's a will, there's a way," and "If you believe it, then you can achieve it." Another one of my personal favorites is the Japanese proverb I just mentioned above, "Fall down seven times; get up eight." No matter how many times you fall down, the only way to make it is to get straight back up again— and again and again. Mountain climbers also say that the only way to reach the summit is to take one step for every two you get knocked back.

The bottom line is this: If you want something strongly enough, you will never take *no* for an answer. Rejection is not an option. Now, that doesn't mean there won't be any rejections along the way. On the contrary; there could be many, and at the very least, most likely several.

Rejection is simply a fact of life in our business. You just can't take it personally. Another way to look at it might be to take it seriously, just don't take it personally. In many cases, it's not you they were rejecting; not your style or your shape or your form or your commitment. You simply were not what they were looking for on that particular day.

How can that possibly have anything to do with *you*? It's purely the nature of the business, and you can't be right for every part or be everything to everyone. Once you learn to accept this, the rest is a piece of cake.

In the big picture, it's all just part of the process. The sooner you understand and accept certain realities about this business you have chosen, the better equipped you will be to set out on your journey. How interesting would this journey be if everything was just handed to you on a silver platter, and at the end of the day you had no war stories to tell?

You know as well as I do that everyone loves a little drama—particularly entertainers—and it's much more fun for the performer in you to reenact the story. So enjoy the journey and the many stories that you will gather and tell along the way. On the other hand, I'm not saying that it never comes easy; it's simply a fact that more often than not, you're going to take several knocks before you land on your feet.

Some people moan and groan every step of the way; they look at every hiccup as a stumbling block or, even worse, a roadblock. I prefer to think of these hiccups as building blocks—and suggest that you do the same. The choice is yours. You can make this really hard on yourself by taking every knock and every blow and allowing them to slowly crush you along the way, or you can set out on your path to success by standing firm in your conviction and thereby enjoying this incredible journey. (And yes, that does mean taking the bad with the good.)

ENCORE:
The bottom line is this: If you want something strongly enough, you will never take no for an answer. Rejection is not an option.

TWO QUESTIONS TO UNLOCK YOUR SECRET DESIRE

With the right attitude, clear-set goals, and total commitment, this can be the most amazing journey you will ever take. Ask yourself these two questions:

1. What are your aspirations? This is where I want you to be totally honest with yourself and as specific as you can be. Be very clear about where you want to end up. What is your ultimate destination? Don't worry about how you are going to get there; just define what that final destination is, how it looks, and how it feels. The clearer your picture is, the more specific your goals can be.

2. Are you willing to break down walls to get to where you want to be? If you have talent and the kind of passion and conviction that it takes to persist, even when rejection is staring you in the face, then you *will* succeed. We can't all star in our own Broadway show or be the next pop idol or film icon, but with all those ingredients, you not only will find your way within the industry; you will find *your* place—a place where you can shine.

In order to help you define your process, I will address some of the various opportunities for building blocks and how you can utilize them to your advantage. Remember, a dream alone is great, but it's not enough. We must add goals and commitment to the recipe to make our dreams become reality.

Opportunity is all around you; even when something seems like a failure, it can really be success in disguise. Don't believe me? I want you to take into account every single class, every audition, every rejection (and every success), every compliment, every correction, every criticism, and every accomplishment. By approaching all these various opportunities in a positive way, you will be building a strong character and stamina with a great attitude—all-around good habits—all of which contribute to building a solid foundation for your career.

The truth is, they can all be accomplishments, every single one; it just depends on how you look at them. At the end of the day, it's all about perception. We can sit in our lonely rooms and dwell on the negative all day long, but where would that get us? Worry, regret, and negativity are three of life's biggest time wasters. Just imagine how positive, uplifting, and hopeful your life could be if you got rid of all three.

You *can* get rid of them, you know. Think of a polishing stone; the more you rub it—the more you polish it—the shinier and more beautiful it becomes. It simply continues to get better and better, closer and closer to perfection with every loving touch. Sure, I can hear those negative little voices already: "That's easier said than done." But the truth is no one ever said it was going to be easy. However, with the right outlook and a good game plan, the road will keep getting smoother every step of the way.

I remind you, it is absolutely essential to set goals; they are the building blocks of our dreams. As Lewis Carroll (author of *Alice in Wonderland* and *Through the Looking-Glass*) said, "If you don't know where you are going, any road will get you there." I love that expression! To that I will add, "If you don't know where you are going, you certainly don't know where you are going to end up—and you may not like it once you get there!"

So remember to set clear goals. Again, I ask you, what is your ultimate destination? Setting goals will get you through the rough patches, and your commitment to those goals is what will get you to your final destination. Never take your eyes off the prize, and one step at a time you will just keep getting closer and the big picture will become clearer and clearer. I've said it before and I will say it again: It's your dream; how much do you want it? This is your journey; do you want a smooth path or a rocky road? You choose.

I will guarantee you this: If you choose a positive and nurturing approach, you will have a much healthier and happier journey. Along the way, you will make your path smoother by simply having the right outlook, and that in itself is a huge success. And no matter how big or small, make it a habit to acknowledge your successes, each and every one of them. Never underestimate the power that comes with each little success. Sometimes it's the exact push you need to get you to the next step, which could then catapult you to your ultimate goal. Besides which, life is simply a better and happier place if you acknowledge yourself for a job well-done.

As I keep saying, the truth is it all comes right back down to your outlook. You can walk out of an audition and say to yourself, "*Wow!* What a great audition! I learned a fabulous routine, did a great job of performing it, and I made some new contacts, which might bring future possibilities." Or you can walk out of that same audition discouraged and berating yourself, saying, "How could I blow it so badly? I completely messed up the routine . . . they hated me . . . I'll never get this gig."

Once again, the bottom line is this: You will have a much more positive experience if you simply look for the good in every situation. It truly is that simple. Look for everything that you did great in each situation, be it a class, an audition, or a meeting.

Don't dwell on your failures; dwell on your successes. You will feel so much better about yourself, which, in turn, will build self-esteem and confidence, both of which are absolute necessities in this business—not to mention in life.

> ENCORE:
> *Opportunity is all around you. Even when something seems like a failure it can really be success in disguise.*

THE (NOT SO) IMPOSSIBLE DREAM

When commencing rehearsals of a new production, or working with a new cast for the first time, I start out with an orientation. This is a great opportunity for everyone to meet each other and for the cast to know what they can expect and what will be expected of them. This interaction could be the most important interaction I will ever have with a cast; I always look forward to it.

One of the first things I say is something I feel very strongly about, and that is that we are an extremely privileged group of people. As dancers, singers, actors, and performers, we get to do what many of us have dreamt of our whole lives. How many people never get to fulfill their dreams? How many people go through their entire lives settling because they were too fearful to follow their dreams?

Take a look around you. How many people do you know in your own life who have either been stuck in that fear, just didn't believe in themselves enough to go for it, or, even worse, had others discourage them from pursuing their dreams? How many people don't even know that the power to fulfill their dreams is really within them? They wouldn't even know where or how to begin. Some even forget how to dream because their goal or passion has been suppressed within them for so long.

The mere fact that you had a dream and you went for it makes you very special indeed. Many of the world's great motivational speakers and authors would say that this decision alone separates you from about 90 percent of the population. Take heart and be grateful for the fact that actually going for those desires and dreams puts you in a very small, unique group that represents only 10 percent of the population. The fact that you can take your dreams and turn them into goals, and commit to the journey, is an incredible achievement. In fact, turning your dream into a goal *creates* your commitment. Once committed, it is a one-way street, with no U-turns and no turning back.

Remember: Stay the course; your commitment is what will get you there. Your talent is a gift, something so unique and so special that you must never lose sight of it or take it for granted. As one dancer to another, I ask that you please nurture your talent, respect your talent, and respect the business and the people in it. This business is full of very special people and once-in-a-lifetime moments just waiting to happen. Always be grateful for this life; although it is sometimes difficult, it is, in fact, a very extraordinary life.

ENCORE:

Your talent is a gift, something so unique and so special that you must never lose sight of it or take it for granted.

NOTES

I'd like to say it was all fun and games! Production team, Umbro Licensing
Show, Montreal, Canada

Chapter Two
Inspiration—Trusting Personal Heroes and Mentors

"Great dancers are not great because of their technique; they are great because of their passion."
~ **Martha Graham**

This chapter is called "Inspiration" for a reason, and that simple reason is this: Inspiration is at the heart of dance. It is the essence of dance. It may take blood, sweat, and tears to train ourselves to perform at peak physical perfection on-stage, in front of an audience, but inspiration is the fuel that drives our dreams.

To be truly inspired requires a lot of soul-searching and asking of very personal questions, such as: What inspires you? What inspired you to dance as a young child? What magical moment created in you this most incredible desire to dance or to pursue a career in dance?

Then think back to a time when you were very young, and remember: Was it one particular performance? A big sister or brother who danced? A famous dancer or choreographer who knocked you off your feet? (Or "onto your feet," as the case may be?) A movie musical? A music video? A Broadway show? Or was it simply an innate need to express yourself through the creative outlet of dance?

Whatever that inspiration was, it was obviously strong enough to keep you dancing, or interested in dance, and to find yourself reading this book. Whatever that initial inspiration was, it created your love for dance and your desire to dance. It is so important to remember that; to keep in mind how incredibly inspired you were, and what you've accomplished so far *because* of that inspiration.

They say that when the student is ready, the teacher will appear. Inspiration can teach us many things, but only if we are ready to be moved by it. If you look back over your years of training, you probably will find that there were different inspirations at different times of your life, each one of them fulfilling a purpose and oftentimes taking you to the next level. So where are you today? Are you just starting out in your professional career? Are you training and dreaming of a career in dance? Or are you already well on your way in your performing career?

Regardless of whether you are just starting out or you are a seasoned professional, inspiration plays a big role in the key to your success. Go ahead and look back into your own life and training and bear in mind why you started and why you continued. Chances are you'll find that your greatest accomplishments were in those very moments in which you were most inspired.

First, though, let's define inspiration so you and I are both on the same page:

> Inspiration (*noun*): *The action or power of moving the intellect or emotions.*

I love this definition because it's so specific: *moving the intellect or emotions.* Isn't that a great phrase? How often have we watched a wonderful dance routine, listened to a beautiful musical score, or felt the dancer's emotions ring through their footwork and were "moved"?

The beauty of inspiration is that it works on two levels: our intellect and our emotions. When it comes to our intellect, we can be inspired to be rational and logical about planning our success. We can watch a dancer or dance, be inspired and think, rationally or logically, "I can do that; with training and persistence, I can be up there doing that."

Emotionally, we can be inspired to provoke our feelings of passion and intensity, both of which are so desperately needed on our long road to success. In the first chapter, I talked about setting goals and meeting them; in this chapter, I will talk about what inspires you and how to tap into that inspiration to sustain your desire long enough to reach your goals.

So, what moves you today? Where are you at this very moment? What is it that you want more than anything else in the world, and what is it that inspires you to set that goal and actually reach it?

The answers to these questions are just as important as asking the questions themselves; find your inspiration and you will find your way. Most people don't ever give this step any thought, but very often inspiration is the overriding force behind one's motivation to do most anything in life.

That's why I've dedicated an entire chapter to it.

> **ENCORE:**
> *Inspiration is at the heart of dance. It is the essence of dance.*

MENTORS + TRUST = INSPIRATION

Mentors are synonymous with inspiration. And when you look up to your mentors and trust them to guide you with experience and wisdom, you can be doubly inspired to achieve all your dancing goals. That's because being inspired follows a simple formula: Mentors + Trust = Inspiration.

- Whom do you look up to?
- Who are your personal, everyday life heroes?
- Who are your mentors?

I would like to take this opportunity to tell you about some of my own mentors, the importance of having them in our lives, and the significance of recognizing them. As I mentioned in my dedication, I always knew how fortunate I was in my life and along my own path to dancing. Specifically, so much of that has to do with the people who have touched my life and helped me along the way.

When I was very young, I remember thinking to myself that if I could have just the right balance of my mother's strength and my father's sensitivity, I would have a great start in life. And guess what? Here I am many years later to say that I pretty much got what I asked for. Had I known back then how truly powerful those thoughts were to become in reaching my goals, the list might have been a bit longer!

I'm sure you've heard the saying, "Be careful of what you ask for in life because you're liable to get it." And to that I add what a very dear girlfriend of mine always said, "When doing the asking, make sure that you are very specific and *ask for exactly what you want*." Don't leave out any details; make sure the list is complete. Keep in mind that this is your list and you can change it or add to it whenever—or whatever—you want. For me, it all started way back, with my mother and father, as I would guess it does for many of us.

My parents were both wonderful, hardworking, honest people with high morals and values. They were great role models, each in their own way and in their own specific areas. They inadvertently taught me to be independent while instilling the importance of family values and integrity. In a large family, one

13

learns the importance of sharing and being a team player, which is not so different to being in a cast or a dance company. Being independent and yet knowing how to be a team player are both extremely important traits to possess in the entertainment industry. My parents were both very creative and perfectionists in all that they did. As a kid, I remember admiring these qualities in them and thinking that I would like to possess such qualities when I grew up. This seemed a pretty solid foundation from which to start. And, if life is, in fact, about the choices we make, then who better to emulate than two people I respected and loved so dearly?

Next were my siblings, I grew up with four big sisters and two big brothers; I was the baby, and much younger than the rest. In my earliest memories, my sisters were either married, had moved away from home or were teenagers. It was almost like two separate families and, although my brothers and I were closer in age, by the time I was eleven or twelve, they had moved away as well. Inevitably, this made me somewhat of an "only child."

My sisters, being so much older than I, were a strong influence in my upbringing. At such a young age, I got to take part in their adult and teenage lives, so my conscious lessons started early. As a result, I learned about influences and making choices. You can imagine growing up at the tail end of all those kids; there were some great life lessons to be learned. It was a bit like being handed my own personal manual on the *do's* and *don'ts* and how to survive just about anything. I won't go into all the details of growing up in such a large family, but I will say that I was very fortunate to have been raised in one; I wouldn't change a single minute of it.

In life, we have choices, and the choices we make along the way help determine and mold our lives and who we become. With six siblings before me, and growing up in the '60s and '70s, to boot, the lessons were invaluable. This lively and caring cast of characters quickly became my early-life personal heroes—and remain so today.

They also became my own personal audience! Before I ever had a single lesson, I was making up dance routines and performing them for my relatives. Formally or informally, I was always dancing around everywhere we went.

The summer that I was nine years old, my Aunt Cletis recommended to my mother that she send me to dance class. So that very September, it was official: off I went to dance school. This was a really big deal! You see with seven children in our family, five being girls, my parents could never have afforded dance lessons, let alone any kind of lessons for all of us. I, being the baby and so much younger than the rest, got lucky. By this time, the others were all grown up and

I was the only one left at home. This was an opportunity for Mom to do for me what she would have loved to, but was never able to do, for all the others. Who could know that this decision would have such an impact on the rest of my life?

The next nine years or so brought some of the best experiences a child, and then teenager, could ever hope for. Luckily for me, my second-oldest sister Joanne was a good friend of the wife of one of the owners of a dance school near to where I grew up. The fact that this school was so renowned, combined with my sister's personal association with an owner's wife, made our search for the perfect school very easy. I still remember that first day, walking up the big wide stairwell to the second floor of the school of performing arts. I was so incredibly excited! Mom signed me up, bought me a pair of tap shoes, and another of the owners, Mrs. G., whisked me off to my first tap and jazz class.

It was the beginning of one very long, and satisfying, love affair with dance . . .

ENCORE:
Mentors are synonymous with inspiration. And when you look up to your mentors and trust them to guide you with experience and wisdom, you can be doubly inspired to achieve all your dancing goals.

"YOU'LL NEVER WALK ALONE"

Who will your mentors be? Let me start out by saying that owners of dance studios, dance teachers, and directors can be a huge influence—and have a great impact—on your career, as well as your life. If there are any parents reading this book to help guide your young aspiring talent, please remember how important it is to choose studios wisely.

Do your research: know who these people are, know their reputation, their background, and their experience. Inquire about the possibilities of viewing a class or two. If taking up dance is something that you have been thinking about for some time, try planning far enough in advance so that you can see recitals or performances of the schools you may be considering. Although most schools hold recitals near the end of the school year, from May through June, some studios may perform at local events throughout the year. A quick phone call to the schools that you are interested in can get you that information.

My first year of dance classes was very exciting and a great experience. Aside from my regular weekly class, I had been chosen to participate in a semi-private class and a choreography competition, in which I would perform my own dance at the end-of-year dance recital.

My mother and I were invited to the annual showcase, a spectacular performance of the school's dance and performing arts company. In order to get into the company, one had to audition—or be chosen. This was a wonderful opportunity for any young, aspiring talent as the company had such an excellent reputation and was known for its travel and performances throughout the country and abroad. Formed in the '60s, this performing arts company was quite innovative for its time, from its artistic presentations and the creativity demonstrated in performances to its company philosophy and structure. There was nothing like it around, definitely not for children, not in an amateur arena, and certainly not in Sudbury, Ontario. For that matter, I don't imagine many professional companies could boast performances to such foreign audiences, but least likely of all, this small company of young amateur dancers from Northern Ontario.

The opportunity to see this performance was so very exciting for me; I had never been to a show like this before. Off we went, Mom and I, and to this day, I remember that performance like it was yesterday. I swear that my mother could barely keep me from standing and dancing in my seat. I was so taken by their performances and thought to myself, "*Wow!* These dancers are fabulous." All I wanted was to be up there on that stage with them. If I wasn't already hooked, by the opening number I was a goner. I knew my destiny now; this was it and there was no turning back.

A week or so after the company's showcase, my dance recital took place. It was now my turn to be on stage, and I couldn't wait. This was my first recital and I was ten years old. I performed my class routines and then, finally, the jazz routine that I had choreographed. As I was exiting the stage, the director of the company was standing in the wings. Unbeknownst to me, I had just auditioned for his company! Suddenly, he shook my hand and congratulated me; I had just been accepted in Training School (this was the youngest student body of the company). To me, it was all so grown-up and professional, as though I had just been offered a role in some great big Broadway show.

That evening, I received the Dancer of the Year award and a scholarship for the following year in the company. This was huge for me, as my parents certainly didn't have the kind of money to afford all that was involved in taking company classes. Yet, my mother would, and did, over the years to come, everything she could in order for me to dance. She made costumes for the dance company, and she even cleaned the dance studio at night to help pay for my lessons. Between my mother's relentless energy, all her hard work, and the many scholarships given to me by my studio, I was able to have the experience that some kids only dream about. In fact, it was the professionalism of the studio and the experience that I gained through my director and teachers that aroused in me the desire to pursue my career in dance.

> ENCORE:
> *I knew my destiny; this was it and there was no turning back.*

YOU SHOULD BE DANCIN'

If I were to recount one single moment that solidified that desire, I would have to say that it was the night I went to see Bob Fosse's *Dancin'* on Broadway. To me, Bob Fosse was and will go down in history as one of the all-time greats; his choreography and direction have been a huge influence on my own career. That night, as I sat in the audience of this incredibly inspiring show, I remember thinking to myself, *I can do that. I can be that dancer. I know I can. I know that I have what it takes!* And that evening was in fact a turning point in my career; it was that night I decided that if I was going to pursue this career, I would have to leave my hometown and move to the city, where there would be opportunity. The lesson here is simple: first there's the passion, then the conviction, and finally, the commitment. Within a few short years, I was living in Toronto earning a living as a professional dancer and choreographer.

Years later, when I was working in Los Angeles as choreographer of *La Cage Aux Folles*, a famous dinner theatre and place to be seen, Bob Fosse himself, my all-time favorite choreographer, came in to see the show. Unfortunately, I was not there to meet him in person (of all times for me to not be at the show!). Apparently, he came in all dressed in black, just as he was so well known for, on his own, and asked to be seated alone. We often had celebrity guests at *La Cage*, and we always respected their privacy. Upon leaving, he told my producer that he thoroughly enjoyed himself, and he thought the show was great. Wow . . . my hero, Bob Fosse, thought our show was great! That is certainly one of those once-in-a-lifetime moments!

GO TOWARD THE LIGHT!

These moments have such significance to us as children, and I share mine with you because I know that each one of you reading this book has their own "Mrs. G.," a "Gerry," a "Miss Suzie," or a "Len"—that teacher or mentor in your life, whether past or present, who above all the rest made an impact on you. Mentors are like lighthouses along our journey, guiding and gently lighting the way. Sometimes, when just the right light is shed, it can reveal an unknown path; a new path we may otherwise never have discovered. It is very important for our own personal growth to recognize these people and all that they have to offer or teach us along the way.

I believe that it keeps us humble and it keeps us in tune. In our world, the world of performing arts, it's only natural to have these mentors as young children. Most of you, I would imagine, have at least one teacher who is (or was) a personal hero. Not only do I think it is so important to recognize personal heroes and mentors from our youth, but I also want to emphasize the importance of having such a presence throughout our lifetime.

The roles that mentors play in our lives can be enormous; they can influence us in such positive ways and teach us through their own experiences. They can be an incredible wealth of information for you to draw from and can help make your path a lot easier—*if* you are willing to be open and learn by their examples and from their know-how. Although there is nothing quite like personal experience to solidify a life lesson, there is nothing wrong with making your life a tiny bit easier by learning from those who have been there before you.

After all, why reinvent the wheel?

As a young adult, there was yet another teacher, an amazing teacher who taught me lessons far beyond dance steps. That teacher was a gentleman by the name of Len Gibson. In my opinion, he was one of the best. During a short time studying with him, I learned lessons about the business that have helped carry me through my career. When I had first arrived in Toronto, I immediately looked him up. I knew of his reputation and studio, and I was extremely eager to meet him. I called the studio and spoke with him directly. I introduced myself, told him I had just moved to the city, and would love the opportunity to study with him. He invited me to audit one of his classes; it was the last class of the evening and we could speak afterwards, he said. I, of course, arrived nice and early and was very excited but rather nervous about meeting him. I observed an excellent class! Talk about inspiring—this man did not miss a trick. In a class of fifty or more dancers, you could be in the last row and if your pinky was out of place, he saw it. There I was, about to embark on the first step of my dance career away from home, and I was ready to take on the dance world!

At the end of class, Mr. Gibson tore into a male dancer like nothing I had personally witnessed before. He went up one side and down the other; I was horrified for this poor guy. Talk about intimidating . . . I was shaking in my boots, and now I had to go introduce myself and say hello. *Do I leave now? Maybe he didn't notice me and he'll never know I was here.* I thought to myself. But no, rather than slipping out, I went up to him and introduced myself as the young girl who had called earlier. We shook hands, and he immediately addressed what had just happened. He said to me, "You see that young man? I believe that he has talent, but he needs to get his act together. It's a tough business out there, and if this is the career he wants, then he has to work much harder than what he just did. He has to prove himself. He doesn't know it yet, but I just did him a huge favor. You see, one of two things will come of this: one, he'll never dance again, or two, he'll be in class again tomorrow ready to work and he will become one of the finest dancers you've ever seen. It takes so much to be in this business and he needs to learn now if he is going to succeed." This was certainly an event that made an impression on me, one I never forgot.

I went on to study with Len for the next few years, and I really loved him. He was tough on us, his dancers, but he certainly made me want to work hard for him. He was already an older gentleman at this time, but that never stopped him; he was in amazing physical condition. He demonstrated everything first, it didn't matter what it was—turns, leaps, falls—he did it all. I don't believe he ever asked anything of a dancer that he did not first execute himself. He was extremely inspiring. I only wish I had had the opportunity to work with him from the time I was younger, and for longer. It's always such a reward when a teacher that you love so dearly and respect so much reciprocates and commends you on your work. He was never short of a correction or afraid to rake you over the coals when necessary, but at the same time, if he thought you were talented, he wasn't afraid to praise you. His praise meant the world to me. A real highlight for me was a few years later when I had my own dance studio and he accepted my invitation to come regularly to teach master classes to my students. My studio was a couple of hours away, and as he didn't drive, he would take the train in every two weeks. What an honor this was for me to have this man whom I respected so much give of himself to teach at my school.

Throughout my adult career, I have been blessed with a handful of great mentors. Some were friends from various walks of life, both in and out of the business, while others were teachers like Len, or employers, producers, and promoters with whom I first worked and, from there, developed long-standing friendships.

WHEN A LEFT TURN BECOMES THE *RIGHT* TURN

I would like to share with you a story that truly depicts *the* turning point in my own career. One day while on a promotional job with a dancer friend of mine, she told me of an audition being held on that very day. Apparently, there was an American show from Los Angeles, Las Vegas, Atlantic City, and Miami coming to Toronto to hold auditions for dancers, as it would be opening a production in Toronto in the near future. Although the lead roles would be played by Americans, the chorus would be all Canadian. It was always a big deal when an American company came to Canada to open a show. Back then, around the same time that Toronto was just developing its theatre district, there were not many opportunities like this; American productions in Canada were still quite unheard of.

How we managed it, I'm still not quite sure, but somehow we scheduled our lunch break to coincide with us getting to this audition. We were not going to miss this one. Once at the audition, we were taken through the paces and taught a challenging and well-choreographed routine. Always a good sign of what is to come! We met several of the key players that day: the production and company manager, the set designer, the director, and, of course, the choreographer. I had a great audition and landed the gig! How exciting, as it always is when you get that awaited phone call or offer. As fate would have it, I was exactly where I was supposed to be on that day. This "lunch-break audition" would become the major turning point of my career. Once in rehearsals, I met Lou Paciocco, the creator of the show and a producer from Los Angeles. He was in town and came to rehearsals to meet the cast and check on how things were progressing. No sooner had he arrived when the rumors were already spreading that he was looking for, and interviewing, choreographers for his Los Angeles revue.

Always being pretty attentive, I didn't need to hear that kind of information twice. I immediately inquired and was told that yes, in fact, he was seeing quite a few people in town about the newly available position. I thought to myself, and expressed to him, that if he was considering different local choreographers then he should also see my resume and demo reel of my work as a choreographer. I certainly thought if there was a position up for grabs, I should be considered as well as any other choreographer. After all, my work was very good, and I had a fair bit of experience. Of course, he would never have known this, as I had auditioned for and taken the position of a dancer. Since I was a young girl, my love for choreography was as strong as my love for performing, and from the moment I set out on my own career quest I actively pursued both. Lou showed interest in seeing my work and knowing more about the dance studio that I

20

owned at the time. So I prepared my promotional material to submit to him, and off to dinner and a meeting I went with demo reel and resume in hand. Looking back on that, I'm sure he must have thought this was rather ambitious of me as I was quite a bit younger than some of the more experienced choreographers who were also vying for the position.

About one week after Lou Paciocco had returned to Los Angeles, I received a phone call inviting me to come out there. I would have the opportunity to meet the cast and to discuss the position of resident choreographer of this highly successful musical revue, *La Cage Aux Folles*. I was thrilled and terrified all at the same time. For one thing, I had never been to Los Angeles, and it was miles away from my family and the life that I knew so well, and two, it was a very exciting opportunity that could, and did, change my life completely. That trip to Los Angeles was some twenty years ago, and I never looked back. Not only did I choreograph the Los Angeles show, but I went on to direct and open more than a dozen *La Cage* productions around the world. To this day, I continue to work with one of my best friends and mentor, Lou Paciocco.

For me, there was never an important decision to be made without running it by one of my mentors, if not all of them; and to this day I still make those few important phone calls first. Having left home at quite a young age to pursue my career in dance, and coming from such a large family, being on my own was somewhat difficult for me. I missed my family so much! I was fortunate enough to have a few "big sisters" on the road—they would always give a shoulder to lean on for strength, a pep talk for encouragement, or act as a sounding board if I was blue. To these women and my real big sisters, I am forever grateful.

There are many significant lessons and great memories from my childhood and early career days that have, to a great extent, influenced me. They are some of the best lessons of all, many of which I continue to draw on for inspiration today. And so, although some of these mentors may not be directly involved in my life today, the memories and the lessons they carry will always be with me.

ENCORE:
Mentors are like lighthouses along our journey; guiding and gently lighting the way.

ACCENTUATE THE POSITIVE!

When you are young, it is very important to pay close attention to those lessons that shape you; this isn't always easy. In fact, sometimes it can be downright difficult to decipher the advice and information you are given. You may very well receive conflicting advice from various sources and, therefore, all decisions should be weighed carefully and discussed with trusted sources.

As a side note for parents, I do encourage you to be involved and present in your child's training and/or career. My only caveat is to suggest that you do so without becoming a stereotypical "stage mother." It is so important to encourage and support children while ensuring that they are always in good hands. You want to be there and be in the know without being pushy, as you don't want to hinder their careers, only help them make their own wisest decisions. Fortunately for me, my mother was very involved in all that I did. And as she always said, she knew exactly what was going on without ever having to interfere. Just as I tell the talent to have the right attitude, so must the parents; it simply makes for a better experience all around.

There are many wonderful and talented people who surround us every day in our personal lives and in business. You have absolutely nothing to lose—and everything to gain—by embracing and aligning yourself with these people. You could be meeting them every day, at class, at auditions, working, performing, and through friends of friends. Be aware of your surroundings; the more you put yourself out there, the more opportunities you are creating.

We should constantly be growing; without growth, we become idle and stagnant, which is like a death sentence to creative people. There is so much to learn every day if you just remain flexible, open, and aware. I know this sounds very basic and simple, and the truth is, it is. Unfortunately, so many people walk through life with blinders on; they have no peripheral vision—none of that extrasensory ability that allows them to tap into all the many side trips and journeys life has to offer off the beaten path.

As an artist and performer, you cannot afford this habit. And mentors can be one of the greatest gifts of all. I am going to suggest that if you don't have any mentors in your life at present, keep an open heart and an open mind. These mentors could be people you already know or new acquaintances you seek out. Look for lifestyles, qualities, and accomplishments that you yourself aspire to. A mentor is someone you look up to and respect; someone who will help inspire and motivate you to accomplish your goals and dreams. You may be fortunate enough to have certain mentors all throughout your life, while others will come and go, staying only as long as you need them. Various circumstances in your life will dictate certain needs.

I remind you of the old African proverb that says, "When the student is ready, the teacher shall appear." I know from personal experience that they do appear, as if out of nowhere. It seems that often, a mere realization of the need is enough to fulfill the request. Trust, ask, and you shall receive.

You want to make sure that you are open enough to recognize these golden opportunities and not miss them when they are right in front of you. Once again, I reiterate the importance of being aware and being open—and choosing wisely. The right mentor can make all the difference in the world.

ENCORE:
You may well receive conflicting advice from various sources, and therefore all decisions should be weighed carefully and discussed with people you trust.

"Midnight Train to Georgia," production singers, Celebrity Cruises' *Mercury*

Chapter Three
Triple Threat—Training + Versatility = Options

"I do not try to dance better than anyone else. I only try to dance better than myself."
~ **Mikhail Baryshnikov**

A dancer's training is absolutely crucial to his or her overall career and performance. Training never ends; a dancer is constantly in training. In this ever-changing industry, it is absolutely imperative that dancers continue their education throughout their careers. The business is far too demanding and competitive to sit back on your laurels or think that training doesn't apply to you; you must constantly be growing and developing your talents, continuously ensuring your versatility and depth as a performer.

This is not to say that only the most trained or talented work in the industry; it's not just about talent. In fact, it's just as often about a specific look or a specialty. We all know a dancer or two with natural gifts who either had no formal training or was incredibly stylized in one specific area only and still succeeded in finding work.

Absolutely, this can and does happen very often. However, these careers may inevitably be somewhat limited. It's like anything else in life: you *can* get by in life being a one-trick pony. But what happens when not knowing that second or third trick limits your career?

The hip-hop dancer, the ballerina, or the "hoofer" who chooses not to train in other areas will be limited, working within a very small and specific area of the business. Even within their area of expertise, they still limit themselves, as there are so many incredibly versatile dancers out there today. What's more, these dancers not only do what dancers with only one specialty do as well or better, but they also come with everything else to complete the whole package.

This may have little significance to you if you have already determined that you want to be that specialty performer or the next prima ballerina. You may have your plan laid out and not see the need for any study outside of your forte.

But even if this is the route you are taking, I still strongly suggest that you explore training in other areas as it will only enrich you as a performer in your own specialty. In business, as in life, we can never have too much knowledge, and the more we have, the more we have to offer.

ENCORE:
Training never ends; a dancer is constantly in training.

ARE YOU A QUADRUPLE THREAT?

This chapter is called "Triple Threat," but perhaps we should update that familiar old saying to something more modern: being a "quadruple threat." We talk about being a triple threat like it's something new. However, the truth is that if we go back to the golden era of movie musicals and studio contracts (1930s to 1950s), all actors had to be triple threats.

In other words, they all had to sing, dance, and act.

Of course, within the industry, there has always been the need for the chorus dancer (otherwise known as "the single threat"). Throughout the decades, there has always been some work in film and television for dancers, whether in variety shows, award shows, pageants or commercials, not to mention the big dance feature film every so many years. The fact is that there simply isn't a great deal of that type of work—and certainly not enough to go around. This means it just may not be enough to sustain you.

There are certainly plenty of stage shows, revues, and variety-type shows for specific venues that do not require dancers to sing, but once again, let me remind you of how limited that area will be. For some of you, that may be just what you are looking for and there's absolutely nothing wrong with you wanting to work strictly as a dancer. On the other hand, I just want you to understand the parameters and limitations that this can mean for you.

Let me just add this food for thought: Although you may very well work consistently as a dancer, at some point you will probably decide that it is time to hang up your dance shoes. When this time comes, your versatility as a triple threat will leave you with many more options. I really do want to drive home the importance of being that triple threat. As a director, choreographer, and a producer who has spent a great deal of my career auditioning and hiring talent, let me tell you that versatility is a key factor in my decision-making.

I look for well-rounded dancers, those who can handle anything I throw at them. I can only speak for myself, but I can certainly tell you that many of my friends and acquaintances in the business who do what I do will tell you the exact same thing.

So what does this mean? This should give you an indication of how important it is to be well-trained in all areas of dance: ballet, jazz, modern, contemporary, lyrical, hip-hop, tap, and then some.

> **ENCORE:**
> *At some point, you will probably decide that it is time to hang up your dance shoes. When this time comes, your versatility as a triple threat will leave you with many more options.*

A WELL-ROUNDED DANCER

A well-rounded dancer will have training in as many styles as possible. I understand that your schedule or budget may not always allow for all of that, and I'm not suggesting that you have to be in all of those classes all of the time—or even all at the same time.

What I am suggesting is that if someone is first starting out, either as a young child or an adult, that individual should, at the very minimum, get into ballet and jazz. As you or your child progress, and if your budget allows, you can add various styles and different classes, all in the effort of becoming a more versatile dancer.

There are many performing arts schools and dance studios today that have dance and performing arts companies within; these are a great vehicle in which to maximize your learning opportunities. Most often, dance and performing arts companies will teach several of the above styles of dance as part of the company's class curriculum.

Once again, I do advise that you do your homework. Know all that you need to know about the school and its faculty: who they are, and their background, training and experience. Ask yourself some pertinent questions before you commit, not the least of which should be: Will you be studying with several teachers, each specializing in their own particular area or style of dance, or will you be studying many styles with one teacher?

In either case, you will want to be sure that they have the experience and versatility that you seek. What is your specialty? What are your strengths and weaknesses? Be clear on what your goals are so that you can ensure that you are getting the right training to support those goals. If you are fortunate enough to be involved in a performing arts school or company, then you may have the added bonus of taking acting or singing, or both, as part of the company's curriculum.

ENCORE:
There are many performing arts schools and dance studios today that have companies within; these are a great vehicle in which to maximize your learning opportunities.

"EVERYTHING OLD IS NEW AGAIN"

Let's talk strictly dance for a moment. The first mentioned is ballet—ah! The importance of ballet cannot be debated, while the passion of it often leaves readers debating. Some of you love it and some of you love to hate it.

I know the story well; I've heard it all too often. I'm here to tell you, if you don't know this already, that you had best find something about it that you can like and appreciate, or at the very least learn to endure. Ballet is your core foundation; it is the basis for all that you do as a dancer. It gives you your technique, strength, and power; your center, alignment, grace, and poise.

Many young dancers often ask me what they can do to help prepare for their careers. One of the first things I ask them is if they are studying ballet. If not, I suggest that they immediately begin taking classes. If you are a young adult setting out in your career as a professional and you have not had any ballet training, then I suggest you get yourself into ballet class *now*.

The technique and strength that you develop will support you in all areas of dance. I'm not saying that dancers of other disciplines cannot be equally as strong or technical; I am simply saying that where technique and strength are necessary as a dancer, you can be certain to get them from good ballet training.

Jazz dance, which is often the favorite with so many young dancers, also offers you a strong technique as well as style and much versatility. One of the great things about studying jazz dance is that you will cover a wide variety of music and styles. Specifically, if you train with some excellent and stylistically versatile teachers, you can then cover an incredible amount of dance styles within a strong jazz syllabus.

The more variety there is in choreography and style, the more stylized and versatile the dancer will be. These are all things to take into consideration when you are choosing a school, a studio, teachers, and/or coaches. Hip-hop, which may include street, funk, popping or locking, or b-boying ("breaking," as it is commonly known), is also a very popular class and offers great variety and versatility of style, not to mention some pretty impressive tricks.

Tap speaks for itself and is always an asset. Not every show will require it, but many will have the one token tap number. Modern and contemporary, once again, offer strength and technique, captivated with intense emotion while lyrical offers a more graceful, lingering, emotive style of dance. Latin, ballroom, belly dance, and other ethnic styles of dance simply add to your versatility. Any and all different types of dance you can study will only help to enhance your abilities and your performance.

For me, it's all about style, technique, and performance—plus the perfect combination and blend of the three. Versatility, versatility, and more versatility; this is the strength of any well-rounded dancer. If musical comedy is not a part of the dance curriculum within your company or within a particular class that you are already taking, make sure to get yourself into a few classes, at the very least.

ENCORE:
Ballet is your core foundation; it is the basis for all that you do as a dancer.

FINDING YOUR VOICE

Next, let's talk about the dreaded (for so many dancers, that is) vocal audition and the importance of singing for a dancer. If you are out there auditioning, or first starting out in your career, and you have not had any vocal lessons as part of your training, find yourself a vocal teacher and start taking some private lessons *ASAP*. Trust me, I do speak from personal experience, both as a dancer who wasn't a strong singer and as a choreographer who has seen many talented dancers not get a gig due to lack of vocal ability.

At twenty-two, I auditioned for the musical *Cats*. I was living in Toronto at the time and this was the first-ever Broadway musical to be produced in Canada, so you can imagine the stir and excitement amongst the industry. There were auditions in several cities, and at the Toronto audition alone, there were over 1,000 dancers, both equity and non-equity. (Actors' Equity Association is a union often referred to as "Equity." You will learn more about this union and others in "Chapter Thirteen: United We Stand.")

This was so very exciting and nerve-racking, and I loved every minute of it. I felt confident, and I did a great dance audition.

Cut after cut, we were narrowed down to eight dancers, and I was so thrilled to be one of the eight. How exciting to have gone from so many down to such a small group; the realization that I had made the cut felt pretty amazing. But, suddenly, I heard those dreadful words, "We are going to have you sing one at a time. Please wait in the hallway for your turn."

Although I knew I would have to sing and came prepared with sheet music and all, I guess there was a part of me that thought surely there must be one cat that doesn't have to sing (or at least I hoped so). I knew in my gut, even though I tried to convince myself otherwise, that it was all over. When my turn came around, dreading every note, I went in to sing, and to make matters worse, I had prepared the song "Home" from *The Wiz*. Hello, is anybody home? What was I thinking? I'm sure the performance was stellar; it was just the sounds that came out that weren't. Needless to say, I took up private vocal lessons immediately after that audition. (By the way, the jury is still out as to whether those lessons actually helped!)

I told you all that to point out that it can be absolutely heartbreaking to be up for a part in your dream show and lose out because you can't carry a tune, or even worse, hold a note. You spent the entire day there, you got through the "cattle call," they've cut and they've cut again and again, you're down to the last few, and now the moment you have either been waiting for—or dreading—is about to determine your fate.

Don't be afraid of it; just prepare for it! If you lack confidence in your singing ability, *do not* allow *this* to keep you from getting the training that you need.

Singing, especially in a private-lesson situation, can be very intimidating to one who lacks the vocal confidence, and many dancers, unfortunately, are notorious for their fear of singing. If you are already confident in this area as either a dancer-singer (or a full-on singer), then you can certainly understand the importance of your vocal training and development. So as I mentioned earlier, if you haven't done so, you absolutely must take singing lessons. Find yourself a private singing coach. Even if you do not have the most amazing voice, you must still do all that you can to train your ear and develop your voice. At the very least, you want to learn to carry a tune. If money holds you back, as it often can when first starting out, consider the most affordable options first. If private lessons are not an option initially, then try to find a choir that you can join. At the very least you might have a friend who is a strong enough singer to help with some vocal exercises and coaching tips to help get you started.

Of course, as we discuss throughout this book, there is a great deal of disappointment in our business. What I hope to accomplish—and help you prevent—is experiencing disappointment based on your lack of preparation. And so I continue to emphasize the importance of ensuring yourself the best shot at every opportunity, which you can accomplish by grasping the importance of—and acting on—the advice given in this chapter.

ENCORE:

If you are out there auditioning or first starting out in your career and you have not had any vocal lessons, find yourself a vocal teacher ASAP.

THEY DON'T CALL IT ACT-ION FOR NOTHING!

Dancing? Check.

Singing? Check.

Acting? Check it out: If you have any dreams or aspirations of performing in musical theatre, whether you are Broadway or West End–bound, or you would like to perform in community, dinner, or regional theatre, you absolutely must *sing* and *act*. Before I segue to the acting portion of our training, I would like to remind you that musical theatre is not the only market that casts dancers who sing. Many variety shows, musical revues, cruise ships, theme parks, and corporate events also hire dancers who sing.

When it comes to acting, it's not only in musical theatre that these skills will be put to the test. How about film and television? How about commercials? Certainly, if you are sent on an audition, a casting call, or a reading for any of the above, there are going to be acting skills required. As a dancer, you could be cast in any number of commercials where movement is a prerequisite.

With the recent rise in popularity of dance over the last several years because of such television shows as *Dancing with the Stars* and *So You Think You Can Dance*, even the most unlikely products have dancers in their commercials. Gap, of course, set the trend some time ago, which propelled so many others to follow suit. This is a great time for the dance world. *So You Think You Can Dance* continues to grow in popularity around the world. Canada, Australia, the U.K., and several other countries have all had their own versions, and the American show added an additional season in the fall of 2009. This was the first time the show aired two seasons back-to-back, and in the same year.

Okay, back to where we were: acting for commercials. It's not always a choreographed routine that you may be asked to perform. You may be required to assume the role of a "young mom" dancing around your kitchen as you prepare the children's lunch or while doing your laundry. Perhaps they are looking for a "dad" to do a little break-dance while repairing his son's bicycle or picking up his new car. What I'm trying to point out here is simply the fact that there will *always* be some acting—and often improvisation—involved, and I want you to be ready for it. I don't believe that there is any kind of performance that would not benefit from acting training.

If you are not already in an acting class, I highly recommend it. At the very least, you want to have a few acting or commercial workshops under your belt. Unfortunately, the truth is that just a few certainly isn't enough, but it's better than none, so do all that you can to get yourself as much training as possible. Do what you have to do to be ready for it, whatever it takes. Many famous film stars and recording artists either first started out in the business as dancers or studied dance as children.

Think of Madonna, Sarah Jessica Parker, Shirley MacLaine, or Patrick Swayze, for example. Madonna moved to New York City to pursue a career in dance. Who could ever have foretold the life, career, and legendary status that this young girl was about to create for herself? Sarah Jessica Parker's family relocated to New Jersey after she was cast in the Broadway production of *The Innocents*. This was only the beginning. Although she is famous for her role in the hit television show *Sex and the City*, which is only one of her many television and film credits, she was first a child star on Broadway. Shirley MacLaine's biography is one to be greatly envied. She also began by studying ballet as a young girl. She then moved from Virginia to New York City straight out of high school to pursue her career. Her first role on Broadway was in *The Pajama Game*, where she understudied the second lead. One evening while performing as understudy, legendary producer Hal Wallis was in the audience and spotted her. This was the catalyst for her incredible film career. Important to note: one never knows who could be in that audience. Patrick Swayze was introduced to dance at a young age by his mother, who was a dance teacher, choreographer, and dance studio owner in Houston, Texas. At the age of twenty, he moved to New York City to pursue his career as a dancer. He studied with the Harkness Ballet School and Joffrey Ballet School. His first professional performance was with *Disney on Parade*, and he debuted on Broadway in *Grease* before going on to Hollywood.

These actors are all so multi-talented; it is hard to put them in any one category: actor, singer, dancer, etc. In short, they are all truly triple threats!

Speaking of triple threats, here is an actor who continues to personify these words: John Travolta. The youngest of six children in an entertainment family, Travolta grew up in Englewood, New Jersey. He dropped out of school and moved to New York City at the age of sixteen to pursue his acting career. Having already studied voice, dancing, and acting at drama school, he went on to win many roles that featured all of those talents. He gave the characters he portrayed in such movie musicals as *Saturday Night Fever* and *Grease* their definition. If you haven't already seen *Hairspray*, be sure to do so. He gives yet another outstanding performance as Edna Turnblad.

This next star may not have started out as a dancer, but when it comes to triple threats, Queen Latifah says it all. And although her biography may not have "dancer" next to singer/actor, she certainly has all the moves. Her performances in the movie musicals *Chicago* and *Hairspray* are, in my opinion, unrivaled. These are two of my favorites, but only two specific performances in a long list of her fabulous credits.

The simple truth of this business is if you get that bug for entertaining, there is usually no denying it, whether you get it from a dance class, a play that you've been to, or singing for Mom and Dad.

So, back to where I started with all of this. Even if you are not aspiring to pursue film and television, what I am pointing out is simply the fact that you never know where your love for dance might take you. And so, if you have a desire to perform, then you must consider all training possible. Any and all classes or workshops that offer you yet another skill or help to develop existing or hidden talent, or even stir interest, are all excellent vehicles to help further create the performer and "triple threat" in you.

ENCORE:
How many famous film stars or recording artists do we know of today who either first started out in the business as dancers or studied dance as children?

DON'T WAIT FOR OPPORTUNITY TO COME TO YOU

As we wrap up this chapter on becoming a more multi-layered performer, I would like to take a moment to address a few questions that have come up time and time again, mostly from young talent first looking to pursue their interest in show business. If you find yourself living in an area that doesn't offer much in the way of training and lessons, then what do you do? First things first: Find out what is available to you in the town or city that you live in. Next, find out what is available to you that might be close by.

Some of you may find yourself with an incredible desire and natural talent but with few options available in the way of training. First and foremost, get yourself enrolled in the best available classes and then start considering all the various options outside of formal training that may be right at your fingertips. You are after all an artist and, therefore, have special abilities, one of which is the ability to improvise. So be innovative by creating your own tools and activities and establishing your own practices; study music videos, movie musicals, and dance movies.

Try to find yourself a good, reputable series of instructional dance DVDs. Check with the most trusted sources first. Some of the most well-known studios carry their own line of instructional DVDs, which can often be purchased online. I would start by checking out Broadway Dance Center in New York City. The center produces and sells its own line of instructional DVDs, which it adds to all the time. How about forming a dance troupe or theatre group with friends who have these same interests? Read everything you can get your hands on that relates to your talent, your interest, and the industry, and the people who have made it in the industry. Who are some of your favorite performers? Find out where they studied and who they studied with.

Create your own commercial practice ritual by tearing advertisements from magazines and even recording television commercials. All magazines, from beauty and fashion to business and homemaking, contain ads which, along with your recordings, can be turned into a mini-commercial workshop.

Don't forget your local library and bookstores! There are hundreds of books on monologues, cold readings, and scene study available from a variety of sources. In today's world, you have a wealth of information readily available, thanks to the luxury of the Internet. Web surfing allows you to locate and purchase an abundance of information in the form of books and videos, and lets you indulge—for free—in a tremendous amount of educational information in the form of articles, write-ups, or reviews on just about every facet of the business.

As for vocals, I would be willing to bet that you will have no problem finding yourself a private singing teacher or coach. Start by inquiring with your neighborhood school's music department or your local church choir. So while you may not have Broadway Dance Center or Screen Actors Studio right down the street, there are certainly plenty of things you can do to help yourself along the way, at least until you reach the point when you have greater access to the right learning institutions.

I hope that in this chapter I have clearly conveyed to you not only the importance of being a triple threat, but also the importance of choosing wisely when considering all your training needs and the many affordable and creative ways in which you can help yourself. I leave you with this thought: If the choice is yours to make, why would you *not* choose to have *everything* you need?

Don't cut yourself short—go for it all! You can always find a way!

"I don't see my dancing or acting as two separate things. More than anything I love being on stage and performing."
~Bebe Neuwirth *(TV & film actress, singer, and dancer)*

It's all about teamwork. Dancers rehearsing their vocals off to the side, Opryland Productions, Nashville, Tennessee

Chapter Four

Dancing for a Degree—To College or Not to College?

I was under the impression that I could do anything.
~ **Alvin Ailey**

For those of you who are currently in high school and have decided that you do, in fact, want to pursue a professional career in dance, you are now facing some very important decisions: decisions about college, decisions about your career, and, of course, the age-old question—should one go to college for dance? How does that question apply to you?

Throughout my book, I explore the many possibilities within the dance and entertainment industry, from where to work to how to get the gig. You may already have decided in what capacity and specific area within the dance world you would like to work, and some of these areas will benefit greatly from a college degree in dance while others may not necessarily. I personally believe that you will always benefit from a college degree; it's more a matter of whether it will benefit your chosen career path. After all, a degree in dance won't necessarily land you the lead in a Broadway show. However, if you are looking to teach dance within the school system, whether at an elementary, middle, or high school, or at the college or university level, a degree will not only be of tremendous benefit; in some cases, it will be mandatory.

There are many career options beyond performance that will benefit tremendously from a degree. Various management positions in a theatre, dance company, or performing arts center, entertainment-related press agent, dance and performing arts critic, and editor are just a few examples. Be certain when considering college to keep in mind those other related careers for a time when you may no longer be able to or want to perform. We will discuss this at greater length in "Chapter Fifteen: Life after the Stage—Career Transitions," where I will introduce you to several friends and industry acquaintances who will share their stories with us.

As a young dancer, I was taught that one did not go to college for dance. It was somewhat ridiculed, so it was embedded in my brain that the two just didn't go together.

When it was time for me to decide about furthering my education, I sat down with my high school guidance counselor to discuss my options. My dilemma was whether to go to college or to just get out there and start my career as a dancer/choreographer, which was ultimately my dream. Some people believe it's best to follow your dream wholeheartedly without any deviation, insinuating if you have a plan B you are not fully committed to plan A. However, others believe it's important to have a backup plan. Ultimately, this is your decision, and only you can make that choice. My guidance counselor's advice to me, as someone who was fully aware of my already young career—as a dancer, teacher, and choreographer—was this. He said: "We are very fortunate here in North America. You can always go to school any time. You have a great talent in dance, and it can be a short-lived career. I suggest you get out there and pursue your career first. You can always go to school later."

My father desperately wanted me to go to university and the thought of me trading in a university education for a career as a dancer was absolutely ludicrous to him. "What will you do when you can no longer dance? What if you become injured and your career ends prematurely?" He would say, "Get a university degree as insurance for your future." This was all excellent, sound advice, but in the end, the desire to dance seemed to me the only choice. Dance was my true passion and I couldn't deny it, nor did I want to put it on hold. And as I've already mentioned, the idea of going to college for dance was not even a conversation, or so I had been convinced.

On that note, I will say this: college programs in dance have come a long way in the past several decades. Twenty-five or thirty years ago, going to college for dance was relatively unheard of. Today, there are more than 600 college and university dance degree programs to consider, and yet it is still a topic that brings out all the skeptics, or should I say often invites a debate. Some topics evoke much emotion, and this is certainly one of them, at least within the dance circle: Do dance and a college degree go hand in hand? Ask the question and you will get an abundance of opinions, all different, yet equally valid. The simple truth is that this is a very personal and individual decision, and at the end of the day, what's right for one may not be for another. There is a great deal to consider, and you want to make the best choice for you.

A college degree is a wonderful advantage to have and to fall back on; it can benefit you in your present career path and in any future career transitions. Although it may or may not make a difference at your audition or be the deciding factor as to whether or not you get that gig, it certainly won't inhibit you, and it will definitely be an asset in your career and in life in general. There are obvious career paths that you can take where a dance degree will make all the difference in the world; others where it will not make a bit of difference. In order to make the right decision for yourself, you will want to consider closely where and how you see yourself working in the industry. This will be important in helping you to decide whether or not a dance degree is right for you, and if so, what program will be best suited to you. Following is a work sheet that you can use to help you in your career path decisions.

ENCORE:

A college degree is a wonderful advantage to have and to fall back on; it can benefit you in your present career path and in any future career transitions.

THE DANCE OF SELF DISCOVERY

Goals and Aspirations

- List all your dreams and desires—everything and anything you ever imagined being as far back as you can remember.
- When you were a child, did you dream of becoming famous? If yes, how did you see yourself being famous? Please describe briefly.
- If there was no possibility of rejection or failure, what would you most want to do or be today? No limits, no holds barred.
- What do you think you most need to work on to achieve such goals and dreams?
- If you could make your mark in the world, what would it be?
- Does your dance training assist you with that goal?
- List ten things you most want to do in your lifetime.

39

Evaluation

- What do you like most about yourself?
- What do you dislike most about yourself?
- What are your strongest assets as a dancer? (e.g., technique, style, passion, creativity, performance ability, musicality, retention, etc.)
- What are your weaknesses as a dancer?
- What are your personal strengths?
- What are your personal weaknesses?
- What other strengths or skills do you possess that could help you in your career or in business?
- What disadvantages do you have that might work against you, and how can you transform them into advantages?
- What would your teachers, parents, and fellow dancers say are your strengths in dance, in business, and on a personal level?
- What natural talents do you possess that you may have discovered along the way? Not things that you've been taught, but rather abilities that just came naturally to you. For example, you might be a natural-born leader, a great organizer, you might hear music and envision the steps, or maybe you have a great imagination and can instantly create a story line.
- Are you a natural-born teacher, creator, or performer?
- Do you see yourself as a business owner? (This could be a dance studio, a talent agency, a theatre or production company, etc.)
- Do you like to help others, and if so, what areas could someone call on you to help out with?

Personal Interests

- What makes you happy?
- What are your favorite pastimes, hobbies, or activities?
- Whom do you most like to spend time with?
- What activities did you most enjoy as a young child?
- If you could travel anywhere in the world, where would it be and why?

Personal Inspirations

- What first inspired you to dance?
- What show, book, or movie most inspires you?
- Who are your heroes or idols?

- Whom do you most admire or respect in the entertainment industry and why?
- Who are the people who most influenced you in a positive way in your training or in your career, and how? (This could be a parent, teacher, coach, employer, etc.)

Now that you have taken this time to ponder the above questions and reflect on your needs, your desires, your strengths, and your weaknesses, I ask you to complete one final and very important task. Go ahead and write down a brief paragraph—a summary of what you see in your answers. Is there a set pattern that you see repeating itself? Do the same desires keep coming up time and time again, and do the same key words find themselves in various areas? Are there weaknesses that might inhibit you or that you feel could benefit from study at college or other modes of additional training? You get the idea! Careful consideration of the above questions and your summary will allow you to take a closer look at the decision you must make and will help you create a road map or action plan. If, in fact, college has an immediate place in your future, you will want to pay close attention to the next section.

COLLEGE OR BUST

Once you have made the decision to go off to college, there will be much more for you to think about and to explore. You will want to be meticulous with your research, considering all your needs, interests, talents, strengths, weaknesses, and, of course, finances. The above questionnaire will already have addressed some of these very important considerations.

Where to study and what program is best suited to you will be your first and most difficult choices, as there are numerous and varied programs available today. I will give you much to think about in the following pages. However, I will only skim the surface; much more than a chapter is needed to assist you in your ultimate decision. This will be an excellent introduction, but there are books specifically devoted to college programs for dance and other performing arts. These books will not only give you very detailed information about the various programs and degrees, their areas of concentration, and whether they are performance or education oriented, but they'll also give you contact details, the do's and don'ts, and great advice on the "how to" process.

I suggest that you learn all that you can about the different colleges and universities that you are interested in, and the dance programs they offer. College for dance can be a wonderful arena in which to grow and experiment, to make contacts, and it will help you determine your place, both in your early career and for what lies ahead should a career transition be necessary. The right choice is paramount. Here are a few additional things to keep in mind as you make your decision.

- Is it important to be close to home or not?
- What is your main interest? Once again consider your strengths and weaknesses. Are the programs offered in line with your needs?
- What diplomas or degrees are offered?
- What is the program's curriculum and what is its focus and objective?
- Who is on the faculty, and what are their backgrounds?
- What are the studio facilities like?
- Are there any performance opportunities?
- Are there any affiliations with dance companies?
- What famous alumni went through their program?
- What have their alumni gone on to accomplish?

Careful research and consideration of these questions will be very helpful in assisting you in your quest to compile your preliminary list of colleges. This list should be consistent with your ultimate career goals, having considered both your immediate and long-term plans. A performance career can be short-lived, so it is a good idea to look ahead to any potential career change.

The range of bachelor of arts degrees and master's degrees is endless, and the only way you can really get to the bottom of this decision is through careful consideration of exactly what the various programs have to offer. The differences are so varied, you will want to take everything into account—your academic likes and dislikes and your personal needs. Be honest as you evaluate the many pieces of the puzzle. If you're not one who likes to write essays or if there are certain studies that you just never want to be subjected to again, be certain that you are not wasting your time with programs that may require the very thing you want to avoid. Be mindful of what is required within the programs themselves. All your in-depth research from various institutions' websites, any additional information you may have requested from them directly, and all that we have touched on in this chapter will help you in narrowing your choices. The recommended college guides in the section "Where Do I Begin? The College Search" will be invaluable tools for you from the get-go and will be very useful in helping you to compare those colleges and universities you are considering, at a quick glance, all in one book.

You will find similar questions to the ones above in other chapters. After all, whether you are deciding on college, or a move away from home to pursue a career in dance, you will want to ask the same questions of yourself. A combination of all these considerations will help you in your final determination.

FOLLOW YOUR HEART

Following your heart is key to being happy and feeling fulfilled in your life and career. If you do not follow your heart, you will never be truly happy. Ask yourself these two very important questions: "Is dance the one thing that I absolutely want to do more than anything in life? Is there anything else that I would be happier doing?" And there you have it—your answer. That, by the way, applies to dance in college or dance as a profession. I mentioned earlier in "Chapter One: Born to Dance," if you don't have passion, what is the point? There are much easier ways to earn a living than a career in dance or show business. Essentially, asking yourself this one question can help you to determine where your true passion lies, and if it's not 100 percent in dance, you should save yourself the heartache. Now, if in fact there is only one path for you and there is no turning back, please read on!

> **ENCORE:**
> *There is so much to consider, take everything into account—your academic likes and dislikes and your personal needs.*

WHERE DO I BEGIN? THE COLLEGE SEARCH

One of the first things I recommend is to pick up one of the following college guides. These books will offer you a concise list of the various programs available, all in one location, and help you create an initial list of colleges to consider and to compare to each other. *Dance Magazine's College Guide*, published and updated yearly, lists the various college dance programs and also features articles about the topic of college for dance. You can visit the website at www.dancemagazine.com. *Peterson's College Guide for Performing Arts Majors* is very comprehensive, and also an excellent choice. It includes a selected listing of dance programs broken down into the following categories: Most Highly Recommended Programs, Recommended Programs, and Other Noteworthy Programs. Peterson's also has a website loaded with information and wonderful articles that will answer so many of your questions. I'm sure that you will find it very useful: www.petersons.com. Both guides can be purchased online at their respective websites, and at some of the online bookstores, such as Amazon and

STARTING YOUR CAREER AS A DANCER

Barnesandnoble.com. Some of the major bookstores will carry them on their shelves; if not, they may be able to special order them for you. I have found that *Dance Magazine's College Guide* is more difficult to locate, and your best bet may be ordering it directly from the website. You can always check at your local library as well.

Next, you will want to visit the various college websites. There is an abundance of information available online, from entire catalogs to virtual tours. Be sure to take full advantage of the many different marketing tools available, such as their websites, viewbooks, and videos, all of which are helpful and should be utilized. You can also request additional information from the school directly, either online or by writing to the director of admissions. If you write, be sure to give your name, address, date of birth, and main interest or area of concentration. They may also require your Social Security number as this might later be used as a way of identifying you. For obvious safety issues, check first whether or not to include your Social Security number in your correspondence. With more than 600 different degree programs available, it can seem a daunting task.

Keeping yourself organized—much like the advice and tips I give in "Chapter Twelve: No More Starving Artist"—will be very important as you create a college organizer for yourself. Just as you would with any task to be organized, you will first want to create a plan. I recommend a "to do" list and a checklist to keep track of your progress. You will also want different sections to record details of your emails and letters; any telephone conversations, when and with whom you spoke; any important information you may have been given; and your first impressions of the school. This is very important to reflect back on. After several conversations or inquiries, you will appreciate this journal to help keep the abundance of information straight.

Careful reading of the school catalogs will give you detailed information about the different programs, which will, in turn, help you to narrow your list. Campus visits, if possible, are indisputably the best means to get a full picture, but that's not until you've narrowed your list to your few final choices. This is a huge decision, and you want to give yourself the most complete picture in order to make the best decision possible.

NARROWING THE SEARCH

Once you've gathered and read through the catalogs or visited the various websites of those colleges that you have serious interest in, you can begin to narrow down the list. Your list should include a "wish list"—this will be a list of your ultimate dream colleges; a "safe list"—those colleges you feel pretty certain you will

44

be accepted to; and a "possibly list"—those colleges you would also love to attend and feel you have a good shot at. Ultimately, you want to give yourself options.

As I've previously mentioned, mentors can play an extremely important role in our decision process, and this would be an excellent opportunity to take advantage of these advisors. Speak to your dance teachers, mentors, and guidance counselors; they often will present just the right food for thought. Sometimes when we are too close to the subject, a mentor can show us a different angle or way of viewing our options. A combination of their advice, your own heart, and careful examination of the information you've gathered will be a good way to filter your process. Speak to other students from your high school, your area, or your dance studio who have been or are presently in college for dance. Asking them about their process of elimination and their final decision will offer yet another form of tried-and-tested advice. Better yet, if there are any students from your studio who are attending any colleges you are considering applying to, try to get as much information from them as you possibly can. One very important question to ask them is whether they are happy with their choice, and if they would have chosen the same college in hindsight.

Lastly, I recommend that you find out about upcoming college fairs. This information can be acquired from the National Association for College Admission Counseling. You can visit their website, www.nacacnet.org, for a complete list of upcoming fairs. This is a perfect time for you to learn about educational opportunities, admission and financial aid, and audition and entrance requirements. When you visit the fairs, you can speak with the admissions representatives. This is a great time to ask questions, so go prepared with questions in hand. You will gain a real sense of what the colleges and specific programs you are interested in are like.

CAMPUS VISITS

Once you've narrowed your search to your final choices, you may want to visit a campus or two, depending on what is realistic. If an interview is required, you should be prepared and try to plan it in advance, thereby combining your visit and interview. This will prove to be very efficient, from both a time and financial viewpoint. The opportunity to visit gives you a sneak preview of life on campus. You will be able to meet other students and audit classes. This is an excellent time to gain feedback from those living in the environment, and lastly, the occasion to see if, in fact, this is where you envision yourself.

Be sure to plan your campus visit before the application deadline; this way, if you absolutely fall in love and decide that this is where you ultimately want to be, you will not have missed your window of opportunity. If you are unable to visit due to financial restrictions, contact the admissions department and find out if there are any alumni or students from your area whom you might be able to contact and meet. If you have not already looked into the college fairs schedule, ask the admissions department if they have any admissions reps coming through your area for any college fairs or presentations.

HOW TO PLAN YOUR VISIT

In order to get the most out of your visit, be sure to find out what is happening on campus. You want to make sure that your visit is not at a time when there is so much going on that you cannot meet with the appropriate people and/or accomplish what you went there for. At the same time, you will want to know the class schedule and if there are any concerts or rehearsals that you can attend. Is staying overnight an option? This is a fine way to maximize your visit. Make sure that the time you choose is favorable for the school; make sure that the admissions department is not inundated with placement so that you can benefit from meeting them and asking questions.

Prepare a list of all questions. Think about everything you want to know about the school, about their studio facilities, the faculty backgrounds and experience, the student body, and the social life. Consider all questions as you would with any first move away from home—questions that relate to living arrangements and the neighborhood. Is the campus safe? What are the crime statistics? You can never ask too many questions, and you must consider everything that could be a concern to you. After all, you intend to spend the next several years living in this environment, and you want to make sure up-front that this is going be a comfortable place for you.

Just as with the advice I gave about auditioning for jobs in the professional scene, be certain to use the same respect and thoughtful gestures with all personal contact, especially once you have made your visit. Make sure to send a thank you note to your interviewer and to your host if you stayed over. This small gesture will be appreciated and will not go unnoticed; it may very well become part of your file.

HOW TO BEST PREPARE AND SHINE AT YOUR INTERVIEW: *THE DOS AND DON'TS*

First of all, find out if interviews are required or optional. Often you will find that the interview process will be optional due to staff restrictions, and travel or financial difficulties. If you are planning a visit to a campus, I believe it would be in your best interest to set up an interview even when it is optional. Nothing makes as important an impression as a face-to-face meeting. Do not confuse the interview with the audition, which is a completely different matter. An audition will almost always be required. Some institutions will hold live auditions, while some will accept video submissions. Audition requirements will be different for each institution, and you should learn about this in the admissions information when doing your research.

I will not proceed to list all the "do not's" as some are simply common sense: e.g., don't chew gum, don't use inappropriate language, don't speak in a negative manner, etc. This is your opportunity to make a good first impression, so you want to present yourself in the best possible light—you want to be someone whom this establishment would be proud to have in its student body. When it comes to attire you will want to dress appropriately. Just as I suggested earlier, you want to appeal to your audience and not offend anyone. You can still be fashionable and current while in good taste. I suggest that you check with the individual colleges for their specific dress requirements and recommendations.

During your interview, take this opportunity to share information about yourself, your family, your background, your interests, and experiences. This is your moment to sell yourself in a positive way without being too boastful or coming off as arrogant. It is also not a time to be overly modest; it is a perfect time to share with your interviewer any special accomplishments or interests you may have.

APPLICATION REQUIREMENTS

Application requirements could include the following: high school transcripts for freshmen or college transcripts if you are transferring, a personal profile that could include extracurricular activities, recommendations from teachers or guidance counselors, and essays. An essay is a good opportunity for you to let the admissions office get to know you. Even if it is optional, write one. And, of course, last, but certainly not least, your audition. College auditions will differ somewhat from professional auditions. You will want to consider everything there is to learn from "Chapter Seven: The Audition," but keep in mind that the attire will be considerably different. Check with the establishment you're auditioning for on restrictions, guidelines, etc. As with all advice I give, I will reiterate that you want to be fully prepared for your audition, so again, make sure that you know exactly what to expect by reading the audition guidelines thoroughly. Where live auditions are concerned, some establishments will teach a class or two, whereas others will ask you to prepare an audition piece. Some will do both, teach class and ask you to present an audition piece. Whether you choreograph your routine or have someone choreograph it for you, be prepared to introduce yourself and speak about the piece that you will be performing. Composure, courtesy, and respect should always be standard behavior in any presentation.

If you are performing a set audition piece, make sure that you are well rehearsed. Set up a mock audition where you perform your piece before an audience: invite your teachers, guidance counselors, and a few family members or friends. Ask your teacher to critique your performance, and then plan to perform it for them again at a later date a little closer to your actual audition. Be sure to videotape these trial runs so that you can view your performance and critique yourself. This is an excellent learning tool, so take advantage in order to best prepare yourself. The more rehearsed you are, the more confident you will be, and the less chance for your nerves to interfere. You want to exude a certain self-confidence and poise and allow your talent to shine through. Very important: Remember to begin the application process well in advance of audition and interview dates. These take place months before the courses start and you want to ensure that you have plenty of time to prepare fully.

FINANCIAL AID

When it comes to financial assistance, you will want to check all avenues. Several books are available to help guide you. There are various grants, stipends, scholarships, and awards available. The first thing you will do is fill out your Free Application for Federal Student Aid (FAFSA) form. The U.S. Department of Education will determine your eligibility based on your answers. FAFSA is the form used by virtually all two- and four-year colleges, universities, and career schools to award federal student aid, and most state and college aid. Please make sure to visit their website at http://studentaid.ed.gov.

This website will assist you in so many ways. First and foremost is your FAFSA; however, you will also find tons of information on the long list of scholarships available to you. There are so many avenues you must consider; colleges and universities also offer scholarships for certain *specific* programs. There are scholarships offered through various organizations, including state government, the federal government, and private associations. As you have heard repeatedly, do not leave any stone unturned. Check with your local religious groups, professional associations, private companies, employers, and last but not least, individuals. There are individuals who like to support the arts and will allocate certain monies to assist young artists to pay for their college education. You never know who is offering what, and if you don't ask, you don't get. You may be surprised at the sources that are willing to support individuals looking to better themselves and further their education. Many people who have a passion in these specific areas look to help new fresh talent along. Sometimes, it's a way of giving back, and sometimes it's simply a passion that they get to fulfill. Explore all avenues. What could you possibly have to lose?

IN CLOSING

As I mentioned at the beginning of this chapter, my intention for this section was to introduce the idea of college for dance and to give you an overview of what you will need to consider in making this decision. In closing, I would like to remind you of something that I have repeatedly driven home, and that is not to throw anything away. Treat your education as you would your professional career. Every experience is an opportunity to learn something that you will carry with you throughout your lifetime and career as a dancer. There will be many challenges along the way. It is an extremely competitive field and in college, just as in the professional world, you will have to earn your place and work hard to *keep* your place. This is a wonderful arena in which to experiment and grow, so take full advantage and don't be afraid to put yourself out there. Go for it and grow from it!

Gain as much outside experience as possible, bearing in mind that each establishment will have its own set of rules about extracurricular activities, such as classes and auditions. When and where it is allowed, be sure to attend as many shows and classes as possible, observe as many auditions as you can, and attend any that do not interfere with your college program. These are fine learning opportunities and a great way to keep current and informed about what is going on in the industry. So take full advantage; you can only gain greater knowledge from these experiences.

If you do decide to go to college, go with an optimistic attitude about all the wonders that await you, take hold of all that is in your path, and give it everything you've got. Don't miss one single opportunity. As the Latin saying goes, "*Carpe diem!*" (Seize the day!)

ENCORE:
Every experience is an opportunity to learn something that you will carry with you throughout your lifetime and career as a dancer.

If you're going to do it, do it 100 percent! "Think," *La Cage* opening night at the Blue Angel, New York City

Chapter Five

Leave Your Attitude Where It Belongs— At the Door!

"The one important thing that I have learned over the years is the difference between taking one's work seriously and taking one's self seriously. The first is imperative and the second is disastrous."
~ **Margot Fonteyn**

What kind of attitude do you need to make it in the field of entertainment, in general, and dancing in particular? The right attitude—a positive outlook, that is—is the only kind of attitude to have in this industry. You might think it's a big industry, but it's a small world, and it is, therefore, very important to create good, strong, and lasting relationships.

Since there is so much more talent than there is work, who do you think are getting the gigs? Could it be the pleasant and consummate pros who are grateful to have the work? Or do you believe it's the divas who think that you should feel lucky just to have them working for you? Be the kind of performer that a producer, director, or choreographer wants to spend hours on end with. Be that person, the one they want to call in for their next gig.

We've all known what I charitably call "big personalities," who are more about the drama and the demands than they are the performance and the professionalism. While some of these dancers are talented enough to be forgiven their egos, the rest of us simply can't get away with that. Burn enough bridges in an industry like ours, and soon enough you'll have nowhere left to audition.

I've been in this business a long time, and I think that I can fairly say that no one wants to work with a diva. When you love what you do then you should simply

51

give 100 percent plus to every rehearsal, every show, every production, and every run. If I have one pet peeve, it is a person with a bad attitude; it is the one thing that can really put me off. And with all the talent out there dying for your gig, it is the one thing that most producers or choreographers will not accept from anyone. Whenever starting a new production or working with a new cast, I always like to make my expectations clear from the get-go. I look at it this way: At the very least I expect the cast and production team to give to me as much as I give to them. I am extremely passionate about my creative work and about the outcome.

There is so much that goes on behind the scenes; so much that the cast is not needed for and oftentimes not privy to. As a choreographer, I like to prepare the majority of my work in advance in order not to waste any precious rehearsal time. Sometimes, when the cast is first arriving to rehearsal, I have already been there for several hours, so it is extremely important to me to get the most out of the time that I have with a cast during rehearsal.

Work ethics and morals are at the top of my list. I want everyone to work hard, and I want everyone to enjoy themselves. When it comes to the gig, I like to keep it simple; I have *three* rules:

1. Always be on time.
2. Check your attitude at the door.
3. Give me 100 percent, *100 percent* of the time.

If we all respect these three simple rules, we will *get on famously!* Not unlike most choreographers, I want to see a great performance; I want to know what I have before me. I want to know what my cast is made of, and I want to know that on opening night they will deliver the goods. I don't think that is too much for any choreographer or director to ask.

It is my responsibility as the creative person—and my mission as a producer or director/choreographer—to always deliver a fabulous show on opening night. I want to know that it's all going to be there. I may be considered by some to be a bit of a taskmaster; however, my intention is never to overtax anyone in rehearsal. It's simply to prepare the best talent and the best shows and, in the end, that will be to everyone's benefit.

If we all give *100 percent*, then I know exactly where we are, what we have to do, and what it will take to get there. I will always keep the show's and cast members' best interests at heart, I will give all that it takes to make you shine on opening night, and all I expect in return is that the cast do the same.

Does that sound like the right attitude to you?

ENCORE:
The right attitude—a positive outlook, that is—is the only kind of attitude to have in this industry.

ATTITUDE ADJUSTMENT

So, let's get back to attitude and asking you to check it at the door. My reason for this is simple: there is no room for it in rehearsal, and I have neither the time nor the patience for bad attitudes and prima donnas. I personally will not tolerate it and know that most people in this business won't. Depending on the size of the production, we could end up living together for the next several weeks or months, and I value my time and life way too much to spend it in bad company.

The rehearsal period and opening of a production are extremely intense processes that are very involved and can be both physically and emotionally exhausting. We spend many long hours together, so it is absolutely essential to have the right blend of personalities in order to form a cohesive group and make for a harmonious time together.

As far as I'm concerned, *everyone in the cast is an equal.* I don't have time for negativity or for any moaning and groaning. If someone is not up to the task, they shouldn't waste my time—or anyone else's, for that matter. We must all have one common goal, and that is to work together to mount the most amazing production possible, one that we can all feel proud of and the cast will love to perform.

What we do is very intimate and specialized; we should be able to enjoy the process. I don't know about you, but I certainly did not go into this business to have a miserable time. I trust that you also chose to go into this business because you wanted to work at something you love.

I don't know too many producers, directors, or choreographers who would want anything less considering the amount of time involved, not to mention the time we spend together in such close quarters. The only people you may spend as much time with, or you may be as intimate with, is a spouse or your family.

I often tell young dancers I work with that the friendships they make today may be friendships that last a lifetime. Some of my dearest friends are people I met through dancing. To this day, some of my best friends are either friends I danced with when we were first starting out in the business or friends I've met along the way.

So attitude is clearly something that transcends both our personal and professional lives. In other words, a positive attitude helps both, while a negative attitude robs one from the other.

53

"BEST FOOT FORWARD"

It's easy for us to lose our good attitudes in a challenging profession, but it's imperative that if you've lost your positivity, you get it back. I've known many a dancer who started out as cheerily optimistic, only to be rejected one too many times and ended up pessimistic and bitter. Maybe that never happened to you, or maybe you're somewhere in the middle.

Either way, I would like you to think back to the very beginning and how this all started. What were your reasons for choosing this profession? I would imagine that it was an undeniable love for dancing, for performing and being on stage. So how do you keep that positivity even when times get tough and jobs are hard to find?

Let me put it in a few words that might help you further on down the line: Do everything within your power to ensure a positive journey. In spite of its ups and downs and complexities, this is a great profession, so be intelligent about your choices and how you handle yourself. Have some fun and enjoy the ride. Your ride is the process, and the process is an integral part of the big picture. Well-traveled, the process can be as great as the final destination. After all, the final destination—however grand—is only one moment in time.

Of course, there will be times that try your patience, and even worse, there will be people who push your buttons. There may be days when you wonder why you do it at all or whether you really have it in you. And that's positively okay; it's normal. It's life and "stuff happens," as they say; just always consider the outcome first.

The truth is that life can and sometimes does deal us what we would consider an unfair hand. It is almost certain that you will have some serious difficulties along the way, so what you must try to do is ease those rough times with a little preventative known as a positive attitude. This way, at least you can be ready for or better equipped to make the most of all that comes your way.

You have the ability to choose how you react in any given situation; make it the right outcome for yourself—and your career. Fast-forward the movie and look ahead at the various possible endings: If I react or behave in a certain manner, this will happen. What are the possible endings? Play the tape through all the way to the end and pick your ending; don't leave it to the audience or, even worse, to chance.

If you don't like the outcome, then make a different choice. Make a better choice—one with a happier ending. This is not to say that if you are in a bad situation, you should just accept it and adjust your attitude. No, of course not. Should you ever find yourself in a compromising situation, then you need to take a closer look at the reality of the circumstances and determine what is right for you.

54

Accept only what you can commit to and will fulfill. Don't ever compromise your integrity; once you *do* commit, be true to your word. Your word is the one thing that no one can ever take away from you. All you can do is have the best outlook possible and go in with great energy and a positive attitude. That, in itself, will always help you make the best choices.

There will be so many choices for you to make along the way—whether it's how you react to a potentially negative situation, or whether it's a decision on what move to make next. This is all part of life; more importantly, this is *your* life. How do you want your role in it to play out? Perhaps you've heard the expression, "It's a small business, don't burn any bridges." I cannot emphasize this strongly enough.

Life is a journey, but don't be afraid to ask for directions. Specifically, if at times you're just not sure what's correct or acceptable, don't be afraid to ask. We are constantly learning throughout our lives; always remain open to the lessons. Be a sponge—learn from everyone and every situation. Take what's good and throw away what's not. Be aware of everything around you, turn on your extra-sensory potential, and be in touch. You are constantly fine-tuning.

A very dear friend and mentor always told me, "It is important in life to be flexible." You mustn't be so rigid in your ways that it interferes with your growth. If you stay flexible, your chances of gaining the most from every experience are much greater. Sometimes, the greatest gifts of all come from those moments that might otherwise be overlooked; fall in love with the surprises along the way. There are often those moments in life when we just can't understand why we are going through something, only to find that, in the end, the outcome is fabulous after all.

You never know what's waiting for you just ahead; positivity opens you up to seeing the good in the bad and knowing the difference between the two. There have been situations in my own career that may not have felt the most pleasant or rewarding at the time. However, I look back on them now and am grateful for the experiences because of the gifts that came with them, often in the form of lifelong relationships.

Don't miss out on an amazing opportunity because of your shortsightedness. Your life will be so much more fruitful, so much more balanced, so much more fulfilled if you always keep a positive attitude and remain open and flexible.

"Life is what we make it, always has been, always will be."
~ **Grandma Moses**

And all that jazz! Cast of the *Constellation*, Celebrity Cruises

Chapter Six

Markets and Venues—Where and How to Find a Gig

"What success I achieved in the theatre is due to the fact that I have always worked just as hard when there were ten people in the house as when there were thousands. Just as hard in Springfield, Illinois as on Broadway."
~ Bill "Bojangles" Robinson

For some of you, this chapter will be a complete revelation; a discovery of what this profession really has to offer you, while others will already be familiar with its content and will have given the industry and its offerings a great deal of thought. You may already know exactly what market or type of venue you want to work in.

You may have your heart set on being in a dance company or on Broadway or in the West End. You may choose Hollywood for the movies, while others will prefer pop videos and tours, not to mention some of the other desirable markets, such as Las Vegas, cruise ships, theme parks and last, but not least, corporate entertainment. Then again, some of you may not want to wander too far from home; you may have aspirations of owning your own studio, or you may be excited at the potential of creating additional opportunities for yourself, right there in your local market.

In this chapter, I will touch on all of these markets and some of the situations you might encounter when working in them. As I said before, show business truly is a great business. It's also a huge industry; but I do believe there is room for anyone who has the passion and determination. It's definitely not the easiest business to be in, but I'm sure you've heard that from other sources as well. The good news is that there are many different markets and types of venues as well as various capacities within the industry in which one can work. It's just a matter of finding your place within it.

Not all dancers solely want to perform; some of you may prefer to be behind the scenes—you may aspire to be a producer, director, or choreographer. Your passion may be in teaching, coaching, or developing talent. Or for some of you, it could be all about production support. You may start out with a strong desire to perform, yet for various reasons, find a new direction or passion along the way. One never knows what hidden talent can be developed or what feelings can be stirred up from the magic of being around show business.

I personally am a "gypsy" at heart and always have been. I absolutely love to dance, but I love to choreograph even more. As far back as I can remember, I believed I was destined to be in show business. I adored performing as a young dancer, and as much as I loved being on stage, I had an equal affinity with the creative and cherished the responsibility of putting it all together. Before I even knew what the word "choreography" meant, I was making up routines at home, a true choreographer in the making. By the time I was twelve years old and training regularly, I was already experimenting with my choreography on other dancers. I had already decided at this young age that this was what I wanted to do in life. The reason I share this with you is simply because I do believe that decisions we make, however young we might be, in the end help determine our destiny.

A male teacher once told me that women do not make good choreographers. Today, with professional choreography credits representing over seventy production revues, hundreds of corporate events, and a smattering of television and film, I say to you, *do not let anyone*, I don't care who they are, take your dreams from you. Was his an attempt to shatter my hopes and dreams or merely a test to see if I had what it takes? It could have been either. The truth is, not everyone you meet will be well-wishers or cheerleaders, but sometimes that opposition or lack of encouragement and support is just what you need to turn things upside down.

ENCORE:
I trust that you also chose to go into this business because you wanted to work at something you love.

THE WORK IS OUT THERE—YOU JUST HAVE TO FIND IT

So, do you know where you are heading, or are you looking for some guidance? Is this something you've given a lot of thought to or are you still searching and not sure what options are really available to you? Following is a list that will help clarify some of your questions.

This list of markets and venues will help you to identify areas in which you can find work as a dancer. I suggest you look it over and give some thought to where you see yourself. What is your forte? What area of performance do you feel most passionate about? Once you've looked over the list, take a moment and create a new list of your own.

Write down the areas that are of interest to you, and make a note of what you like most about each of them. This list can become a useful tool in helping you to make decisions about your career path.

- Broadway and the West End
- Broadway touring companies
- Cabaret
- Community and regional theatre
- Corporate entertainment (conventions, conferences, and trade shows)
- Cruise ships
- Dance companies
- Dinner theatre
- Film and television
- Hotels and resorts
- Las Vegas and other casino or entertainment cities
- Musical revues and variety shows
- Music videos
- Concert tours
- Theme parks

Many young dancers with stars in their eyes have their sights set on the likes of Broadway and Hollywood, and why shouldn't they? Both are huge entertainment capitals and exciting cities. These two markets, along with professional dance companies, are probably by far the most popular and most obvious aspirations for young dancers in the United States. However, as promised, I will introduce you to a plethora of other markets and venues and hopefully create excitement about the many possibilities available to you within this industry. With all of this newfound information and knowledge, you will be able to make informed choices about where you might want to live, the business, and your place within it.

NEW YORK VERSUS LOS ANGELES: A TALE OF TWO CITIES

New York City and Los Angeles are two very exciting cities and incredible markets for dancers, both buzzing with mind-boggling energy and more than enough to satiate any performer's appetite. However exciting they both are, New York City and Los Angeles are extremely different from each other. First of all, they have two very different main entertainment markets, i.e. stage in New York City versus film and television in Los Angeles. Secondly, the lifestyles are as opposite as "chalk and cheese." A. L. Gordon, of *The New York Sun*, said, "New Yorkers revel in good works and historic institutions. In Los Angeles, people revel in the beauty, clothing, love affairs, and talent of the entertainment industry." This common belief translates into the dance world as well; some teachers tend to encourage their students to choose New York City over Los Angeles, intimating that New York City has more to offer the serious dancer, while Los Angeles is about trends, glamour, and glitz. For this very reason I will compare the two, and I will also follow this with a third entertainment city that is often overlooked when making career choices, Las Vegas. Having worked and lived in all three cities, I can tell you that each has much to offer. At the end of the day, it all comes down to your personal tastes, needs, and desires. What are your career goals, what are your personal goals, and what does each city have to offer you in relationship to those goals? What your heart longs for first and foremost is ultimately what you must pursue.

NEW YORK CITY

New York City and Broadway are synonymous. Loaded with culture and diversity, New York is a fabulous destination plain and simple, but for a singer, dancer, or actor, it can be the ultimate destination. Why is it that the Broadway stage always beckons even the most accomplished and highly sought after Hollywood movie stars? "Home sweet home," and just as the stage is home to actors, it is also home to dancers. It's where we started out, and it's where we gained our first experiences. I believe that there is no greater sensation or more gratifying recognition than an audience's applause. Nothing can truly replace the exhilaration of a live performance, especially on *Broadway*!

As I am completing this book, there are currently forty Broadway theatres. There are currently twenty-six musicals and fifteen plays on Broadway. Off-Broadway and off-off Broadway theatres will present well over 100 different productions, some with short runs ranging from two weeks to six weeks, and a few with longer runs ranging from three months to twelve months. The

Broadway League is the trade association of the Broadway industry. Its members consist of theatre owners and operators, producers, presenters, and general managers of Broadway and touring Broadway productions as well as suppliers to this industry. To learn more about the Broadway League you can visit their website at www.broadwayleague.com. According to the league's end-of-season statistics for the 2010-2011 Broadway season (which began May 24, 2010 and ended May 29, 2011), forty-two new productions opened on Broadway—fourteen new musicals, twenty-five new plays, and three specials.

LOS ANGELES

Hollywood, with its celebrities and all the glamour, can be very enticing; the idea of rubbing elbows with "the who's who—the cream of the crop" can be rather alluring. One most often chooses Los Angeles when his or her interests lean more toward film and television or music videos and concert tours. With the whole world having a newfound love affair with dance thanks to those shows I mentioned earlier—*So You Think You Can Dance* and *Dancing with the Stars*—Los Angeles is certainly an exciting place to be. Not only have we seen so many dance-related reality TV shows over the last few years, but many advertisers are featuring dancers in their television commercials. Just as live work brings great exhilaration and a sense of accomplishment, so does seeing yourself on the big screen. Let's face it—most people would love the opportunity. For many it would be a dream come true.

ENCORE:
New York City and Los Angeles are two very exciting cities and incredible markets for dancers, both buzzing with mind-boggling energy and more than enough to satiate any performer's appetite.

LAS VEGAS

When you think of Las Vegas, you might think of casinos and variety shows or hundreds of showgirls in larger-than-life musical extravaganzas. Las Vegas is all that and more. It is a huge entertainment city with a great market for all types of performers; a place that aspiring performers relocate to all the time. (Though other gambling cities may also have live entertainment, they simply do not have as much work to offer. Dancers don't usually relocate to these smaller centers in the hopes of finding work, but rather move there for a particular contract.)

Las Vegas is home to forty-plus headliners and approximately fifty production shows, including several *Cirque du Soleil*–style shows. However, it doesn't stop there; Vegas has also been the West Coast home to several Broadway shows. There have been many attempts to bring Broadway to the Las Vegas Strip, some of which have been more successful than others. *Avenue Q*, Steve Wynn's first big attempt at bringing the Broadway musical to Vegas, opened at Wynn Las Vegas and closed after a nine-month run. Steve Wynn is one of the world's most famous casino and resort developers, credited with spearheading the expansion of the Las Vegas Strip back in the 1990s. Next, *Hairspray* ran for only four months at the Luxor in 2007. *Mamma Mia!* however, holds the record as the longest running Broadway show in Vegas. It ran almost six years at the Mandalay Bay and closed at the end of summer 2008. May 2009 brought a new "King" to town and his name was Simba. Disney's *The Lion King*, a true phenomenon on stage, played at the Mandalay Bay for two years and seven months. Its farewell performance was on December 30, 2011. *Phantom* has been reconceived for the Las Vegas Strip and is playing at The Venetian in a $40 million custom-built theatre. It opened in 2006. *Jersey Boys* took up residency at the Palazzo and enjoyed great success. Last, but certainly not least, Broadway's award-winning smash hit *Spamalot* had a very successful fifteen-month run at the Wynn Las Vegas and closed July 13, 2008. Also in the lineup are a few off-Broadway hits, *Stomp Out Loud*, a newer, bigger version than the original *Stomp*, *Blue Man Group*, and *Menopause the Musical*. Although the complete fate of Broadway shows in Las Vegas has not yet been determined, the attempts to give theatre its place out West persist.

There are currently seven *Cirque du Soleil* shows playing: *O, Mystère, Zumanity, The Beatles LOVE, Ka*, and more recently added: *Criss Angel – Believe* and *Viva Elvis*. Michael Jackson – *The World Immortal Tour* was scheduled for Vegas in December 2011, and last but certainly not least is the *Cirque*-style show, *Le Rêve*. These are all extravagant productions performed in multi-million dollar theatres built to specification. A certain extent of *Cirque's* popularity was brought on, in part, by a need for something new and innovative, and it is absolutely fabulous what they have done. The intense demand and interest that has been created is absolutely genius.

With so many *Cirque*-style shows in town, there may not be quite as much work for dancers right now, but no one can dispute that Las Vegas certainly still offers it all. It offers you everything from showgirls to trapeze artists, magicians to comedians, impressionists to impersonators, and musical theatre to huge celebrities such as Elton John, Cher, Prince, Janet Jackson, Tim McGraw, and Gwen Stefani, to name just a few. Dancers who choose to pursue work in either musical theatre or revue type work can find themselves equally at home. If you love the excitement of a city built around entertainment, Las Vegas could be just the city for you.

WHERE WILL YOU LAND?

Regardless of whether you are deciding between New York City and Los Angeles or considering any other city, I want to point out some very real concerns that you must address when planning any potential relocation. Since there is no guarantee that you'll get the first Broadway show, musical revue, feature film, or music video you audition for, you must consider the following:

1. How will you live while waiting for the perfect gig to come along?
2. How will you survive between gigs?

Let's face it, the glamour of show business will fade quite quickly if you are consistently redefining the "starving artist" role. We will discuss more on that topic a little later in our "No More Starving Artist" chapter.

You may want to have your pen and paper handy; here are a few more key questions you should ask yourself:

- Do you have any friends or relatives living in the city or cities that you are considering who could help make your transition a little easier?
- How much money will you need to make the move?
- How much money will you need to survive until you find steady work?
- What job skills other than dance do you possess?
- What is the average cost of living, and what can you anticipate spending on an apartment?
- Will you live on your own or share an apartment with fellow performers?
- Where will you study? Do you have your heart set on studying with any specific teachers or at any particular studios? There is certainly no shortage of great teachers on either coast; many are even bi-coastal.
- What will your monthly training costs be? Consider all classes—dance, acting, and vocal.
- What will transportation to and from auditions and classes cost?

63

Obviously, these are all good considerations whenever relocating from home. Not all aspiring talent is lucky enough to grow up in a city, let alone an entertainment city! Many aspiring performers must relocate in order to pursue their dreams. It is important to have a solid plan, and considering the above questions carefully can help you to strategize how you will get there and how you will survive. This pre-planning will give you the optimal shot at success.

ENCORE:

Let's face it, the glamour of show business will fade quite quickly if you are consistently redefining the "starving artist" role.

CITY LIGHTS

Having grown up in Northern Ontario, I decided to move to Toronto at nineteen years of age to pursue my career in dance. I knew that in order to fulfill my dreams of working as a professional dancer and choreographer, I had to leave my hometown and move to the "city." My goals had been long determined; I was excited for the adventure, but sad to be leaving my family. Once in Toronto, the first thing I did was get myself into dance classes at the best and most popular studios in town. This was great; I immediately started meeting other dancers and finding out who was who. Who were the working choreographers, and which were the best local production companies? I would constantly check the audition postings at the studios as well as the weekly entertainment columns in the various newspapers. I quickly learned which magazine was the number one place to find audition notices, and between word of mouth and these notices, I was soon off on every audition that had the word dance in it.

Now as you make your final decision, I remind you to be honest with yourself. No one knows you better than you, and it is you who must consider what positions you can slot into most comfortably and most naturally based on your talent type and your goals. One of the big differences between New York City and Los Angeles is the different type of work that each city has to offer and, consequently, the different types of talent recruited for that work.

If you haven't already done so, it would be a good idea to subscribe in advance to several of the "industry rags" or periodicals. This can help you to identify and learn about prospective agents, studios, dance companies, and various production companies, in addition to the obvious: "What is happening in the industry?" "Who is holding auditions?" and "What new shows are coming to town?" *Backstage* has been the New York actors' resource for over forty-five years and has two different publications, *Backstage East* (New York City) and

Backstage West (Los Angeles). Once known as *Dirt Alert, Callback News* covers the industry happenings in Las Vegas. And a newer online service called VegasAuditions.com is well-regarded by industry professionals. For any of you living in Europe, *The Stage* publication, which covers the industry throughout Europe and predominantly London, has long been the number one resource for dancers. *Dance* magazine, for the young dancer and professional dancer, has been an industry leader since 1927, and *Dance Spirit*, their newer addition, is known as the young dancer's resource. Both offer an excess of educational and informative articles to help keep you in the know. These industry resources can also be accessed online. Additionally, there are numerous Internet-only resources that are great ways to find out what is going on in the industry.

These materials, along with an honest and fair consideration of the above questions, should give you a reasonably clear indication of the market you are best suited for and which one will offer you the most longevity. Keep in mind some of what we discussed in earlier chapters on the importance of being a triple threat. Clearly, as a triple threat, you not only create more diversity and, therefore, broaden your markets, but you also increase your career opportunities. Think about who you see on Broadway and who you see doing the latest concert tours and music videos. Are you that type? Do you see yourself working in that market? These are important questions, and you need to consider all of them when making your decisions.

Although much emphasis has been placed on New York City and Los Angeles, these are by no means the only significant markets; as prefaced earlier, they are simply the two largest and most popularized dance markets. There is an entire dance and performing arts world waiting for you to discover, and you need only read on!

ENCORE:
No one knows you better than you, and it is you who must consider what positions you can slot into most comfortably and most naturally based on your talent type and your goals. Be completely honest with yourself.

GIVE ME SOMEBODY TO DANCE FOR

When it comes to seeking employment with specific venues or independent production companies, do your homework first, as you should in any situation. Some venues that have ongoing or long-running shows will hire independent production companies to produce their shows, while others will produce them in-house. More often than not, when holding open auditions, such venues and/ or production companies will post their audition notices at various dance studios as well as advertise in trade papers, magazines, and on various casting or audition websites. Some may choose to go through casting directors or call on talent and dance agents directly.

Today there are many sites that post auditions; you can find them by simply doing a search online for castings, auditions, or dance jobs. Keep in mind that the various publications mentioned previously will often have an Internet presence as well, and it is always good to go with those most trusted sources first—those that have been around for many years and/or those endorsed by trusted sources and sponsors. When considering a new website, if there is a contact number call to find out how they verify the accuracy of such postings and their advertisers.

Many production companies will accept photos and resumes throughout the year. They may also accept video/DVD submissions to have on hand in the event of a need for a sudden replacement. Some companies have been known to handle their entire casting needs via snail mail or email, hence cutting the costs of live auditions.

Prior to sending out a promo package or photo and resume, it is always a good idea to make a phone call to introduce yourself first. A dancer would normally be expected to send out a photo and resume. A choreographer, a director, a specialty act, a performing group, or a production company are a few examples of those who would send out promotional packages when soliciting new clients or business. Such promo packages might include a DVD and bio, press reviews, and any special promo pieces. This would normally be packaged in a press kit folder, with a cover letter to introduce the act, the group, or the company. And today with so much business taking place online, many people will only accept promo packages or photos and résumés in electronic format.

When calling to introduce yourself, you should ask if there is an entertainment director, a head choreographer, or an in-house person in charge of casting with whom you can speak. Find out if they accept talent submissions via mail, and if so, to whom your submission should be addressed. This call will give you the opportunity to establish personal contact and identify a secretary or administrative assistant should you be unable to speak directly to the person in charge. For future calls, an established contact can go a long way; you will be able to address the person directly and remind her or him of your initial call, thereby creating some affinity. My advice to you is to be polite, courteous, and respectful at all times when dealing with people and to always be appreciative of any assistance given to you. You always want to make a good impression, especially on the person answering the telephone. Our business is so personable, and first impressions are very important. Your attitude can make it or break it; it can be the deciding factor as to whether your call gets put through to the person in charge or whether you come up against a roadblock. And, of course, this last bit of advice applies to any and all contacts you make, regardless of the market or venue: You must always present yourself in the most professional manner. On that topic, I would like to add a side note—do not allow your professionalism to be influenced or altered negatively by the lack of respect that we see so often on television today in certain reality TV shows. Although the over-the-top auditions in the early stages of some of these shows may sell airtime, the truth is, if anyone ever spoke to a producer that way (the cursing, talking back, and belligerence as so many of these contestants are encouraged to do), they not only would get themselves thrown out of the audition, but there is a great chance that they would *never* work in the industry. Sensationalism may get John Q. Public interested from season to season, but it just doesn't cut it in the real world, so don't believe for one second that this demeaning and often ridiculous behavior you see in the early stages of some of these shows is normal or acceptable.

ENCORE:
When it comes to seeking employment with specific venues or independent production companies, always do your homework first.

DANCE AGENTS AND TALENT AGENTS

Although we will discuss agents in further detail in our "No More Starving Artist" chapter, I would like to take this opportunity to mention the tremendous role that agents can play in your career. As they relate to markets and venues, there is no greater resource than an agent to find you work. Yes, many auditions are advertised, and open calls are exactly that—open to the public—but there are a great number of castings that go on every day that a dancer without agency representation would not be privy to.

Plain and simple is the fact that some production companies have no interest in going outside the inner circle. Therefore, dance agents and talent agents play an important role in our industry and can play an important role in landing many of the jobs we are discussing in this very chapter.

As you will see throughout this chapter, the topic of markets and venues is very much intertwined. Most large entertainment cities will have an assortment of venues, all with varied entertainment needs. What follows is an overview of the most often pursued commercial markets, in addition to the cities outlined earlier.

ENCORE:

There is no greater resource than an agent to find you work.

CORPORATE ENTERTAINMENT

Most large cities, especially tourist and convention destinations, have a vast corporate entertainment market. Las Vegas and Orlando are great examples of such cities, as they both thrive on their tourism and their convention business. Therefore, there is a need for corporate entertainment, and that can be a very lucrative market for you, the performer. For those of you who are not familiar with corporate entertainment companies, these are production companies that provide entertainment to various corporate clients.

This could mean anything from a new product launch to business theatre, or an awards presentation and a gala evening. The clients can be as diverse as a group of doctors, to an automobile company or a chain of grocery stores, to a software company. Your job as a performer might involve introducing new products through song and dance, meeting and greeting guests, presenting awards, or performing in a full-blown musical revue for a company's or an organization's final gala celebration. You may be involved in only one aspect of the convention, conference, or trade show, or you may be involved in various activities throughout the weeklong meetings, seminars, or sessions. The shows are often fun and always upbeat. They may not always be the most challenging artistically, but they will usually be enjoyable. And, obviously, the better the production company, the better the production. Rehearsals and the performances can run from as little as a few days to a few weeks, depending on the client, the size of the show, and the nature of the presentation.

As a young dancer, I did a great deal of corporate entertainment work between long-running shows. Some corporate work was during daytime hours, which was a bonus as I was often able to do both, the corporate gig and my evening show. When a contract was coming to an end, I would start planning ahead. I would contact the various corporate entertainment companies to let them know that I would be available for work or to find out if there were any auditions coming up. I first contacted those companies by telephone that I had already been working with, and then sent out promotional materials to new companies I had not yet worked for. This way, I was not only securing work through my usual channels, but I was also making new contacts for future opportunities. I have always enjoyed working in corporate entertainment. As a dancer, there were always new shows to learn, which made it interesting, and it kept me busy performing when I didn't have a steady show. As a choreographer, they kept me busy creating a variety of new material.

Unfortunately, there is no one industry resource that will list all corporate entertainment production companies. So put on your thinking caps; this is where you get to be creative networkers and promoters. Your best bet is always to learn of these companies from fellow dancers, choreographers, and through the studios. This will allow you to learn more about them and verify their reputations through tried and true experiences of others.

It goes without saying that the Internet has become the number one resource for information worldwide; once again, you just need to be creative with your searches. Especially if you don't know anyone in the industry, this is a great place to start. There is no limit to what you can access online. And such companies can be found under different headings: production companies, entertainment production companies, entertainment agencies and bureaus, talent agencies, and several other entertainment-related headings. Although this is a very good starting point, I must warn you that you will need to check them out through other reputable sources in the business. At the very least, you will want to call the companies in order to determine what type of work they do and whether or not they even employ performers, specifically dancers. If they hire dancers, make sure you are clear on what kind of dancers they hire.

I learned that lesson very early on, and although my example comes from having answered an ad in the local newspaper, the point of the lesson is nevertheless the same. Having just arrived in the city and eager to get to work, I responded to an audition notice looking for dancers. However when I arrived at the venue and was greeted by a cocktail server wearing a thong and a couple of pasties, I quickly gathered that they were looking for a *different* type of dancer. Needless to say, I hightailed it out of there. At that moment, I promised myself to do my homework and to check things out before wasting my time going to every call that said "dancers wanted."

FYI—"production company" can mean everything from stage builders to video production, while the title "entertainment company" or "entertainment agency" can mean anything from show producers to escort services. So be sure to check them out. Some production companies that do use dancers in their presentations may often refer to outside sources for hiring this talent; i.e. casting agents, dance agents and managers, and/or dance companies and studios. So again, do your homework thoroughly.

Production guides, which are known predominantly as resources for film, television, and commercial work, will sometimes list corporate entertainment producers under their "production companies" category with different subheadings, such as live events or corporate events. You may also find some production companies listed under meeting planners and party planners.

Most importantly, if you are new to a city, pick up the local industry paper, see what auditions are going on, and get yourself to class and start meeting other dancers. This method alone can be the most valuable means of getting to know the business. It will be a wonderful network for you to tap into immediately and get to know your new market, as well as make some friends. From there, you should find out which choreographers are doing most of the work and see if they are teaching any classes or workshops; then attend them.

ENCORE:

It goes without saying that the Internet has become the number one resource for information worldwide; once again, you just need to be creative with your searches.

MUSICAL REVUES AND VARIETY SHOWS

Musical revues and variety shows represent a very large market as there are so many different venues in which these shows can be presented. This genre is a personal favorite of mine. I've spent the last twenty-five years choreographing and directing musical revues throughout the United States and abroad. I love this genre of production because of its variety and the versatility of the material. If you enjoy a wide range of music and styles of dance, then these shows can be great fun and might just be perfect for you.

In any one revue, you could find yourself covering material from your favorite Broadway show to your favorite pop star's repertoire. And the markets and venues are often just as varied. Some contracts will offer great travel opportunities and exciting experiences; i.e., a touring company, a cruise ship, or an engagement abroad. Each venue or production company will have its own contract standards and lengths of runs. Often, you will be hired as an employee, rather than an independent contractor, when signing on with a large corporation for a long-running show. When dealing with major corporations such as some of the big hotel chains or theme parks, you may also receive employee benefits. The following is a list of some of the types of venues in which you will find musical revues and/or variety shows:

Resorts, Hotels, and Showrooms

Many hotels and resorts, especially those in tourist destinations, have showrooms and theatres that present long-running musical revues or variety shows. These venues can be found all over the world.

In the United States, you have several gambling or entertainment cities; the mecca, of course, being Las Vegas which has more than 100 casinos. Other popular gambling cities that are also known for their entertainment are: Atlantic City, New Jersey; South Lake Tahoe, California; Reno, Nevada; Laughlin, Nevada; and Mashantucket, Connecticut (home of Foxwoods Resort and Casino) and Uncasville, Connecticut (home of Mohegan Sun Casino).

There are more than 700 cities in the United States with casinos. Now that's not to say that every casino will have a show, but you can be sure that a great percentage will have some form of entertainment. This should give you an idea of how vast the employment opportunities truly are.

The city of Branson, Missouri, is a huge entertainment market with over sixty shows in town—everything from magic shows to country-western style productions, celebrity artists to musical revues. Branson is all about the entertainment; there is no gambling.

Myrtle Beach, South Carolina, and Pigeon Forge, Tennessee, are also great destination cities. Myrtle Beach is full of golf resorts and numerous entertainment venues, while Pigeon Forge is more of a family vacation destination with several theatres dedicated to family entertainment.

Theme Parks

In this section, I will mention a few of the largest and most popular theme parks. Many dancers who have worked for me have spent years working in these establishments. The reviews are often mixed. Some dancers absolutely love it; these are the dancers who stay on for years, while others may do one contract and not care to return. Working in a theme park can be a fabulous ongoing gig. However, it can also be very demanding. You probably will work long days doing several shows per day, often outdoors, in very hot temperatures. But looking on the brighter side, this can be an incredible way to earn a steady livelihood and a terrific experience living somewhere new and exciting, and meeting people from all over the world. You will be performing daily while gaining invaluable experience that you will take with you throughout your career. What great fun to be able to do what you love and get paid for it! For some, these gigs will be a stepping stone, and for others, a place they are happy to settle into and call home. As you can see, working in a theme park can be very rewarding for many reasons.

You are generally hired as an employee, not as an independent contractor. As an employee, you are most likely eligible for a benefits package. These benefits will vary and can be determined by the number of hours in a workweek or the amount of time you have worked for the company. There are usually different levels with different packages.

In the United States, the opposite of being hired as an employee (W-2 tax form) is to be hired as an independent contractor (1099 tax form). There are certain guidelines that dictate this classification. If you meet these guidelines and are hired as an independent contractor, you are responsible for yourself. You will be responsible for filing and paying your own taxes, and very often, you will also be responsible for your own health insurance. As an independent contractor, you have the ability to act as your own company, and you will have many deductions that can help reduce the amount of taxes you pay. Deductions such as the cost of travel to and from work, makeup, dancewear, and classes are just a few. I discuss the advantages of working as an independent contractor in greater detail in "Chapter Twelve: No More Starving Artist," and "Chapter Fourteen: Money Makes the World Go Round."

Some theme parks will allow you to swing out of shows as long as your track (your position or part) is covered. Some companies promote this as a way to keep cast members long-term. They understand that a little flexibility keeps things interesting and fresh. As long as the show does not suffer and your position is adequately filled, they encourage a little moonlighting. Some will even allow you to take a leave of absence. This is a very nice bonus in the event that another great opportunity comes along. What a wonderful incentive to know that you can always come back to steady work!

Don't lose sight of the fact that you are doing what you love and that you have steady employment, which is not too shabby in this business. But don't get caught up with the paycheck unless it comes with happiness and fulfillment. Always remember why you went into this business. I find nothing more heartbreaking than seeing talent wasted or turned bitter. I am not saying that you shouldn't take a job for the steady paycheck and wonderful perks that it offers; on the contrary, these are all excellent reasons to take the job. What you mustn't do is grow tired, stale, or bitter. I believe that as long as you keep your attitude in check, always look for the good in every situation, and create an excitement for yourself with every new performance, you can have the best of both worlds: doing what you love and earning a steady paycheck. And for the record, that goes for any job you take. After all, there's so much to love about what you do. Never compromise your integrity, your employer, the business, or the audience by putting yourself in a situation in which you cannot fulfill your obligations.

Here is a list of theme parks you may want to consider researching and learning more about. As you will see, some of them have several locations, and I have listed them with the name of the group or corporation in bold type.

- **Busch Gardens:**
  Tampa, Florida
  Williamsburg, Virginia
- **Cedar Fair, L.P. & Paramount Parks:**
  California's Great America—Santa Clara, California
  Carowinds—Charlotte, North Carolina
  Cedar Point—Sandusky, Ohio
  Dorney Park and Wild Water Kingdom—Allentown, Pennsylvania
  Gilroy Gardens—Gilroy, California
  Kings Dominion—Doswell, Virginia (near Richmond)
  Kings Island—Kings Mills, Ohio (near Cincinnati)
  Knott's Berry Farms—Buena Park, California (near Los Angeles)
  Michigan's Adventure—Muskegon, Michigan
  Valleyfair—Shakopee, Minnesota (near Minneapolis-St. Paul)
  Wildwater Kingdom—Aurora, Ohio
  Worlds of Fun and Oceans of Fun—Kansas City, Missouri
- **Cedar Fair International:**
  Canada's Wonderland—just outside of Toronto
- **Disney Parks:**
  Disneyland Resort—Anaheim, California
      Disneyland Park
      Disney California Adventure Park
  Walt Disney World Resort—Lake Buena Vista, Florida
      Magic Kingdom
      Epcot Center
      Disney's Hollywood Studios (formerly known as Disney-MGM Studios)

Disney's Animal Kingdom
Tokyo Disney Resort—Urayasu, Chiba, Japan
Disneyland
Disney Sea
Disneyland Resort Paris—Marne La Valle, France
Disneyland
Walt Disney Studios
Hong Kong Disneyland—Penny's Bay, Lantau Island
Shanghai Disney Resort—Pudong, Shanghai (Scheduled to open 2016)

- **Dollywood:**
  Pigeon Forge, Tennessee
- **Hershey Park:**
  Hershey, Pennsylvania
- **SeaWorld:**
  Orlando, Florida
  San Antonio, Texas
  San Diego, California
- **Six Flags:**
  California
    Six Flags Discovery Kingdom—Vallejo
    Six Flags Magic Mountain—Los Angeles
  Georgia
    Six Flags Over Georgia—Atlanta
  Illinois
    Six Flags Great America—Gurnee (near Chicago)
  Maryland
    Six Flags America—Baltimore
  Massachusetts
    Six Flags New England—Springfield
  Missouri
    Six Flags St. Louis—St. Louis
  New Jersey
    Six Flags Great Adventure—Jackson
    Six Flags Wild Safari—Jackson
  New York
    The Great Escape and Splash Water Kingdom—Lake George
  Texas

Six Flags Fiesta Texas—San Antonio
Six Flags Over Texas—Arlington
- **Six Flags International:**
  Canada—La Ronde, Montreal
  Mexico—Six Flags Mexico, Mexico City
- **Universal Studios:**
  Universal Studios Orlando—Orlando, Florida
  Universal's Island of Adventure and The Wizarding World of Harry
  Potter—Orlando, Florida
  Universal Studios Hollywood—Universal City, California
  Universal Studios Japan—Osaka, Japan

As you can see, the list is endless. There are theme parks throughout the United States, some larger than others, all offering multiple shows. Aside from Disney, Paramount, and Six Flags, I haven't even touched on the international market of theme parks. The bottom line is that there is no shortage of theme parks for anyone interested in opportunities in this type of venue.

CRUISE LINES

Cruise lines employ staff from around the world and, therefore, are accustomed to all that it takes to obtain any necessary visas or work permits. Should you need a visa or work permit, depending on your citizenship, the ship's country of origin, or your travel itinerary, the cruise line will be able to guide you and assist you with any process necessary.

The cruise ship industry is one of the fastest growing industries today. Over the past fifteen years, I have done a great deal of work with the cruise industry. I have worked for several lines and watched the industry grow. In the past ten to twelve years, it has grown by leaps and bounds, with every cruise line trying to outdo the other. It's a bit like keeping up with the Joneses: who will have the latest and the greatest? Each new ship is more luxurious and spectacular than the last. The entertainment facilities on board some of these ships are not to be believed. The theatres are state-of-the-art with every special effect and gimmick available today, from hydraulic stages to intelligent lighting. The scenic elements even rival some of the grandest Disney productions and Broadway stages.

Having said this, you should be aware that not all ships are equal. There are some smaller ships that also have lovely showrooms and theatres, but they may not be on as grand a scale as the newer, larger ships. Then you have some of the more luxurious cruise liners which are, in fact, known for their smaller ships. There are older ships, both small and large, which will normally have more standard showrooms. All ships and contracts offer different experiences. Some staff members much prefer the smaller lines or ships as there is a comfortable and often friendlier atmosphere. Others prefer the larger or more lavish ships for their size and grand showrooms.

As always, you must do your homework and get to know your ships and cruise lines. The industry is so huge today; if you are interested in auditioning for, or have been offered a contract with a cruise line, it is very easy for you to access information about the company and even the ship itself. Chances are, if you don't know someone who has worked on board, someone you know will. So ask around, and make sure you speak to several people. You want as much feedback as possible on individual experiences with a variety of cruise lines. As a mentor once told me, one person can be wrong but an audience never is.

From a performer's viewpoint, working on a cruise ship can be a very enticing prospect with all that ships have to offer: steady work with contracts that range anywhere from six to nine months, free food and accommodations, very few expenses, travel with exciting itineraries to foreign and exotic places, and a variety of shows from Broadway style to rock and roll and everything in between. As with theme parks, theatres, and some showrooms, you have the opportunity to do multiple contracts, though not necessarily always back-to-back. Life on board can be very demanding, and most cruise lines understand the importance of having a break from life at sea. If you enjoy the work and you do a great job, you can always have future work. For some people, working on a cruise ship is an ideal situation; they do a six-month contract, take a break, and come back again. Some performers choose to stay with one cruise line and will move around from ship to ship and itinerary to itinerary, while others will work for a variety of cruise lines. Just as all ships are not created equal, nor are their contracts.

Some cruise ship companies are better than others to work for. They can be as different as night and day. Some produce their own shows in-house, while others contract independent production companies. As a result of the numerous variables, not all shows are of the same standard. From what I have seen, some onboard productions, whether produced in-house or by outside producers, can be fabulous, while others can be mediocre. Of course, this does not apply to the cruise ship industry alone; it applies to show business, in general.

Most importantly, remember to do your homework; I cannot emphasize this enough. Learn about the business you want to be in. Who are the top producers and the best cruise lines to work for? A lot of what I am pointing out here applies to the industry at large. Which are the best cruise lines, the best Las Vegas showrooms, the best theatres, the best theme parks, and the best corporate entertainment companies? *Which are they?* Ask around, read the reviews and company profiles, get to know who is producing what and where. Who are the people you want to work for? The more you know about this industry the better equipped you will be to make intelligent choices, which will allow you to improve your overall performance and to gain the best experiences.

I will tell you exactly what I have told countless numbers of dancers and singers who have worked for me on board various ships. Working on a cruise ship is a completely different venue than any other venue you will work in. Life on board is not for everyone. Some people love it and make entire careers out of performing from one ship to the next, while others simply cannot adhere to the conformity of onboard life or handle the confinement of a ship. A ship that appears overwhelming in size when you first step on board will, over time, become smaller and smaller. Then there is always the consideration of motion sickness. Not everyone is a good sailor; not everyone can handle the motion of the ocean. I have had some people work for me who just never got used to it, while others were never affected by it.

If you are not one who likes rules and regulations, you probably will not appreciate the military structure and attitude of the cruise ship. Since life at sea is not to be taken lightly, there are many safety rules and regulations, as well as training and responsibilities that could be a mandatory part of your contract. Some cruise lines may include cruise-staff duties in your contract; some companies pay you extra for these additional duties, while others don't. Some companies do not require cruise-staff duties from any of their performers. The bottom line is, if you are offered a contract, make sure to read it thoroughly, ask questions and clarify. Know and understand what you are getting into.

I've had some wonderful experiences working at sea; I've also had some not so wonderful ones. But as you're about to find out, some of my greatest memories and life-changing moments are all thanks to ships. After all, this is how I met my husband! So, as I've said on many occasions, be grateful for all experiences, for you never know what gifts they bear or what lies just ahead. I've been very fortunate to have produced, directed, and choreographed my work on some incredible ships, with some exceptional theatres and showrooms. I have also had the great pleasure of working with some fabulous creative people and some extremely talented performers. I've enjoyed many fantastic moments, both in and out of rehearsals, while putting on these various productions. Some of my favorite people and memories are from my time in the cruise industry.

77

As I've told countless performers, I do think that working on ships can be an excellent experience. Aside from the steady work and travel opportunities, one of the best aspects of all is the family-like ties that you create. It's your home away from home, and you will build friendships that can last a lifetime. To this day, many performers who have worked for me are still the best of friends with each other ten and fifteen years later. It's always such a pleasure to hear that one of them is coming through town and the old gang is planning a get-together. Whenever I travel back to New York City, Los Angeles, England, or Canada to hold auditions, I always manage a get-together with those same special friends of mine who live there.

One thing that I haven't mentioned yet is rehearsals, and in the case of cruise ships, just how grueling they can sometimes be. Then again, I don't want to put you off entirely. After all, the purpose of this information is to enlighten you as to the many wonderful opportunities. I will say this, though: just be prepared to work hard. The rehearsals can seem endless, especially when you are rehearsing on board, and every day you arrive in a new port only to watch the passengers disembark as you head to the showroom. This is sometimes the only opportunity you have to work on the stage as rehearsal space and time can be limited. There is a ship full of passengers needing to be entertained, as well as other artists who must also rehearse. Keep in mind that once the shows are up and running, you will have plenty of time to enjoy these lovely ports of call.

Always remember this; you get out of life what you put in, and the same applies to your work. If you are going to perform a show night after night, I am certain that you want it to be a fabulous show, one that you can be proud to be a part of. As the saying goes, "Practice (or in our case, rehearsal) makes perfect" and a well-rehearsed show and timely opening make for a smooth run and a very happy choreographer.

The following is a list of several (but not all) of the most popular cruise lines:

- Carnival Cruise Lines
- Celebrity Cruises
- Costa Cruises
- Cunard Line
- Crystal Cruises
- Disney Cruise Line
- Holland America Line
- Norwegian Cruise Line
- Princess Cruises

- Regent Seven Seas Cruises (formerly known as Radisson Seven Seas Cruises)
- Royal Caribbean Cruise Lines
- Silversea Cruises

ENCORE:

If you are offered a contract, make sure to read it thoroughly, ask questions and clarify. Know and understand what you are getting into.

CROSSOVER IN MARKETS AND VENUES

Many of the same types of shows that you could be hired for will cross over into different markets and venues. For example, the many musical revues (or Las Vegas–style revues as they are sometimes referred to) will be found in various markets and venues, from gambling cities to tourist destinations around the world, whether in a small cabaret-style room or a large several thousand-seat theatre.

When it comes to theatre, other than the obvious markets of Broadway, the West End in London, and, of course, the theatre districts in some of the larger cities across the United States and Canada, there are additional opportunities in local dinner theatre and regional theatre.

Film, television, and commercials are not only produced in Hollywood, although it certainly is the mecca. There are many other major cities in which you can pursue this genre of work; it's just that there won't be as much work produced. Chances are, there won't be as large a pool of talent vying for the same roles, either. I'm sure that by now you get the idea of the crossover in both markets and venues available to you.

Last, but certainly not least, I will touch lightly on the various types of jobs in which one can work within our industry. After all, not everyone who is captured by the industry's magic grows up wanting to be on the stage. You may have aspirations of becoming a director, choreographer, or producer, teacher, agent, or manager. You may have additional talents and creative abilities in other areas of the business, such as costume design, makeup artistry, music, writing, lighting and audio design, or scenic design. Each of these departments offers yet another list of possibilities, from assistants to all of these various positions mentioned above, to stage managers, dressers, and various stylists.

The world of entertainment and show business is such a fascinating business to be involved in that I want all of you who have a love for it to be aware of all the opportunities that it holds. And very important is to know how truly wonderful these opportunities can be, and how significant your role will be, whether you choose to be onstage or offstage, in production support, or the producer. No production can come to realization and be a spectacular work of art without the team. And every team player is of equal importance.

Las Vegas, Los Angeles, Hollywood, and New York City have all, at various times, been known as "the entertainment capital of the world." Where will your dreams take you? Wherever your passion lies, whichever genre or specialty you choose, do it for all of the right reasons and chances are you will have a fabulous experience.

NOTES

It's not just about the steps; it's about the whole package. Script and vocal study, Opryland Productions, Nashville, Tennessee

Chapter Seven
The Audition—What It Takes to Get the Gig

"The more auditions you go on, the more you will learn not to take it personally."
~ Paula Abdul

It is my sincere desire to help educate and prepare you for the audition process and the career possibilities that lie ahead. I aspire to teach the do's and don'ts, what to expect, how to present yourself, and how to have the best shot at a career in dance. We've all been there; we've all been in your shoes before.

We know how scary the other side of that table can be, all the while having to contend with your own fan club or not-so fan club, the cheering, heckling, bashing, and berating, as you stand there trying desperately to remain calm, cool, and collected while not letting them see you sweat.

You know the fan club I'm talking about—those thousands of little voices in your head telling you: "They love me." "They hate me." "Why did I come here?" "What do they think of me?" "What are they saying?" And so on and so on.

I believe one of the first and most important things you need to know and remember is that we want you to succeed. It is our utmost desire as producers, directors, and choreographers to find talent. So in essence, we need you. Keep in mind that we are on your side. We want you to dance your backside off and perform as if it's your last performance. If you have the talent and are the person we need, then show us. If you do your job and let us see this, then we all walk away successful. It is in both our best interests for you to be your best. As badly as you want the gig, we want to find the right talent.

Now I do realize that no two auditions are exactly alike. We all have our own way and style of handling different situations, and no two people will handle their audition in the exact same manner. However, I feel quite certain in saying that for the most part, they are truly on your side. So if you go into the audition *confident* and *deliver* the goods, chances are you will walk away feeling great about your performance. I often take the time during my own auditions to remind the talent of why I'm there and to let them know that I am rooting for them and want to see them succeed. Yes, of course I want to see a top-notch performance, and I expect them to turn it on and kick some ass—after all, they are auditioning and therefore up against everyone else. So when you walk into an audition I want you to do your talent justice, both from a technical standpoint and a performance standpoint, and the only way you can really do that is to simply give it your all. You must prove to the person auditioning you that you are, in fact, that talent they went in there looking for.

It is your job at an audition to sell yourself to the people auditioning you. If you give one of those "I can't be bothered" performances then you will walk away disappointed. Could you possibly expect anything else? If you do not give it everything that you're made of, then you don't deserve the gig. You have spent so much time training, taking a variety of classes, and perhaps even performing—some of you professionally and some of you in local productions or school recitals, and now you stand before a panel of people who can make it or break it for you. Don't waste their time or yours, for that matter. Whether it's your first audition or your one hundredth, don't sell yourself short; don't deprive yourself of this opportunity to be anything but your very best. Don't give less than 100 percent ever! After everything you have worked toward, everything you have been preparing for, here you are! This is your moment; you have only one shot at this job, don't blow it.

Let's start at the beginning: How did you hear about the audition? Was it an ad? If so, what did it say? Did it specify attire, shoes, makeup? What are they looking for? Who is the production company? Who will be holding the audition? Do your homework, do your research, know what you are auditioning for, know whom you are auditioning for. Is this a pop video, a Broadway show or tour, a theme park or cruise ship, a commercial, a feature film, or a Las Vegas revue? You need this key information in order to determine how to dress, what your overall look should be, and what shoes to wear. As for shoes, bring them all: heels, dance sneakers, tap shoes, ballet slippers, pointe shoes, and jazz shoes; you want to be prepared for it all. You may even want to have your Rollerblades in the trunk of your car. You just never know, so expect the unexpected, and be ready for it.

ENCORE:
Whether it's your first audition or your one hundredth, don't sell yourself short; don't deprive yourself of this opportunity to be anything but your very best. Don't give less than 100 percent ever!

DRESS TO IMPRESS

Okay, you've done your research the best you possibly can and hopefully you now have a general idea of what to expect. When it comes to attire, unless a specific look is asked for, keep it simple; dress nice and look your best. Dance attire of course is always best. Wear something fitted, something body-conscious and flattering. We want to see you move. You may want to add something different and unique that will make you stand out, whether it's a bright color, a bandanna, a special belt, or something in your hair—you don't want to simply blend into a sea of dancers.

If the audition is more specific; for example, a particular role in a Broadway show, then once again, do your homework and find out what the character is like. How would he or she dress or wear their hair? Take on that role and let the audition team see you as that person. If it is a chorus position, then stick to dance attire and let them see your movement and your lines—all things important to a dancer and the choreography. Be sensible in your choice of outfits. You want to impress them, and you don't want to offend anyone. As I said in the beginning, no two auditions are identical, and no two audition teams will have the same view. So when I say be sensible, consider the wide range of people you could be auditioning for and try to appeal to the masses. You want to look your best, have your hair done and makeup on. Choose dancewear that you like, that you feel good in; something that is a bit fun and stylish, yet fitting. Remember, we want to see you dance. It is so important for us to see those lines. If you're wearing big, baggy clothing or layers upon layers, how will the choreographer be able to see what they need to see? Don't forget to add that little something special to help you stand out.

If you are auditioning for a music video or concert tour, then we're talking about a whole different subject matter. Consider the group or artist, consider their style, and choose appropriately. Find out all that you can about the look that they are looking for. Girls, as for makeup, in this case less may be more. Eyes and lips—let them see your natural beauty, let them see what they have to work with. Accentuate your eyes with a little liner and mascara, and you can't go wrong by choosing a light and natural color for your lips.

If you are in Las Vegas auditioning as a showgirl, then you had better pull out the old high-cut body suit or trunks. Although high-cut isn't exactly the *style-du-jour* today, show some leg. You know what I mean: Get out your fishnet stockings and heels. Oh, and while you are at it, you may want to put on your false eyelashes. Talk to other dancers to find out if anyone you know has ever auditioned for this particular venue, artist, or show. Maybe they know the production company; maybe they know the choreographer. Don't be afraid to ask. Someone may be able to give you a heads-up and the exact information or advice you need to help you best prepare.

ENCORE:
Choose dancewear that you like, that you feel good in; something that is a bit fun and stylish, yet fitting. Remember, we want to see you dance. It is so important for us to see those lines.

LOCATION, LOCATION, LOCATION

Next, the location. As part of your research, you should have mapped out where you're going and how long it will take you to get there. Very important: Always be sure you have enough time to get there, taking into account the time of day, rush hour, etc. Always arrive early. Give yourself plenty of time for a thorough warm-up, which means time to prepare both mentally and physically for your audition. As you approach the audition location, turn it on and keep it on. It's showtime! You never know who is who and you want to make a great first impression.

You never know who you are first meeting; the person signing you in could be your future employer. Be professional, be pleasant and courteous to all when introducing yourself. In the end, you could be working alongside any number of the people you encounter throughout this day. Make yourself memorable. Be a dancer's dancer; be that someone whom a producer, director, or choreographer would want to spend hours and hours a day with. The work we do is intimate. We can spend days or weeks on end together, first in rehearsals and then depending on the gig itself, we could spend weeks, months, or years working on the same production. So be that someone special on- and offstage whom other cast members want to work with and spend time with.

When you first arrive, introduce yourself and ask if and where you should sign in. Usually, there will be a sign-in sheet, and you will often be given a number and an audition form. You could be asked to fill out the form and have a photo and resume ready to be handed in at some point during the audition, perhaps after an initial typecasting or cut. Sometimes they will ask for them straight up front; other times they will wait until a final cut. And on that note, make sure you have a professional head shot that looks like you, and a professionally laid-out resume that is truly your resume. *You* are your resume, so *be* your resume. Remember the famous line from *A Chorus Line*, "Who am I anyway? Am I my resume?" *This is not the time to be borrowing* from someone else! Yes, you will have to spend money in this area; you absolutely must keep current, changing your photos as often as needed. This is your business and these promotional pieces are essential. You never want to give anyone a photo that does not look like you.

As for your resume, it should be no more than one page in length and should be updated constantly, making sure that all contact information is accurate. If you are first starting out and are concerned about not having any professional experience, you can list any local performances with your school, performing arts schools, or dance studios, as well as any awards or accomplishments and hobbies you may have. If you have not had much experience in the area of performances, you may prefer to write a simple biography about who you are and any special interests or personal accomplishments.

Okay, let's get back to sign in. Once you have signed in and the room is accessible, go on in, put your dance bag and resume aside, and give yourself that full complete warm-up we talked about earlier. Once again, make sure you've given yourself plenty of time to be physically warmed up and mentally prepared. Focus on why you are there; focus on your confidence, strengths, and ability to give an excellent performance and audition—*visualize* a great outcome. Your mind is a powerful tool, so use it to your advantage. Rather than allowing useless non-productive chatter, (remember that fan club we talked about earlier), why not envision a fabulous ending to this day? How do you envision it? It's your story; you can write it any way you like.

Bill Bartmann, a highly successful entrepreneur and motivational speaker, talks about reverse worry. Simply put, he says, "If your mind can worry, why can't it imagine? Worry is looking into the future and seeing the worst possible outcome. If you have a 50/50 shot, why not expect something good instead of bad?" Is the glass half-full or is it half-empty? Your thoughts can be supportive and constructive, or they can be negative and damaging. It's your choice.

Once the audition has begun, be present and attentive; be there completely in mind, body, and spirit. You could be asked to state your name and number, or name and agency; demonstrate confidence, maturity, and personality. You want to be captured in a good light. Videos sometimes have a way of hanging around for a long time and besides which, the person who ultimately makes the decision may not be at the audition. They could be meeting you for the first time on video. Keep in mind that they could be seeing hundreds of people this day, so you want to make yourself memorable both on and off the camera.

ENCORE:
It's your story; you can write it any way you like.

PRACTICE MAKES PERFECT

Once again, be aware of everything and everyone around you. Get that extra-sensory capacity working for you; a dancer must be able to feel another dancer's energy next to him or her. There could be hundreds of dancers in one room at the same time all trying to learn the same routine. You could start out in the tenth row. I personally would make sure I was front and center, and I suggest you do the same, especially since you did arrive so nice and early. More often than not the choreographer or person teaching the routine will rotate the rows so that everyone has the opportunity to pick up the choreography as well as be seen. So if you should find yourself in the tenth row, don't fret; you will have your turn front and center. In the meantime, be courteous and patient and most important, stay present.

Dancers often express to me their concerns about not being able to pick up the routines fast enough. This is certainly a dancer's worst nightmare. Let's face it, when you only have a short time to pick up the routine and your nervous system is already working on overtime, the last thing you need is for your speed and accuracy to fail you. However, let me offer you two different thoughts on that note. Some choreographers base decisions on looks, personality, and overall dance ability rather than speed at picking up. Others will definitely want to know right then and there that you can cut it when it comes to picking up quickly, as rehearsal time is often pressed, and there can be a great deal to learn in a short time. Here are a couple of simple recommendations that can help. First of all, get yourself into a variety of classes with as many different teachers and choreographers as possible. The more exposure you have to a wide variety of choreographers and styles, the more opportunities you give yourself to pick up different combinations on a regular basis. Some teachers will offer choreography classes. These are great for practicing speed and accuracy.

We've all been told that practice makes perfect, so let me give you another suggestion, a little trick that I once learned from a great teacher. Partner up with some friends and fellow dancers. Call it a jam session of sorts. Play some of your favorite music and just start dancing. You'll want to mix things up a bit to get the most out of your session, so make sure you have plenty of music in a wide range of styles. You can start out with one person leading the dance, and everyone else following along, trying to pick up the routine as he or she freestyles, or you can break it down into partners, one leading while the other follows and then switching roles.

This is a great little exercise that you can have some fun doing while sharpening your skills on picking up quickly and accurately. Remember, variety is the key. Audition workshops can be of enormous benefit to you. The more opportunity you get to practice in lifelike auditions without standing the chance of blowing the gig, the better equipped you will be to handle the real deal. Get out those dance and music DVDs; don't stop and rewind, just follow. Every single opportunity you take to learn choreography on the spot the quicker you become at picking up.

One of your other goals should be to develop an ability to walk into any audition and feel right at home, picking up any number of styles. As a choreographer, I can tell you that it is extremely important to me that a dancer be stylized. All choreographers have their own unique styles and believe me, if they are teaching you a routine, they expect you to get the style right. This is their creation, and there is a reason for their every move. Ultimately, they want it executed just the way they do it, so your job in an audition, when learning a routine, is to ensure that you are mimicking the person teaching. You want to watch their every move. Be exact! Where is that pinky? What angle is their head at, and what is the attitude of the dance? The goal is to look just like them. So as mentioned earlier, be extremely attentive to every little detail. Get that routine down, get that style down, and then perform it like it's your last. Give it everything you've got and show them what you're made of. Performance, in my opinion, is huge; I want to see you sell it, period. If you can't sell it in the audition, how can I know or trust what your performance will be like at showtime?

ENCORE:
One of your goals should be to develop an ability to walk into any audition and feel right at home, picking up any number of styles.

ALWAYS TAKE IT PROFESSIONALLY, NEVER TAKE IT PERSONALLY

There is so much that goes into casting. Producers, directors, and choreographers usually know going in what they are looking for. Sometimes it's about a particular type or look, sometimes it's a specific style, sometimes it's all about technique. Other times, it's all about performance, and sometimes it's about the perfect blend of all of the aforementioned. And every now and then, we go in thinking we know exactly what we want only to be blown away by someone, and we end up rewriting the role or requirements. Unfortunately, you cannot be everything to everyone, so you go in as geared up as you can, confident of your dance ability, and give your very best performance. That is all you can do. Believe me, if you go in there and give it your very best shot you will walk away feeling great about what you did, and so you should.

Let me backtrack for a minute; let's revisit that whole learning process. Very often during auditions you will not have a great amount of time to learn the routine; however, the process of the audition itself can be quite lengthy, so there's no need to panic. Not all auditions will have masses of dancers, but certainly some of them will, so be prepared. In this event, once the routine has been taught, the choreographer will have to break the large group down into smaller ones. Sometimes you'll be asked to leave the room while other groups have the opportunity to perform; this is an opportunity for you to review the choreography. Other times, they may choose to keep everyone in the room and rotate one group after another. Throughout the process, be mindful and respectful of those dancers who are performing; don't be in the sidelines practicing, as this can be distracting for the audition team and not fair to fellow dancers. This would be the time for you to review the routine in your mind, quietly visualizing the choreography. This can be an excellent exercise to calm you and help prepare you for your turn as well. You can be certain that someone is always watching and will make a note of how you handle yourself on the sidelines and how you interact with others. You will have the opportunity to strut your stuff center stage, so give your peers their moment to shine.

There will be times at large open calls when, in actuality, you may not have the opportunity to learn a routine. Some audition teams will do typecasting or a quick process of elimination by asking you to perform something as simple as pirouettes on both sides. This could be as much of the audition as you get to see. Now, if they are typecasting and you are not asked to stay past the initial lineup, you mustn't take this personally; it could be as simple as you not being the look that they are casting for. This is only one gig, and it certainly doesn't mean that there will not be plenty of other parts that you could be perfect for.

Dancers often get their nose out of joint over this process, and I do understand that no one wants to be rejected before having the opportunity to dance. But what you must try to remember is that this is only one audition out of the many that you will go up for. In addition, the truth of it is there are often hundreds of dancers who turn out to audition for a gig that has very few positions available. It can be a very long and difficult process, and some audition teams choose different procedures of elimination in order to maximize the time available for finding the exact talent that they are looking for. You will appreciate that additional time when you are that talent.

Some auditions will eliminate after an initial lineup or after asking for a specific technique to be executed, while others will eliminate after teaching a quick combination, all for the purpose of narrowing down to a smaller pool of talent with whom they can then spend more time. If you are chosen to stay on and learn a combination, the audition will normally continue with some sort of a cut process.

When I hold an audition, I personally like to see everyone dance, so I will often start my auditions with a lineup and ask for pirouettes on the right and left sides, and with both a jazz and a ballet preparation. However, I will usually teach the routine, or at least a section of it, to everyone. From there, I will break down into smaller groups and see everyone perform at least once. At this point, I usually do my first cut. Depending on the number of dancers, there could be several more cuts before we end up with that small chosen pool of talent. My reason for giving you this information is to reiterate how important first impressions are, and to emphasize how important your performance is from the minute you walk into the room. You may not get a second chance to perform, so you had better give 100 percent right from the get-go.

ENCORE:
You can't be everything to everyone, so you go in as geared up as you can, confident of your dance ability, and give your very best performance.
The rest will take care of itself.

FINAL CUT

Okay, so let's say you've spent the day auditioning, and you've made it to the final cut. At this point, you could be offered a job or you could be asked to come to a callback. As if all that wasn't nerve-wracking enough, you could be dismissed and simply told that you will receive a telephone call if, in fact, you got the gig. When you've made it this far, some companies will call to let you know either way, whether or not you got the gig, but not always.

If you are asked to return for a callback, this is fantastic; you are now one step closer to where you want to be. Now I want you to consider everything, as you did for your original audition. This time, you may have more specific details, as to a particular type, style, look, or character that they are looking for. They may even make a special request of you by asking you to dress or look a certain part. Pay attention, and just as you did the first time out, let them see you as that person they want in their company. If no special request was made, then dress to impress, and give them a performance that will seal the deal.

You may be performing the same routine as the last time, or they may choose to challenge you with yet another combination or a different style altogether. If this is a straight dance position, you could be asked to perform any special technique or tricks that you do, i.e., tumbling, jumps, leaps, or turns. If you are auditioning for a chorus position and have not already been asked to do so, be prepared to sing. I will stress one more time the importance of being a triple threat. However, I am not suggesting that you cannot work strictly as a dancer; I'm just saying that you will limit your opportunities and your marketability.

Today's market is so much stronger, with the competition getting better and better every day. Dancers do everything nowadays; they just keep coming up with much superior technique and bigger tricks. Therefore, in order to remain on top of your game, it is extremely important for you to not only equip yourself with all of the various techniques and styles, but also to add vocals and acting to your repertoire. This will make you a much more versatile performer. So if you do not consider yourself to be the next Andrea Bocelli, Celine Dion, Michael Jackson, or Beyoncé, I would strongly suggest that you get yourself a vocal coach ASAP. I know I'm repeating myself, but I just want to make sure you got it. By the way, this in no way implies the caliber of vocals that is required of a dancer; however, you do want to be able to at least carry a tune.

When preparing for your vocal auditions, plan to have at least two songs available: one up-tempo and one ballad. You can purchase a cheat book from any good book or music store. A cheat book or fake book is a large book full of sheet music. This will give you a long list of songs to choose from, or if you prefer, you can purchase an individual songbook or sheet music for a particular piece. You will want to have your sheet music transposed in the proper key. Although some accompanists can do this on the spot, it is always best to be prepared in advance. It is also a great idea to have copies of your sheet music already taped together so that it can be easily laid out for the accompanist. It should be neat and easily accessible in a book or folder.

Here's a quick tip: A three-ring binder can be a great and easy way to organize your audition collection as it grows. Simply keep each song taped and prepared in clear sheet protectors. This will keep it in good condition and always available. This will also come in handy in the event that they would like to hear you sing more. Initially, you will probably be asked to sing only sixteen bars. Some auditioners will want to hear no more and no less, but then again, they may want to hear a different style of music than what you had originally chosen. Just as with your dance audition, do your homework—know what style of music the auditioners will most likely want to hear from you. It's best to always be prepared.

When entering the room, be confident and go directly to the piano. Have your sheet music ready, and hand it to the accompanist. Show him or her the exact sixteen bars you intend to sing, and give any specific requests at this time. Step away, and very important, don't forget to breathe! Greet the audition team and tell them which song you have chosen to sing for them. The idea again is to present yourself as a true professional, and by now, you should have demonstrated a strong sense of efficiency and confidence. It all comes down to first impressions. If for any reason you miss a note or a lyric, just carry on; there is no need to draw more attention to it. Maintaining your composure and the performance you give will show them how you work under pressure, and it will be appreciated.

Same goes when preparing for an acting call. Are you reading for a commercial, a television show, or a feature film? Are you predominantly portraying the role of a dancer, or is it mostly acting with some movement involved? You will want to know as much detail as possible in order to best be prepared. If it is a commercial, you will want to do a little research on the product; especially if this is a new or unfamiliar product, you will want to be knowledgeable. As for all readings, you will want to know what type they are looking for so that you can dress the part and prepare mentally for the character. If you are reading for a part in a television show or a movie, you could be given the script in advance or you may be asked to do a cold reading. This is when you are handed the script at the audition itself. With commercials, you are often given the script right then and there.

Last, but certainly not least, how about the audition when they ask you to improvise? This can come up in many situations, but it seems to be a favorite for dancers, especially in commercials where there is only one character doing all the dancing. When looking for individuals as opposed to a group of dancers, there isn't always a choreographer on hand, and sometimes even if there is, he or she may still prefer to see you improvise in order to see your character come through. So, as I recommended in "Chapter Three: Triple Threat," you should now better understand the significance of preparing through proper training. What you don't want to do is blow several auditions in order to learn the process. I've heard a few naive young performers say that they would prefer to learn from their own experience; however, when experience costs you a national spot or a television show or role in the next best dance movie, trust me, you would prefer to have been better prepared.

The industry is full of great expertise, and you should take advantage of all that is available. You can often find workshops advertised in your local industry trade paper or posted at dance studios and acting schools. Ask around—find out from fellow dancers and your teachers who is offering what and where. Good audition, commercial, and acting workshops are absolutely invaluable in helping you to prepare for auditions. The better prepared you are, the more professional you will come off and, therefore, the more favorable your results. Remember, it's one thing to walk out of an audition that you prepared for and felt confident about, and it's another thing altogether to walk out of an audition disappointed because you didn't do all that you could to prepare.

In closing on the audition process, I would like to sum it up by saying that there are many factors that come into play, some of which are beyond your control. In order to really get the most out of your experience in this business, you truly must learn to keep a cool head about you. Do not take things personally, and understand the difference between "being serious and getting down to business," and "not taking things too seriously." As mentioned so many times earlier in this book, making it in this business is a lot about balance. You must be flexible enough to grow, yet strong enough to stand firm for what you believe in; be secure enough to share in your colleagues' triumphs, while being centered enough to recognize your own successes, even in those moments that sometimes look like defeat.

I don't know that anything in life is ever completely perfect, but there's nothing wrong with striving for perfection and doing all that we can along the way to keep ourselves in check and create the healthiest lifestyle we can, both in business and in play.

So, a quick recap: Do your homework, understand what you are up against, show up early, be mentally and physically prepared, be kind and courteous to everyone you meet, and be present and attentive always. Most importantly, dance, sing, act, and perform like it's your one and only chance. Have some fun with it, and don't forget to *thank* the audition team on your way out.

ENCORE:
In order to really get the most out of your experience in this business, you truly must learn to keep a cool head about you.

Play it again, Sam! "Mr. Zoot Suit," *Swing Train*, Celebrity Cruises' *Mercury*

Chapter Eight
It's Showtime, Folks!—Let the Fun Begin

"And my goal in life is to give to the world what I was lucky to receive: the ecstasy of divine union through my music and my dance."
~ **Michael Jackson**

Congratulations! You got the gig. Now what? This is the time to put to use all that good stuff you just learned. Are you up to the challenge? Are you ready to put into practice and make a part of your daily existence your newly acquired qualities and traits, especially those covered in detail in the previous chapter, "The Audition"? Most importantly, are you ready to be that person, that dancer, that performer, the one your choreographer and employers want to spend days on end with? That is really a key issue here. If you focus your efforts on being the best talent and the best employee you can be, then you should have all of your bases covered. Once again, just as you did for the audition (here I go with one final review), you will want to be early and be prepared both mentally and physically, be focused and attentive, be pleasant, courteous and respectful, work hard, give them 100 percent, leave any attitude behind, and last but certainly not least, perform like it's your last. Let them see you at your best; this is your opportunity to prove to them that they made the right decision in choosing you. Remind them of why they hired you, and let them be thrilled that they did.

At this point, I would like to touch on the rehearsal process and tell you a little bit more about what you might expect. If you don't already know, rehearsals can at times be very long and involved, they can be difficult and exhausting, and sometimes downright grueling. There is so much to learn and take in on all levels.

You will be learning new choreography and staging while getting to know your new castmates and production team, as well as learning the do's and don'ts of this particular gig and any rules and regulations of the venue in which you will be performing your contract. This can all be very emotionally taxing. To cut to the chase, the rehearsal process will be by far the hardest part of the job. You need to be in your best form both physically and mentally.

We need you to be up for the task, so make sure that you are taking proper care of yourself, and that you are resting enough and eating properly. A well-balanced and nutritious diet is essential, especially now during rehearsals when you will be exerting so much energy in the long days to come. The length of your rehearsals will vary and ultimately be dictated by the production company, the demands of the show, and the type of contract.

A portion of your rehearsal time will be in the studio working in the mirrors, learning and perfecting choreography as well as learning any vocals necessary. You may also learn some of your blocking (your placement within the routines) and stage entrances and exits while learning the choreography, or you may have separate rehearsal time on stage for that process. Everyone works differently. I always like to teach as much of my staging and blocking as possible up front. This helps in making a smooth transition to the stage.

As all rehearsals are different, there is no set time you will spend in the studio and no set time you will spend on stage or on the set. When it comes to working in live stage productions, the size of the stage, the technology, any special effects, and the size of the production will determine how much time is needed to nail down the blocking and all other technical aspects of the production. The larger the production, and the more bells and whistles, the more time that will be needed on stage for the blocking and to ensure everyone's safety on deck.

Once the cast members have had this time on stage and safety issues have been addressed, then there will be time for lighting rehearsals, sound checks, costume runs, makeup and hair requirements, dress rehearsals, and full technical rehearsals. Often with various productions you will find that you can work just as hard offstage, with all of the costume changes and the need for costume presets as you do onstage. Presets are a very big part of your track in a theatrical production or revue-style show. You will have to determine where each costume will live backstage during the show in order to facilitate any quick changes with your entrances and exits and yet not interfere with other cast members. *Beware*—the number one backstage rule is, *never ever* touch another cast member's preset, the consequences could be catastrophic!

> ENCORE:
> *Always remember this: you get out of life what you put in, and the same applies to your work.*

PERFORMANCE ATTITUDE

As you know, "attitude" is extremely important; so much so that I dedicated an entire chapter to it ("Chapter Five: Leave Your Attitude Where It Belongs—At the Door"). In that chapter, I addressed how crucial it is to have the right attitude when it comes to your career and the day-to-day life within the business. Here, I would like to address your performance attitude; this is the one time you will be given full license to give as much attitude as you want!

This is your opportunity to be a diva (or divo) and strut your stuff. All of those years of training are about to pay off! This is where you get to put that training and muscle memory to work for you. Throw away your thinking cap and any inhibitions, and bring it on. I want to see you sell it like nobody's business. I want you to take that nervous energy and use it, turn it around to make *it* work for you, and tear up that dance floor. I want you to perform like there is no tomorrow, and I want you to do this every time you walk out onstage.

I've probably said it a few times already, but I do not want you to forget why you are here in the first place. This is so basic, but if you want to live the life and last in the game, then you better always remember where and how this journey began, and most importantly, *why* it began. That is what will drive you to give the ultimate performance at *every* performance and walk away proud and loving what you do. We talked about what it takes to turn your childhood dreams into your reality; we talked about your love for dance and your passion for performing *and voila!* Here you now stand on opening night, just as every great performer did on their opening night. "Places" has been called, and the curtain is about to rise. You're so excited, and maybe even a bit scared—maybe a lot scared and probably more than anything just plain nervous. Finally, after all you have been through—all the hard work, the training, the sacrifices, the doubts, the fear, and the rejection—you have at long last made it. So get out there and show them what you're made of!

Understand this: once you are there, you must continuously earn your place in order to keep your place. There is no shortage of dancers vying for your position; they are waiting in line, and your producers have plenty of choices. You must have the same attitude as the pro athlete and know that every performance is a make or break performance. So even if you might find yourself comfortable in a long-running show, don't ever become complacent in your performance. If you don't go in with the right attitude every time, it could be your last time.

Let's go back for a moment and revisit a little of what I talked about in the first chapter, turning stumbling blocks into building blocks. I want to remind you of the importance of those building blocks; all of those otherwise frustrating moments that you must learn to chalk up as experience. All of this will help prepare you for the many opening nights and jobs to come and give you the stamina required to constantly compete with yourself, reaching new performance heights every time. Without that process, you may never even get to the stage. You may never get to see the audience from this side of the curtain; you may never get to experience the amazing sensation one gets from a standing ovation or the stir from a fully charged audience. And that would be so unfortunate; after all, is this not a great measurement of what we as entertainers live for—the applause and the recognition? Is this not in some part a validation of our success and the long, often hard, road we've been down? Every one of those lessons along the way that you choose to turn into a positive experience will only make the journey so much more gratifying—the stage your home, and the business your life.

ENCORE:
I want to remind you of the importance of those building blocks, all of those otherwise frustrating moments that you must learn to chalk up as experience.

AN ATTITUDE OF GRATITUDE

Ever since I was a little girl, I said that fame and fortune, "the Fred and Gingers or the John Travoltas" of this world were few and far between, but I always believed that there was a place for me in the business. I knew that I would be happy if I could simply earn a living doing what I loved most. I thought what a special privilege this would be. I believe that I was given a wonderful gift, a God-given talent, and to be able to share this talent and use it to bring a certain joy and happiness to others is a magnificent honor.

What greater accomplishment is there than to do what you love most? Your talent truly is a special gift, and to have the ability to share it is an honor and a privilege not to be taken for granted; one to hold true to and always be grateful for. This passion and love that I have for dance and show business is what got me through years of learning, growing, falling down, and getting back up.

And because of this conviction, I implore you: Don't ever throw away a performance, not one single moment. The truth is you never get it back.

Furthermore, you never know who could be sitting in the audience. You never know how a lackluster performance by one cast member can affect the overall impact of the show and the cast, or for that matter, an audience member's experience. One night while sitting in the audience of a hit Broadway show, I was absolutely shocked by one very unprofessional young lady. She was continuously disruptive throughout the show, making gestures to her castmates on stage and basically having a laugh at the audience's expense. I'm sure that she thought she was being very clever and that no one would ever see; however, I was appalled that a performer in such a show would throw away her performance with this lack of professionalism. Unfortunately for her, I wasn't the only person in the audience who noticed it. After the show, I overheard a couple of other people expressing their distaste as well. Can you even imagine having the opportunity to perform on Broadway and not giving it everything you've got?

To give anything less than your very best means that you are cheating not only your audience, your fellow performers, your choreographer, and the people who hired you, but first and foremost, you are cheating *yourself.* You are utterly robbing yourself of your own true potential. This is something that I've always felt very strongly about and continuously drive home to all performers who work with me. On a few occasions, I've had the opportunity to slip into the audience of one of my shows unannounced. This is always interesting because as you can imagine, everyone is on their best performance when they know that you are in the house. Bottom line: There are no shortcuts in performance, and I don't care if there is one person in the house or thousands. Do yourself proud; you've aspired to and worked hard for this opportunity. Every performance should be like opening night; every performance is a first time. In his book *Footnotes,* Tommy Tune says, "A long run becomes a launch pad that allows one to spring higher each time the curtain rises." What a great ambition to have, constantly aspiring to greater heights. If you were, in fact, only as good as your last performance, wouldn't you want each performance to top the last?

ENCORE:

To give anything less than your very best means that you are cheating not only your audience, your fellow performers, your choreographer, and the people who hired you, but first and foremost, you are cheating yourself.

THINKING ON YOUR FEET

These lessons that I am sharing with you apply to all areas of performance, whether live stage, television, or film. In live stage and in live television, you only have one shot at the perfect take. In film and pre-taped television, you have the added luxury of retakes, if necessary; however, as production costs are so exorbitant, you certainly wouldn't want to be the one holding up the show. And so it's really very simple: Don't waste one single moment because you'll never get it back.

Performance is a critical part of your training, both learning about performance and the actual experience of performing. There are so many varied situations that one must be prepared for at all times. Only experience teaches this stuff. Having studied and performed with a children's touring and performing arts company gave me an incredible education about the theatre and its do's and don'ts, both on and off stage. The dance director and choreographer of that company was a brilliant teacher in that respect; he had been a performer on Broadway and was an incredible wealth of information, which he so generously passed on to all of us, his students. He taught us about being in the business and about respect for the business and respect for each other. He taught us about how to respond to unexpected situations that could happen on stage. He would say things like, "What happens if the lights go out? What happens if the music stops? What happens if the scenery falls? What do you do if you drop a prop? What if your hat or wig falls off? What if a piece of your costume comes off? What if you make a mistake or stumble? What if you fall down?" What if, what if, what if? These were ongoing lessons throughout class, throughout rehearsals, and throughout our education in his company.

The bottom line is that everyone reacts differently in a crisis, but in a show, you can imagine that if everyone reacted differently you would have major chaos on stage, which could ruin the show and be very dangerous. You may well be lucky enough to have learned much of this, either through training or through experience, and if so, you can be very grateful. If not, I would imagine that from recital performances alone, you may have encountered a technical glitch or two, and therefore have some idea of what I am talking about. Whenever entering new or unfamiliar territory, don't be afraid to ask for advice. Better to have a little foresight and be prepared than to be surprised and not know how to handle a situation.

Let me share with you a couple of stories that I have experienced. First of all, I will tell you about a situation that happened years ago when I was a young girl performing with my dance company. If I remember correctly, we were probably, on average, about thirteen to fifteen years of age. It was our annual showcase and we were performing a group dance number. During this number, there was a huge prop in the shape of a crystal quartz that was suspended from the ceiling and came down from the fly space. It was motorized and therefore rotated above our heads. At the end of the number the prop was taken up into the fly space again so that it was no longer visible. However, someone forgot to shut the motor down and so this prop, unbeknownst to anyone at the time, continued to rotate high up in the rafters. By the end of the show, with twenty or so dancers on stage, the rope or cable by which it was suspended finally wore out, and this tremendous prop came crashing down in the middle of all of us! First of all, let me just say how lucky we all were, as this accident could have been fatal. The reaction was unbelievable. At the outset, there was a huge gasp from the audience, but not one dancer even so much as flinched. The routine continued completely uninterrupted; no one missed a beat. In the routine, there was a *grand jeté*, a traveling second to the right, and I will never forget seeing the girl who was next to the quartz leap into the air and sail over this prop to land perfectly on the other side of it. You can imagine the audience's reaction. At the end of the number, they were standing on their feet cheering in amazement. This is only one of many stories. It's simple really; we were just all so well drilled on how to expect the unexpected that we were often amazed, ourselves, at the precision with which we got through these situations.

In my early years of performing professionally, I was often quite taken aback to see how poorly some people could react in unexpected situations. Having received such well-rounded training and gained such a vast experience, I was quite shocked to learn that not everyone had that same performance training or upbringing within the business. I assumed that everything I had learned in the company was what all children would learn if they studied dance. These lessons were absolutely invaluable throughout my career as a performer. It certainly made stepping out into the real world and the crossover between child performer and working professional a lot smoother.

Here's another story I'd like to share with you—this one many years later in a show that my husband and I produced and I had also choreographed. There I sat on opening night with my husband on one side and my assistant choreographer on the other. After a long hard rehearsal period with a great cast, we were, as always, very excited and anticipating a great show. The number was "Hello Dolly." The lead singer stepped through the center of the upstage black curtain and onto a platform that would rise up out of the floor elevating her to the top of what would become a staircase. Once at the top, with the dancers in place left and right to greet her, she would then descend the staircase through the center of the dancers. Next thing I knew, she disappeared. Rather than being elevated on this staircase, it came up backwards. Unfortunately, the stage manager had forgotten to reset the turntable after our final dress rehearsal earlier that day. So instead of watching her descend this grand staircase, "Dolly" had to walk up the staircase only to stand on top of a platform with no way down or off. Thank God the dancers were thinking on their feet; the two boys downstage of the platform looked at each other, acknowledged each other, and then walked right over to Dolly. She reached her arms out to them; they gracefully lifted her off the platform to set her down on the stage and continued the choreography, "Well, hello, Dolly, it's so nice to have you back where you belong," as the song goes. Needless to say, I gave them my own standing ovation just for that one move! No one in the audience was ever the wiser; no one knew that was not exactly as it was meant to be. And so there you have it—being well prepared for everything and anything that could go wrong, thinking on your feet, and a little common sense can go a long way.

What about those horrifying moments when you might simply draw a blank on stage? All those long hours of perfecting and cleaning all that choreography only to space it! Oh my, is there anything worse for a dancer? Possibly only falling flat on your face right down front and center. Sad but true, it happens to the best, so whatever it is, don't let them see you sweat. You carry on like nothing ever happened, and if it's a fall, make it a grand one, and if you mess up do it with conviction. Then you will be so convincing in your performance that the audience will be certain that the rest of the cast went wrong. The truth is, even when they are aware, they appreciate your professionalism and don't give the so-called embarrassment another thought, but rather commend you for your performance.

LIFE IN THE REAL WORLD

The transition into the real world is the beginning of yet another series of lessons. Throughout our careers, as in life, we are constantly learning. All my years in the business have been a continuous learning process. Along the way, there were definitely some lessons less pleasant than others, there were some people less pleasant than others, but overall, I somehow always trusted in the bigger picture, believing that some good would come of it. It was all just part of the test.

If ever there were times when I lost sight of this, there was always someone there to remind me that the lessons, however difficult and painful at the time, were in fact necessary. As I look back, I'm sure that they were well-deserved lessons. Life has a way of knocking us around a bit; sometimes when we least expect it, and often when we need it most. Sometimes it's a gentle nudge, a simple reminder when we should have known better. Other times, it's a bit of a push, maybe an eye-opening experience when we were in need of a new lesson. And then there are those times when life smacks us right in the face because we just needed to be told off or put in our place. The important thing is not to stay down, but to get right back up again. Time and experience are wonderful teachers, and although there's nothing quite like personal experience, the lessons that they teach can be passed on through others, and there is certainly nothing wrong with making the learning process a little bit easier on ourselves. We undoubtedly can learn a thing or two from the experiences of others. Besides which, you might save yourself a few of those knocks and blows. So, graciously accept all the lessons offered or handed down, take them and put them to good use in your life, in your career, and in every single performance.

ENCORE:
Life has a way of knocking us around a bit; sometimes when we least expect it and often when we need it most.

Strike a pose. "Vogue," *La Cage*, the Blue Angel, New York City

Chapter Nine
Fit to Dance—You Are What You Eat

"The wise man should consider that health is the greatest of human blessings.
Let food be thy medicine."
~ **Hippocrates**

In this next section, I would like to discuss the significance of keeping fit and healthy, thereby giving you, the dancer, the best possible shot at preventing injury and creating longevity for your career. We will also address what to do should you become injured and the importance of proper care and recovery.

Through my own experiences and research I have learned the importance of keeping healthy and fit, and believe me, I'm still learning. It is truly a never-ending process. There are always new studies taking place and, therefore, new discoveries. In order for you to stay on top of your game as a dancer and per-former, it is crucial for you to be informed. Read everything you can about your business. Taking care of yourself is a huge part of your business; after all, your body is your business, and if you don't take care of it, you won't be in business for very long.

Please understand that the information in this section is merely meant as suggestions with the intent of helping you find the correct path in your own quest for optimal health and fitness. There are many wonderful books and web-sites that will help substantiate and elaborate on what we discuss here as well as offer you other great ideas that may be suited to your own ideals. It is so very important to remember that when we talk about "diet" we are talking about nutrition as a way of life and not some fad diet that you go on for a week or two at a time.

In an effort to further educate myself and to be able to offer the best possible advice in the area of health and fitness, I sought the help of a very dear friend of mine, Dr. Spencer H. Baron. He is a highly revered chiropractor and sports injury specialist, not only in his field of chiropractic, but also in the world of athletics and dance.

He has held many prominent titles and has been the treating physician for many Broadway shows, including *Cats, Crazy for You,* and *Les Misérables* to name a few, not to mention every show I ever had come through town here in Miami. Dr. Baron has been appointed the team chiropractic physician for the Miami Dolphins and the Florida Marlins. Additionally, he's treated players for the New York Mets, the San Francisco Giants, the Colorado Rockies, and the Florida Panthers. Dr. Baron is the author of *Secrets of the Game: What Superstar Athletes Can Teach You About Health, Peak Performance and Getting Results.* You can visit Dr. Baron's website at www.spencerbaron.com.

YOUR HEALTH PYRAMID

Much of this section on health and fitness will revolve around what we will refer to as the *health pyramid.* Simply put, Dr. Baron asks us to view our health as having three sides—nutritional, physical, and mental; thus the comparison to a pyramid. He points out that the pyramid is one of the most stable and balanced geometric structures in the world, and in order for us to have the same stability and balance in our health, we need all three areas—nutritional, physical, and mental—to be in balance. In terms of health, this is what we call homeostasis, and it is of paramount importance to any athlete, including dancers.

It is essential for you to realize that all three of these areas are integrated and extremely intimate with each other. Any faltering of one of these three categories and you could end up with an injury, if not this time, almost certainly in the future. It's almost like a trickle-down effect: if you weaken one side, the others will eventually follow. When you understand the importance of homeostasis, you can go a long way toward avoiding this and preventing both injury and illness.

GOOD NUTRITION—A WAY OF LIFE

Good nutrition is the foundation of good health. As previously mentioned, it is so very important to remember that when we talk about diet, we are talking about nutrition as a way of life and not some fad diet that you go on for a week or two at a time. When it comes to creating an actual diet plan for yourself, you will want to have a good understanding of what a healthy diet should consist of. First of all, the food and the quality of the food you are putting into your body— and whether or not you are getting the proper balance of water, carbohydrates, proteins, and fats—should be within the correct amount of calories necessary to counter and/or support your activity level.

You will also want to consider whether you are getting the correct amount of vitamins and minerals and whether you should be taking supplements. Yes, it can all seem a bit daunting, however, the more you learn, the easier it becomes to make intelligent choices for yourself.

ENCORE:
Good nutrition is the foundation of good health.

YOU ARE WHAT YOU EAT?

I'm sure you've all heard the familiar saying "You are what you eat." When I was a young dancer, I certainly heard it many times. I was constantly told what not to eat and which body part it would end up on if I did. However, the one area that I would have liked to learn more about was *proper* nutrition. I'm certain there are teachers and company directors out there teaching about the importance of proper nutrition and good eating habits. Unfortunately, a great number of dancers don't receive this education and adopt many unhealthy habits that can then lead to illnesses or eating disorders.

At twenty years old, 5'3" and 110 pounds, I was told by my producer that I needed to lose weight or it would cost me my job. I was told I had to lose it straight away as I was already in a performance contract, so I did—I lost twelve pounds and my new weight was ninety-eight pounds. Then I was told that I was too thin and needed to put some weight back on. And people wonder why dancers are so obsessed with food and the way they look. I mention this to make a point; this is a minor story, but one of thousands of incidents in which dancers' jobs were on the line for a few pounds. Whether you think that this attitude toward weight and overall picture-perfect body image is right, wrong, or indifferent, you have to admit that in choosing this profession and going into it, you must understand that this attitude is prevalent and goes with the territory. Unfortunately, the people making these calls don't always have a good enough understanding of nutrition to really be of any help to you. They may suggest losing ten pounds when in fact all you need is to drop a few pounds and tone up.

This is why it is so important for you to have a good understanding and grasp of health and nutrition. You should know your ideal performance weight, and what for you is the most nutritionally sound way to achieve a realistic goal. As you well know, it's not always about the numbers you see on the scale but what you see in the mirror. What I want to stress here is that there is a right way—more importantly, a healthy way—to approach weight control.

I say that today with a strong conviction due to many years of trial, error, and overall education. I know now that back when I was that young dancer of twenty and already neurotic about my weight then being told to lose weight, I went about it the wrong way—I either didn't eat at all, or ate very little. It was so easy for me to get caught up in the need to lose weight and ignore the importance of health; something we can all do when we are younger and don't necessarily know any better. Over the years, on several occasions I have had to speak to my own dancers or cast members about weight issues. This is never an easy subject, but I always take a very strong attitude toward them handling it in the right way. For any dance teachers reading this book, I ask you to handle this topic with the utmost sensitivity and to be prepared to help educate your dancers so that they can accomplish their goals in a healthy manner with proper nutrition as the number one focus. We all know that a dancer's work is not only extremely physically demanding, but it can also be emotionally taxing; a balanced diet for optimum physical and emotional health is imperative.

A big concern in this area especially relating to young female dancers is the nutritional deficiencies that often result from eating disorders or even simply from bad eating habits. The combination of such nutritional deficiencies and low body fat can very often cause menstrual irregularities known as *amenorrhea*. When you interrupt the fine hormonal balance of a teen or a young woman in her twenties, you can provoke skeletal abnormalities or conditions that can then cause stress fractures. Needless to say, this is not a good thing for a dancer. Again I want to remind you of the trickle-down effect I mentioned earlier. In this classic example, we have an eating issue, which may have started out as an emotional problem, which turns into a nutritional problem, which turns into a physical problem. Get the picture? It is important to realize that an eating disorder doesn't just mean bulimia or anorexia; these are the full-blown medically diagnosed versions we are all too familiar with. However, in their infancy stages, eating disorders begin when someone is simply missing a few vital nutrients from their diet. Nutritional deficiencies, and specifically eating disorders, can cause a wide range of health complications. In this book, I will not go into all of the possible complications; however, if you or anyone you know has any concerns in this area, please learn all that you can about these illnesses and the possible complications, and seek professional help immediately. There are organizations that deal specifically with these issues; there is much information and help available today. The complications are far too great and too dangerous not to be addressed seriously.

> ENCORE:
> *We all know that a dancer's work is not only extremely physically demanding, but it can also be emotionally taxing; a balanced diet for optimum physical and emotional health is imperative.*

MOTHER KNOWS BEST

Mom knows best! For me, my mother was a huge influence on the healthy habits I later took on in life, from my food choices to alternative therapies. First of all, just about everything we ate growing up was made from scratch—from fresh-baked bread to desserts of every kind. Also, it seemed that Mom always had a natural remedy for just about any ailment; she grew up on a farm during a time when people relied on what was naturally grown—often herbs from their own gardens or from the fields. Although she probably thought I wasn't paying much attention as a teen, something obviously sank in, for when I was old enough to know better I found myself doing the exact things she had recommended to me all those years ago—following a natural, healthy diet and always looking for natural remedies.

> ENCORE:
> *For me, my mother was a huge influence on the healthy habits I later took on in life, from my food choices to alternative therapies.*

MAKING HEALTHY CHOICES

On that note, I will discuss some guidelines for both healthy and not-so-healthy habits. When it comes to proper nutrition, a pretty safe bet would be to start by making healthy *whole food choices*. You know, the foods your parents or maybe your grandparents and great-grandparents ate before the birth of so many preservatives and additives. Making healthy choices is one of the most important things you can do for your overall health and diet. So, what are healthy choices? I am often amazed at the false or misconstrued beliefs many people have when it comes to what is healthy and what is not. The truth is, it often comes down to what we've learned as children, as well as which marketing and advertising

111

ploys the food manufacturers have led us to believe in. I will outline below certain guidelines for you to consider when making food choices. The bottom line is to try to eat whole foods. Think "Mother Nature" foods in their natural state, or as close to their natural state as possible: foods that have not been or have been minimally processed or modified. Granted, this is not always easy to do when a tight schedule has us eating on the run, but this is where a little creativity with food and meal planning is extremely important. It is definitely doable; it simply requires some thought, commitment, and preparation. Always remember that you have everything to gain from your efforts!

I can attest to my own experiences over the years, and I can honestly tell you that I am at my best when my diet is clean and loaded with an assortment of fresh and whole foods: fresh fruits, vegetables, legumes, whole grains, nuts, and seeds. I love fish and try to have it a couple of times a week. I prefer to eat chicken and ground turkey to red meat, but do love a good steak once in a while. I have always been a protein junky, and I have learned the importance of moderating my intake of animal proteins. I do so by having a couple of vegetarian meals every week. I also avoid refined flour and white sugar (except for a chocolate fix, which I allow myself every now and then). Although studies have proven that dark, good-quality chocolate is healthier, I still prefer the taste of good-quality milk chocolate. Again, I am simply sharing with you what I like and what works for me. The variety I'm talking about will give me a good balance of nutrients. One of my very favorite foods is sushi, and it is an excellent way to create a balanced meal. You have your vegetables, such as asparagus, carrots or cucumber, then you have seaweed, which has several vitamins and minerals, lean fish for your protein, and rice for a complex carbohydrate. (I prefer brown rice over white whenever possible.) Plus you have wasabi and ginger, which are huge in antioxidants. So as you can see, sushi can be loaded with goodness!

ENCORE:
Think "Mother Nature" foods in their natural state, or as close to their natural state as possible: foods that have not been or have been minimally processed or modified.

COLORS OF THE RAINBOW

When shopping for food, think of the colors of the rainbow and try to select a wide variety, since many nutrients are associated with various colors. Your richly colored fruits and vegetables are of primary importance to you because they have the most vitamins, antioxidants, and carotenes.

When it comes to salads, you want dark leafy greens. These could be the most important greens of all because they have the most vital nutrients. These include spinach, kale, romaine, and collard greens.

Other great greens include green apples, green grapes, kiwi, broccoli, cabbage, brussels sprouts, watercress, asparagus, green peppers, celery, cucumbers, and the green portions of scallions, chives, and leeks. Although we have given specific mention to those all-important greens, don't forget the rainbow. Make sure to select a wide spectrum of color from deep yellow and orange, deep red, blue and purple, and last but not least, white. Try to eat as many colors as possible, and preferably raw or lightly steamed when it comes to your produce. I love fresh juices, which I prepare at home. I am a big fan of juicing for two reasons. One, this is a great way to ensure that you get your daily recommendations of two to three servings of fruit and three to five servings of vegetables per day; and two, this is a superb way to get some raw food into your diet, thereby ensuring the maximum nutritional value.

- **Deep yellow and orange:** pineapple, nectarines, peaches, yellow apples, yellow peppers, yellow winter squash, spaghetti squash, corn, oranges, melons, tangerines, apricots, papayas, orange peppers, carrots, pumpkin, sweet potato, and yams.
- **Deep red:** red apples, cherries, red grapes, pomegranates, cranberries, watermelon, strawberries, tomatoes, beets, red cabbage, red peppers, radishes, and red onion.
- **Blue and purple:** blackberries, blueberries, purple grapes, raisins, eggplant, and plums.
- **White:** bananas, pears, garlic, onions, white potatoes, mushrooms, turnips, and parsnips.

ENCORE:
When shopping for food, think of the colors of the rainbow and try to select a wide variety, since many nutrients are associated with various colors.

KEEP IT LEAN

When it comes to protein, stick to lean meats, chicken, or fish. Vegetarian choices include beans, tofu, and low-fat cheese such as cottage cheese (most varieties make lower fat or fat-free versions; once again, just read your labels). Your lean protein sources provide you with the essentials that your body needs to build and repair soft tissues like muscle, tendons, and ligaments. When you eat protein, the first thing your body does is break it down into amino acids. Calcium and iron are often derived from a good source of protein, which can help reduce the soreness that you usually experience the day after a workout, and will help improve recovery time. Not just recovery time from an injury; but recovery time from a great performance, a class, or rehearsal without injury. Protein prevents one from becoming easily fatigued by allowing the body to express stamina and energy.

Nuts and seeds, which are also a great source of protein and good fats (the heart-healthy kind), are an excellent and easy-to-take-with-you snack. They are also simple to add to other foods such as salads and cereals, and can be used as a topping for fruit and yogurt. Whole grains are composed of minerals, protein, and carbohydrates and have been the staple food for a wide variety of cultures for thousands of years. When it comes to adding them to your meal planning, consider a good vegetarian or specialty recipe book for a little variety in preparation. Otherwise, the truth is that grains are easy to cook and need little or no preparation. For the most part, all you need to do is to rinse them, add water, and place on low heat. There is much natural goodness to be gained from adding whole grains, such as barley, bran, whole wheat, oats, brown rice and wild rice, corn, millet, buckwheat, and quinoa to your diet.

Let color, whole foods, whole ingredients, organics, (when you can), simple natural goodness, and unrefined and unprocessed be your mantra when shopping.

Stay away from junk food, fast food, and processed food.

The truth is they're *all* the same: *bad for you!* Do your best to exclude them from your diet. They are, for the most part, loaded with artificial or processed ingredients and offer little to no nutritional value whatsoever. Firstly, it's important to understand that the term "fast food" does not just mean the numerous chain restaurants; it also includes things like frozen dinners and the countless prepared meals in a box or can, as well as a candy bar or bag of chips. Fast, yes, but not good for you. I suggest that if it comes in a box or bag with some great big fabulous claim printed across the front, you should immediately read the ingredients on the back. It can be quite shocking. First things first: Start paying attention, and *read those labels!*

Being somewhat of a reformed chocoholic myself, I understand every whim when it comes to having a sweet tooth, and sure, a little cheat once in a while never hurt anyone; just try not to make it a daily habit. On those rare occasions when indulging, you have a choice to make, and that is whether or not to go with a natural and healthier version found in your local health food store—the kind that may be sweetened with organic cane sugar, molasses, apple juice, or honey—or to just simply go for that Snickers or Cadbury bar you've been craving. When it comes to choosing healthier versions, again, read your labels. Just because it is sold in a health food store doesn't mean that it's automatically healthy. Although you will find healthier choices, the same rules still apply. And that I will leave to your discretion and simply remind you that moderation is everything.

If you've never seen the movie *Super Size Me*, be sure to do so. It is both shocking and a real eye-opener! If eating on the road or on the run and Burger King or McDonald's are truly your only choices, then go with a salad—one of their healthier choices. At the end of the day, one big, fat juicy burger once in a while is probably not the end of the world; this is more about your everyday habits. And that is all I will say about fast food specifically.

Processed food, which basically includes everything that is not a whole food in its natural state, can easily be found in abundance. (Processed meaning altered, or added to in some form, and whole food meaning as close to the state in which Mother Nature delivered it to us.) Processed foods have been, and continue to be, defined by people in *many* different ways, and one can certainly get carried away with the topic. So, in an effort to help you understand, I say keep it simple. If a food is not in its natural state, then it has been modified to some extent, and can therefore be considered processed. However, some processing is necessary and some advantageous. You want to stay away from those foods that are over-processed, often with chemicals and mostly loaded with artificial ingredients. These make for very poor choices; some are potentially harmful, and most are nutritionally deficient. Here's a good rule of thumb: If you shop the perimeter of the grocery store, you will avoid many of the over-processed foods as this is where you will find your produce, meats, dairy products, etc. Think about what food items you find in the aisles, in the interior of the grocery store. Not to say that all foods in the aisles are processed, but this is where you will find most of your junk foods and so on. So keep these items to a very minimum, and keep your minimum to the minimally processed when shopping.

One area in particular to try to avoid, and to certainly beware of, is salad dressings and marinades. Dressings can be one the most deceptive areas in a person's diet. How often do you go to a restaurant, and in an effort to do the right thing you order a salad only to then pour an undisclosed dressing all over it? Before you know it, you've added hundreds of calories full of bad fats and sugars to your wonderful healthy choice. How about all of those varieties in the grocery stores? So many to choose from, so I will say it again: first and foremost, *read your labels*. Just because something says fat-free, no sugar added, low-calorie, light, or no carbs doesn't automatically make it the healthiest of choices. When eating in, you can make yourself a lovely healthy salad dressing with a few basic ingredients: a little olive oil and balsamic vinegar or fresh lemon juice, a touch of mustard, and some fresh crushed garlic makes for a great-tasting and healthy choice. Personally, I say the least amount of packaged goods you can buy and consume, the better off you will be.

ENCORE:
Let color, whole foods, whole ingredients, organics (when you can), simple natural goodness, and unrefined and unprocessed be your mantra when shopping.

LOW-FAT OPTIONS AND GOOD FAT VERSUS BAD FAT

It is important to understand that although fat was the first to receive bad press as being the main culprit of obesity and cardiovascular disease issues in the United States, fat is indeed necessary, and when eaten in moderation is important for our body's development and growth and our overall health. However, what you *must know* is the difference between *good fat* and *bad fat*. There are four major categories—monounsaturated fat, polyunsaturated fat, saturated fat, and trans fat.

Trans fats are getting the majority of the media's attention and bad press today. And rightfully so, thanks to the efforts of BanTransFats.com, a California nonprofit corporation that began an international trans fat campaign by suing Kraft in 2003 to eliminate trans fat in Oreo cookies. Trans fat is made when manufacturers add hydrogen to vegetable oil, a process called hydrogenation. It is the worst kind of fat, far worse than saturated fat and should be avoided entirely. These trans fats are often found in products such as margarine and many other packaged foods. Many of these packaged foods are also used in restaurants to prepare or cook other food. These oils are often blamed for contributing to the ever-increasing number of heart disease problems in the world. In December 2006, New York City passed a regulation banning the use of all trans fats in restaurants; in February 2007, Philadelphia followed suit, and today the initiatives by other cities and states have been overwhelming and too numerous to list. If entire cities are banning the use of trans fats, don't you think *you* should?

Generally speaking, you should also try to limit your intake of saturated fats, the kind that are solid at room temperature. Saturated fats occur naturally in many of the foods we consume. They are predominantly found in animal sources, including dairy items, especially whole-fat versions, and in fatty meats, such as beef, veal, lamb, pork, and chicken with the skin on. Many baked goods and fried foods may also contain high levels of saturated fats. Saturated fats are certainly among the most harmful fats in the everyday diet and when consumed in excessive amounts, they can be a major source of bad cholesterol and blood fats that can lead to cardiovascular problems. When it comes to dairy products, consider fat-free and low-fat options.

Monounsaturated fats and polyunsaturated fats don't seem to raise bad cholesterol levels and are beneficial when consumed in moderation. Monounsaturated fats, which are some of the best fats, are extremely important to your diet and can be found mostly in vegetable and nut oils, such as olive oil, canola oil, and peanut oil, as well as avocadoes and many nuts and seeds. You should consider replacing the lesser quality vegetable oils in your diet with olive oil. Olive oil is a staple of the Mediterranean diet, which has been proven time and time again to be one of the healthiest diets.

Polyunsaturated fats are found in a number of vegetable oils, including soybean oil, corn oil, safflower oil, and sunflower oil. Omega 3s, which are a very important group of polyunsaturated fats, are absolutely essential to optimum health and not as abundant in the average everyday diet. Omega 3s can be found in certain fish, especially fatty fish like mackerel, lake trout, herring, sardines, albacore tuna, and salmon, as well as walnuts, hemp seeds, and flax seeds. When purchasing salmon, try to choose wild salmon, not farm-raised and color-enhanced salmon. Aside from the questionable diet farm-raised fish are fed, once you taste the difference you'll understand why.

ENCORE:
Monounsaturated fats and polyunsaturated fats don't seem to raise bad cholesterol levels and are beneficial when consumed in moderation.

FIVE TO SIX MEALS PER DAY

Brace yourself! Here it comes that terrifying five to six meals a day topic. I remember the first time I went to a nutritionist in Los Angeles many years ago. The first thing he said to me was that he wanted me to eat five to six meals per day. I immediately thought to myself, "How can I possibly eat five to six meals a day? I'll be as big as this building!" Like most people I was appalled at the thought. Well, let me tell you that in three short months on this program I went

117

from 17 percent body fat down to 10 percent body fat and learned the importance of food and "fueling the furnace" as he called it. Let's use this analogy of your body being the furnace and your food being the fuel. You have to put fuel into your furnace in order for it to run, same goes for your body, if you don't put any fuel in it, how can you expect it to operate at optimum level. If you don't feed your body regularly it doesn't know when you are going to feed it again, so instead of burning calories it learns to hoard them as a means of preserving itself. This is the worst thing you can do for your metabolism.

First of all, a meal doesn't have to mean one meat and two vegetables. Small meals, more often, are much better for your digestion and overall weight control. You will be most successful if you plan and prepare meals in advance and get creative with your food choices. Five to six meals a day should consist of a good breakfast, lunch, and dinner, a midmorning snack, an afternoon snack, and a light evening snack (if you like), but no later than one hour before you go to bed.

In the morning, before you go to class or rehearsals, make sure that you have a good source of carbohydrates to give you the energy you need. Fruit, a dark or multigrain bagel, oatmeal and other whole-grain cereals, or whole-grain bread are all great sources of complex carbohydrates. When it comes to snacks, nuts and a bottle of water can be a great choice. If you're worried about salted versus unsalted nuts, Dr. Baron actually prefers salted for athletes as they perspire so heavily while in training or performance. Not only is your salt being replaced, but you are also increasing your thirst, so you're more likely to drink more fluids, and this, of course, is a good thing. He doesn't advise this for someone who is sitting at a desk all day, but you, the dancer, are moving; you are active. As a side note, nuts are loaded with good fats, primarily the "heart-healthy" mono-unsaturated and polyunsaturated fats, which are very good for you, so don't let anyone tell you that nuts are not a good diet food. You probably won't want to eat two pounds in one sitting as they are high in calories. That's just common sense, but we all need those little reminders: *portion control is everything*. As for other snacks, try to keep them light and clean; consider your overall daily calorie intake. Here are a few ideas: individual servings of apple sauce (the all-natural, no-sugar-added kind is best) and a couple of graham crackers, a natural brand yogurt, a fruit smoothie made from all fresh ingredients, or a protein shake. Last, but certainly not least, any fresh fruit or vegetable, and for something a little different and refreshing, try freezing some blueberries, grapes, or cherries.

As for lunch and dinner, try to eat a good balance of protein, carbohydrates, and heart-healthy fats. Protein should be lean and no larger than the size of

118

your fist. As for carbohydrates, stick to healthier and cleaner carbohydrates such as vegetables and whole grains as opposed to those over-processed versions we spoke of earlier. Once again, remember your portion control. Lunchtime can be a great time to load up on veggies, especially those dark leafy greens; they make a wonderful base to your salad. Also if you like pastas, which happen to be a good energy source, it's not a bad idea to eat them earlier in the day; just remember to keep your portions smaller, unlike the often heaping servings you might get when ordering in restaurants. Dinner is a good time to load up on protein and choose carbohydrates that are easily digestible, such as steamed vegetables. This will prove especially important if you are having a late-night dinner after a show. Easy reminder: Keep your *protein lean* and your *carbs clean*! Whenever possible, try to keep your last full meal to at least three hours before bedtime.

ENCORE:
You will be most successful if you plan and prepare meals in advance and get creative with your food choices.

READ THE LABELS

I'm sure by now you've gathered that I have never been a fan of processed foods, and anyone who has spent any time around me would likely say that I could make them a bit crazy with reading labels and conversations about ingredients! It's very simple—if you don't know what you're reading, you don't know what you're eating. Luckily for us, the law dictates that food manufacturers list ingredients and outline the nutritional breakdown on the packages of most foods. This is known as the nutrition facts panel and is regulated by the Food and Drug Administration, so take advantage of this feature. Have I said it yet? Read your labels and not just the calorie and fat counts.

Overall calories and the breakdown of fats, proteins, and carbohydrates are all important; however, you will also want to read the ingredients list. What are you eating? Ingredients are listed from the largest quantity to the smallest, so if sugar is first on the list, then that is the number one ingredient in the food item. If it is last on the list, there is a smaller quantity in the product.

So pay attention! Maybe the front label boasts some natural ingredient that is good for your health; however, in the ingredients list, it might be last on the list, and the product could have very little of the one ingredient you thought you were buying, not to mention the fact that it has been processed beyond recognition.

The other area that can prove to be very deceiving is the advertisement and promotion by companies of items for the diet-conscious consumers. "Fat-free" often means loaded with sugar, and "sugar-free" often means chemically processed sweeteners, while "low-carb" could mean loaded with fat, and not necessarily the "good" fat. The truth is that some people can, and will, eliminate all processed foods from their diets, while others will find it difficult. At the very least, do your best to keep these purchases to a minimum. By reading your labels, you can begin to eliminate the worst ingredients first. Refined white sugar and white flour are right up there with hydrogenated oils as ingredients to avoid. Keep in mind that if something is listed near the top of the ingredients list, it means that it is one of the main ingredients.

Over the last century, we have seen food manufacturers use everything possible to get their products out quicker, cheaper, and bigger. Along the way, they have ended up using more and more chemicals for processing and have supplemented diets with growth hormones in order to cut corners.

Research is slowly determining that not only do these procedures reduce the nutritional value of our foods, but they can actually be detrimental to our health. Let's face it, in this day and age, when we witness ever-increasing health issues, one sure fix is to simply go back to basics. Try to obtain foods in as natural a state as possible; you may want to consider shopping at your local health food store, whole food markets, and/or local farmers markets if available.

ENCORE:
It's very simple—if you don't know what you're reading, you don't know what you're eating.

MEAL PREPARATION AND PLANNING

If you truly want to control what you put into your body, one certain way to accomplish this is to plan and prepare your own meals. Yes, this means you will want to brush up on your gourmet flair, and a few great cookbooks could help you with exactly that. Truth is, you can make it as simple or extravagant as you like; most important is simply that you take the time to prepare, make sure you have all those healthy choices on hand, and get a little creative.

VITAMINS AND SUPPLEMENTS

I'm going to touch lightly on this topic merely for the purpose of introduction. When speaking with Dr. Baron I asked him which vitamins and supplements he recommends, and which, in particular, he most recommends for strength and endurance, or for healthy muscles and bones. His response was, "A multivitamin is always important, and having said that, I want to make it clear that what you cannot do is eat a terrible diet and then pop a multivitamin expecting it to be a cure-all. When you are eating properly, you get a lot of nutrients naturally. Unfortunately, unless you eat an absolutely impeccable diet, it will be difficult to get all of your nutrients from food alone—not impossible, but certainly difficult. Therefore, your multivitamin will be important to help supplement your diet.

"If you are interested in taking vitamins, it is a good idea to spend some time reading about the benefits of vitamins made from whole foods versus synthetics. Just as it is recommended that you eat whole foods in as natural a state as possible, you should also try to take good quality vitamins from a trusted brand, that are at best made from certified organic whole food ingredients. If your budget won't allow for certified organic, try to at the very least purchase vitamins made from whole food ingredients.

"Antioxidants naturally occur in all of your fresh fruits and vegetables and are very important to us. They are exactly as they sound, antioxidation; they block or inhibit destructive oxidation reactions. Oxidation is what happens during the aging process. Antioxidants give you the ability to fight off some of that damage. Does it not stand to reason that if antioxidants help to retain the elasticity in the skin, they can also do the same for what lies beneath the skin, our ligaments, tendons, and muscles?"

And that elasticity is so important to a dancer. If you are interested in taking antioxidants in supplement form, I suggest that you do some research as the list can be overwhelming. You will want to learn more in order to determine what is right for you, based on your personal nutritional habits and needs. Most multivitamins should include some antioxidants. ACE is a simple acronym to help you remember a few important antioxidants—vitamins A, C, and E—but the list does not end there.

In reference to our joints, ligaments, and bones, Dr. Baron continued, "Vitamins like E, A, and D, which are oil-based, are very good; E specifically is going to be extremely important because it helps to lubricate the joints. Other supplements that are super and are proven to show merit for arthritic joints are glucosamine, chondroitin, and MSM. Glucosamine and chondroitin are probably the most important arsenal for a dancer, due to the fact that they help repair and support cartilage. After all, the cartilage is what often takes the abuse, constantly absorbing the shock from your landings of all those jumps and leaps, and, therefore, suffers repetitive micro traumas." Some joint formulas or complexes can also be found with ginger and turmeric in them; these additional ingredients are known for their antioxidant properties, anti-inflammatory agents, and pain relief. I have found the combination to work very well for me.

"Papain and bromelain," Dr. Baron continued, "which are enzymes found naturally in papaya and pineapple, are both fantastic for muscle repair. After an injury, it would be a good idea to add some extra papaya and pineapple to your diet. Again, these can also be taken in supplement form."

ENCORE:
Antioxidants naturally occur in all of your fresh fruits and vegetables and are very important to us.

DRINK YOUR WATER

Dr. Baron also stressed the importance of drinking water. "Water constitutes about two-thirds of your body weight. So, what's the best thing for it? Water, *not diet soda*, and *not fruit drinks*, as they are loaded with sugar and can defeat the purpose. Your body needs water. It is extremely important to constantly keep hydrated." Every system in your body depends on water. For example, water flushes toxins out of vital organs, carries nutrients to your cells, and provides a moist environment for ear, nose, and throat tissues. I'm sure you have often heard that you should drink at least eight 8–12 oz. glasses of water per day. The average adult loses more than ten cups of water every day simply by sweating, breathing, and eliminating waste. You also lose electrolytes—minerals such as sodium, potassium, and calcium that maintain the balance of fluid in your body. Normally you can replenish sufficiently through the foods and liquids you consume. However, if you eliminate more than you replace, this can lead to dehydration.

ENCORE:
Your body needs water. It is extremely important to constantly keep hydrated.

EIGHT QUICK REFERENCE TIPS

1. Make healthy choices:
   Eat whole foods as close to their natural state as possible.
   Shop for the colors of the rainbow.
   When it comes to animal protein, keep it lean.

When it comes to carbohydrates, keep them clean.

Good fat versus bad.

Grains are easy to prepare.

Nuts and seeds are easy to pack.

2. Stay away from junk food, fast food, and processed food.

    Bottom line is it's all the same: bad for you!

3. Five to six meals per day:

    Not every meal has to be a meat and two vegetables.

    Don't skip meals.

    Nuts and a bottle of water are a great snack.

    Make sure that your last meal of the day is at least three hours before bedtime.

    A light evening snack should be no later than one hour before bedtime.

4. Portion control:

    Small meals more often, hence the five to six meals.

    Protein portions should be the size of your fist.

    Stop when you are no longer hungry; don't wait until you are stuffed.

5. Read the labels. (Can't stress this one enough):

    If you don't know what you're reading, you don't know what you're eating.

    Ingredients list is important—not just the fat, calories, and carb count.

6. Meal preparation and planning:

    The healthiest meals start in your own kitchen.

    Load up on good-quality ingredients.

    Buy yourself a good "healthy" cookbook.

    Get creative and try new cuisines.

    Take a cue from the Mediterranean, Indian, and Japanese diets.

7. Supplements and vitamins:

    Try adding a daily multivitamin.

    Supplements made from whole foods versus synthetics.

    Read and learn more about antioxidant-rich foods.

8. Water:

    Keep hydrated with a minimum of eight glasses (each 8–12 oz.) of water per day.

ENCORE:

Moms Know Best—isn't that why we refer to Nature as Mother Nature?

Bringing it . . . all together! Cast of Arbitron corporate event—*Toga Party*, Miami Beach, Florida

Chapter Ten
Let's Get Physical—Injury Recognition and Prevention

"The doctor of the future will give no medicine, but will interest his patients in the care of human frame, and in the cause and prevention of disease."
~ **Thomas Alva Edison**

The information transcribed by me and extensive quotes you are about to read in this chapter are the results of an in-depth interview with Dr. Baron, as previously mentioned.

Dr. Baron has always had a special interest in dancers; he refers to dancers as, "One of the ultimate athletes, they are the only athletes that have to present their art using their bodies while making it look beautiful and effortless. If they are in pain, you will never know." He also reminded me of how often I have said to him, "The show must go on," and that, concisely, is why he finds dancers so fascinating. To me the *ultimate dancer* is exactly that, fascinating. When a dancer is driven by passion it's no wonder they can endure just about anything and achieve such great feats. One of my favorite quotes by Albert Einstein sums it up: "Dancers are the athletes of God."

"Recognition and prevention are keys to your longevity as a dancer or an athlete," Dr. Baron says. "And a fail-safe way to really accomplish this is to have an imaginary checklist in each area of your health pyramid—nutritional, physical, and mental. Think about everyday life; emotional upsets tend to create stress. With a dancer, there is always a tremendous amount of pressure, from the need to constantly perform at the same level or better, to vying for a job or specific role at an upcoming audition. Either of these could cause a great deal of stress, and if you are so preoccupied with stress, then your performance will undoubtedly be affected. Here's why: first it creates tension, next you're not sleeping, and before you know it, you're not eating well, or you may not be eating at all. I understand that sometimes you can't help getting stressed. If that's the case, then you have to make up for it and compensate in other areas by taking extra care, and ensuring that you eat properly, and stay away from unhealthy choices. For instance, if you had a bad night's sleep because you were stressed out, and to add insult to injury, all you have for breakfast the next morning is a cup of coffee, where are you going to pull your energy from? If anything, this will provoke more anxiety and more anguish as your system is being driven by poor fuel; hence, you are mentally and physically unstable. One small mistake during a jump, and before you know it, you've landed inaccurately and injured yourself. You can see from this example how integrated and intimate everything is."

ENCORE:
Recognition and prevention are keys to your longevity as a dancer or an athlete.

IN YOUR CONTROL AND OUT OF YOUR CONTROL

The previous paragraph relates to recognition and prevention in areas that are within our control. Next, we want to stress the importance of recognition in areas that are outside our control. Environmental factors, such as a dance floor, a cold and drafty atmosphere, or humidity and high temperatures can often be the cause of injuries. You don't always know the kind of environment you will be working or auditioning in, so at all times, you should be prepared for the worst. Never slack on your footwear; it is your most important piece of equipment. There are many types of flooring that you might encounter at auditions or during rehearsals. Some may not have been originally intended for dancers, so don't cut corners on your footwear. When it comes to a drafty environment, you have to be very careful, especially in hot climates where you have air conditioning.

The air from such systems is cold and dry, so you want to make sure that you are appropriately dressed and properly warmed up; a few extra layers can go a long way towards injury prevention. Something to be aware of in the summer months, and something we see here in Florida year-round, is humidity and high temperatures. This can provoke dehydration, cramps, and exhaustion, so the components of nutrition and rehydration become absolutely imperative. Be sure to eat balanced meals and drink plenty of fresh water.

126

I want to emphasize that preparation is always the best form of defense even when confronted with unfamiliar circumstances. Dr. Baron remembered a story that reiterates this point succinctly. "It was the cast of *Les Misérables* and they were performing on an incredibly raked stage, certainly the worst one the dancers had ever worked on. This was the only time that I ever had to send a dancer to an orthopedic surgeon. Due to the extreme rake in the stage, he lost his footing, and unfortunately injured himself on the spot. Sadly, he ended up having knee surgery."

Of course accidents do happen, but awareness and preparation are key under these circumstances. Sometimes spending just a little extra time familiarizing yourself with your environment can help you prevent such accidents. In fact, think about the dancers working on cruise ships. Very often they are performing on a stage that is moving up and down and side-to-side. The way to handle this is to first of all be open to the situation at hand, and be completely focused so that you are fully aware of exactly what is happening. This will allow your body to compensate and adjust as necessary; your muscles will naturally adjust their tension, motion, and memory, but it does take some time. So you must approach it intelligently, taking the necessary time to become familiar with your new territory.

ENCORE:
Sometimes spending just a little extra time familiarizing yourself with your environment can help you prevent accidents.

CHIROPRACTIC AND THE DANCER

Year in and year out chiropractic has become one of the chosen treatments for athletes and dancers alike. Dr. Baron explains: "Chiropractic offers an understanding of physiology and of biomechanics, so we, as chiropractors, observe the athlete and identify what actually went wrong and why, and then we can treat the injury from that perspective. As chiropractors, we help to create balance and strengthen weak muscles. We work with the way the body naturally heals, so you are not misguided by an impression that you are better when, in fact, you are not.

"Part of the beauty of being a chiropractor with a specialty in sports injury is that we look to identify things that are actually compensations to the original injury. So, for example, let's consider a torn hamstring. In traditional medicine, it would be all about your hamstring, and yes, of course, chiropractors pay attention to the hamstring as well, but we will delve further. What you may not have known is that your injury was due to the fact that your pelvis was out of alignment, or that you had pressure coming off the nerve at L5, 4, or 3 [L stands for lumbar region of the back, while the number relates to the exact vertebrae]. This pressure was slowing down or hindering the full potential of that hamstring muscle, both in strength and coordination. Because it was weak and not operating at optimum level, it became injured. A different scenario could be if the ankle on the opposite leg to the injured hamstring became a problem. Maybe your dance shoe didn't fit properly, and you were compensating for it. Whenever there is an ankle or a foot injury, we always look to the joint above on the opposite side, so a bad ankle on the left can produce a bad right knee, and what is hooked up to the knee but the hamstring? So before you know it, you have a hamstring strain. The problem is this: If you never fix the ankle, you'll constantly have hamstring strains. Now that's putting it so simplistically for the purpose of clarity; however, there is a whole web of other biomechanical compensations. It's like peeling back the skin of an onion to get to the core of the injury."

TRADITIONAL MEDICINE AND YOUR INJURY

"Unfortunately, the primary health care choice that most people know and use is traditional medicine. This is all well and good, but the form of treatment they generally use is medication. Medication is the very short-term approach to getting better, and it's not necessarily getting better; it is simply shutting off the fire alarm and never really addressing the fire. So when a dancer rehearses or performs with the fire alarm shut off, he/she is magnifying the potential for re-injury. They are actually shortening their life span as dancers. Dancers have very strong wills and are already accustomed to and capable of shutting off pain in their mind. Unfortunately, with medication, you have a double whammy: first the dancer shuts it off in their mind, and then the medication shuts off the actual sensation. It's one thing to control the sensation and modulate it; however, to eliminate it artificially is a completely different situation. Together, the two are an extremely dangerous combination for a dancer. Depending on the injury, the other option recommended by traditional medicine is surgery, and when you are a dancer, surgery is not a good thing. It can impose great delays and often it can even be the end of your career. You want to avoid surgery at all cost."

ENCORE:
Medication is the very short-term approach to getting better, and it's not necessarily getting better; it is simply shutting off the fire alarm and never really addressing the fire.

OTHER ALTERNATIVE APPROACHES

"In addition to chiropractic, here is a list of other healing arts that can also be very beneficial. Massage therapy should be a part of your standard practice whenever possible. Pilates is one of the most superior practices for a dancer because it is both a rehab and preventative program. It is perfectly made for the dancer. A physical therapist can be helpful; try to find one that has a specialty in sports injury. Some are meritorious of having the ability to treat conservatively without drugs or surgery. An athletic trainer who is certified in treating pro athletes, a good nutritionist, a dance or sports psychologist, and an acupuncturist might all be helpful. These are all good people to know and to have on hand.

"One other area is osteopathic medicine. The beauty of it is that it's meant to be the combination of the traditional medical doctor who prescribes medicine with the philosophies of manipulation of the spine and extremities, which is what the osteopath does. The only unfortunate thing is that many osteopaths here in the United States have found it easier to put a greater emphasis on prescribing medication than on performing the art of manipulation."

Different practices work for different people, so sometimes you have to try things on for size and see what works best for you and your body's needs. The above list is merely intended to serve as a guideline and provide information to help you in determining what natural approach will be best for you in both injury prevention and rehabilitation. The bottom line is, as I've said previously, your body is your business, and it is your responsibility. You have to ensure its proper care by putting yourself in the right hands in order to sustain the maximum longevity possible.

MINOR INCONVENIENCE, WARNING SIGNAL, OR INJURY

Because of the strong will that dancers have and that innate ability to dance through much pain, I want to pay special attention to the differences between a minor inconvenience, a warning signal, and an actual full-on injury. From the time I was very young, I was taught that what the average person considered pain was simply a minor inconvenience to a dancer. Although I hope that dancers today are more informed and better educated in the area of health and fitness, it is still in their blood as a breed to endure and live by the wonderful old adage, "The show must go on." So how does this same dancer—the one who is capable of shutting off the sensation of pain—understand the difference between a warning signal, an injury, and just a minor inconvenience?

Dr. Baron reiterates the importance of prevention and recognition: "A good warning sign is a weakness in the muscles. For example, if a dancer is on pointe, and she is losing control of her stability, that could be a sign of fatigue. This is usually a sign that there is a potentiating injury ensuing, so you must be aware. There is nobody more body-conscious than a dancer; therefore, I suggest that you learn to use this to your advantage. It is possible to be aware of the pain and still maintain that same mentality so that it will not get you down—"the show must go on" attitude. But you must heed the warning and take care. An even stronger warning would be if you suddenly found that you could not hold a position like you used to. This could also be due to a weakness, and it might be an early warning sign that something is building.

"There is a first sign that people do not heed, and that is called a loss of *proprioceptive skills*. Proprioception is one of the components of nerve conduction; nerve fibers conduct four senses—the sense of pain, the sense of temperature, the sense of pressure, and the sense of proprioception. Proprioceptive fibers allow you to understand where your body is in space without looking, for example, when you land from a jump or leap without looking at the floor. If you begin noticing that you are no longer able to land pinpoint, then you should start questioning your proprioceptive skill, as this is one of your first signs of a potentiating injury. Proprioception is critical to a dancer; it is a sensory perception that everyone has, but is definitely enhanced in dancers; so if you start to see this falter, you should beware.

"This is why in the athletic training camps, you hear more and more about football players learning ballet. It helps them to develop that ability of balance, which is proprioception. When it comes to recovering from an injury, there is much rehabilitation being done today with balance boards for this exact reason. If we can rehabilitate an athlete's balance and proprioceptive skills, we have a much stronger and more stable foundation, and, therefore, can secure far less chance of re-injury. The old way was to simply get them back into the game, or onstage, as quickly as possible with not much foresight as to their overall career longevity. Back then, the reason people were not rehabilitating correctly from ankle strains and similar injuries was because they were not developing their proprioceptive sense. Without developing and re-strengthening that sense, you cannot ensure that you will dance or perform and not do the exact same thing again, hence the constant re-injury. If you cannot feel where the floor is, how are you going to land? Today there is so much more beyond just pain control that can be done for injury rehabilitation."

In the event that you might notice this sort of early warning sign, you should immediately go back, default to your nutritional, physical, or mental checklist, and find out what is going on. You may realize that you are overtraining, or are becoming overtired. You may not be giving your body adequate nutrition. *Something is out of whack*, and this could mean an impending injury. Your checklists are your ways of identifying some of what may be lacking.

ENCORE:

Without developing and re-strengthening your proprioceptive sense, you cannot ensure that when you dance or perform you will not re-injure yourself.

R.I.C.E.

In the event of injury, you cannot go wrong with the acronym *R.I.C.E.:* rest, ice, compression, and elevation. This should be done for the first three days of an acute injury. Current research suggests that one should ice intermittently immediately following an acute strain. For best results, recommended protocols are ten minutes with ice, ten minutes without ice, and ten minutes with ice again, repeating every two hours or as often as you can for those first three days.

After the first three days or so, when all swelling has stopped and has definitely been reduced, then you can start to do a contrast of ice and heat, alternating ice for ten minutes, then heat for ten minutes, and ending with ice. This will serve as a vascular exercise to pump all of the injured or dead blood cells and tissue out of the area. Heat expands and ice contracts; when you alternate heat and ice a couple of times back-to-back, then you create a vascular exercise. Heat re-accommodates the blood vessels to open and forces fluid and nutrients in; ice closes them so you don't cause additional swelling. Swelling is where further injury can happen because it distorts the tissue from the onset of the injury. You can control tissue distortion by suppressing any swelling that is going on. Even though some of it is natural and is supposed to happen, you still need to control it.

There is a time to use heat only, however, and Dr. Baron stresses that you must be very clear on this point. "Heat is good as long as you don't continue to aggravate the situation. So, for example, let's say that you are into day number seven and you are back to doing some moderate performing, moderate levels of activity, or even full performance. Let's take it a step further. Let's say that the original injury was to a shoulder, although this is not a weight-bearing joint. Imagine that every time you do a certain move, you re-aggravate the injury; this is when you must not use heat or you should stop using heat if you have been. When you re-aggravate an injury, you have to use ice again and restart the cycle. Heat you only use if you're not re-aggravating the situation. If you're into day six, seven, or eight, then you should be using heat only to warm up the muscle, without allowing it to swell. Whatever you do, you do not want to re-potentiate the swelling. Here's a good rule of thumb to help you better understand: Because the injury is under the skin, you can't see it, so think of it as a cut on your knee. Every time you feel pain or pulling, you're opening up the wound again. You wouldn't put heat on your wounded knee because it would actually deteriorate the scar tissue (the scab), and it would start to bleed again. So consider that the same is happening below the skin, and the last thing you want to do to a fresh injury or re-injury is to make it bleed. This is why we always use ice first."

ENCORE:
R.I.C.E: rest, ice, compression, and elevation. This should be done for the first three days of an acute injury.

PULL, TEAR, SPRAIN, OR STRAIN?

Dr. Baron explains in layman's terms the difference between a pull or a tear, and a sprain or strain to a muscle, a ligament, or a tendon. "A pull is a word used so freely," he says. "When people say a pull, it is usually a tear. This sounds very aggressive, but all strains and sprains are, in fact, tears to the soft tissue; they are micro-tears. Because the word tear sounds so overwhelming, I don't often use it. A sprain is what happens when the ligament tears, whereas a strain is what happens when the muscle or tendon is injured or tears for the sake of explanation. If you were to take a piece of toilet tissue and not tear it apart, but just start pulling on it to the point where the fibers start to separate, then you would have an idea of what happens to muscles and ligaments and tendons. To further clarify, ligaments are found much deeper than the muscles and tendons; ligaments attach bone to bone and tendons attach muscle to bone. So to connect the tibia to the femur, you have a lot of ligaments. Ligaments provide stability. They do not provide any power, whereas muscle, which turns into tendon and attaches to the bone, provides you with power and propulsion. Many years ago, when soccer players would suffer ligament sprains, surgeons often recommended cutting certain ligaments out. Since the technology for healing ligaments was so inadequate back then, the players just continued to re-injure them, and so the simple solution was 'Let's get rid of them.' It was believed that they didn't really need the ligaments, because one could manage without them. Because soccer players have such incredibly strong leg muscles,

132

and since that is where their propulsion comes from, this very strength is what they relied on to carry them through. But you see the problem is this, when they get older and their muscles get weak, without those ligaments, they are left with a sensational amount of instability." Thankfully, this is no longer common practice.

> ENCORE:
> *Ligaments are found much deeper than the muscles and tendons; ligaments attach bone to bone and tendons attach muscle to bone.*

HEALING TIME

"Why does it always seem to take so much longer to heal a strained muscle or sprained ligaments than to heal a bone fracture?" He answered, "It has often been said, 'I would rather you fracture a body part than strain it.' Why? When something is fractured, we pay a lot of attention to it; we cast it immediately, and it's a big deal. When it comes to a strain or sprain, no matter to what degree, you think that it's only a minor injury, and so you don't take care of it as well; hence the elongated healing time. You simply never really take care of these minor problems with the same concern as a major problem. The truth is, when properly addressed, a muscle or tendon can take four to six weeks to heal, a ligament can take six to eight weeks, whereas a bone can take eight weeks or more.

"With dancers, the most common injuries are stress fractures in the feet. Unfortunately, what usually happens is that we wait until a strain leads to a fracture before we take care of it. The lower extremities are nearly always beaten up from various injuries, but when you let them go on and on and do not take care of them, then they become stress fractures. Bones are strong, and it takes weakened ligaments or tendons to create a lack of support; without that support, the bone takes the brunt of the problem. Usually the first to go is a muscle, then tendon, then ligament, and finally bone." So you can see the importance of paying attention to those early warning signals and properly addressing them before they become debilitating injuries.

> ENCORE:
> *The truth is, when properly addressed, a muscle or tendon can take four to six weeks to heal, a ligament can take six to eight weeks, whereas a bone can take eight weeks or more.*

INJURIES AND SLEEPING PATTERNS

I've had a few dancers over the years with injuries that we discovered were being aggravated in their sleep, although it's difficult to tell which came first, the potential injury and the improper sleeping patterns or the improper sleeping patterns that provoked the injuries. "Allow me to explain: Most important to the aesthetics and performance of a dancer is balance and symmetry. Therefore it only stands to reason that if you were to sleep in awkward or funny positions 365 days or nights out of the year, you would be damaging your balance and symmetry? The worst way you can sleep is belly-down; your head might be turned to one side, with one arm over your head, and one leg in a passé position. Imagine if you are absolutely exhausted and you just don't move from that position all night, when, in fact, our bodies are meant to move countless times throughout the night. Do that all night for six or eight hours and see how you feel! The best way to sleep is on your back with a pillow that provides curve to the neck. Your head should be slightly back with your ears in balance with your shoulders, and maybe a couple of pillows under your legs. The second best way to sleep is on your side in the fetal position with a pillow between your legs and one placed underneath your head. Your shoulder should be slightly forward; you should not be lying on it.

"Bad sleeping habits are hard to break, but because they can be the culprit of chronic aches and pains, they are definitely worth your consideration." How many of you sleep in turn out, passé positions, or legs and arms extended in all angles? Some of you may be doing full-on choreography in your sleep! Give it some thought, and try to retrain yourself to sleep in one of the more favorable positions recommended. I have seen a few dancers, including myself, eliminate a fair bit of pain through a good night's sleep.

ENCORE:

Most important to the aesthetics and performance of a dancer is balance and symmetry.

HOME REHABILITATION

When it comes to at-home rehabilitation and exercises that are best for preventative measures, Dr. Baron strongly recommends Pilates, a method that has been widely embraced by dancers for years. I trust that most of you are familiar with it. It was created in the early 1900s by Joseph Pilates, a performer and boxer who developed his concepts and exercises based on over twenty years of self-study and apprenticeship in yoga, Zen, and ancient Greek and Roman physical regimens. "Pilates is the ideal thing for dancers; it's as though it was made just for them.

"When it comes to rehabilitation, you want to use a non-trauma approach. I wouldn't recommend jogging. I would, however, recommend a therapy ball or if you're looking for more conditioning, I would suggest doing all non-traumatic activities like a recumbent bike, the elliptical machine, and StairMasters rather than jogging or using a treadmill. You want to avoid trauma—you've already done so much of that in your dance."

ENCORE:
When it comes to at-home rehabilitation and exercises that are best for preventative measures, Dr. Baron strongly recommends Pilates.

OFF-SEASON TRAINING

In "Chapter Three: Triple Threat," I talked about the importance of constant training for a dancer. The reason I put so much emphasis on this is because over the years I've seen many dancers develop bad habits. Often, when they are traveling for work and not able to get to class, many are not disciplined enough to give themselves a class or get to the gym. Even worse, when doing a long-running engagement, many think because they are performing every night they don't have to be in class every day, but there is no greater misconception. Although I have stressed the importance of training even when you are in contract, Dr. Baron made special mention of what he refers to as off-season conditioning, or for clarity, out-of-performance-season or out-of-contract training.

"Off-season conditioning is so important because you want to be as close to performance ready as possible without enduring the trauma of what it is like to be in training during performance season. So you really want to gradually ramp up your activities throughout your off-season in order to prepare for performance season or an upcoming contract rather than waiting until the last minute. This could be really simple stuff, because what you don't want to do is suddenly shock the system as that will take its toll on you and defeat the very gradual approach necessary for building your stamina."

I can certainly relate as a choreographer who has spent her career in and out of rehearsals on a regular basis. My dance schedule would change with my rehearsal schedules, and so it has always been important for me—and much more so after I stopped performing—to maintain a strong training and workout schedule.

STRENGTH TRAINING FOR THE DANCER

Over the past twenty years or so, I have studied and trained in the area of muscle conditioning and strength training, and I have found that I'm at my best and strongest when I am doing a good blend of light weight training, low-impact aerobics, yoga, and Pilates. Years ago, it was thought that strength training was bad for dancers and that it went against our grain as dancers. I asked Dr. Baron what his thoughts were about strength training.

"It is a fantastic way of keeping in shape while strengthening your overall muscle tone and providing the body with additional resistance greater than your own body weight. As dancers, you have naturally trained yourselves over the years to endure your own body weight. Strength training can only help to enhance what you do naturally, by adding that additional resistance.

"Your body is an amazing mechanism; its accommodative reflexes are so cool, and we totally take them for granted. Think of calluses on your feet. They are due to repetitive trauma, which is just enough stress to the superficial tissues to make the body go, 'Hey, I need some more skin cells down here.' So what does the body do? It thickens that area and makes it more durable. When you stop doing what caused the irritation in the first place, the calluses go away. That is exactly what is happening to your body when you stress it just enough over a long period of time. The accommodative reflexes add increases of minerals to the bone, ligaments, tendons, and muscles. This strengthens them, so now you become more tolerant of the stresses that you're going to encumber in your performances."

As dancers, we tend to use the same muscle groups over and over again. Think about what happens when you change your routine by starting rehearsals for a new show. How often do you come in the following day stiff and aching, suddenly feeling muscles that you never knew existed? I remember one particular show that I was doing; it was the summer production revue at the Royal York Hotel in Toronto. The first day of rehearsals was so exciting—meeting the new cast, learning the choreography, and getting an overall flavor of what the show was going to be like. Day two, I woke up feeling like a Mack truck had run over me. I was so stiff, it hurt to get out of bed, let alone move my head. My friend and roommate at the time, who was also doing the show with me, woke up feeling pretty much the same. I remember both of us moaning and groaning all the way to rehearsals and lamenting about what horrible shape we must be in, only to arrive at rehearsal and find the entire cast with leg warmers and scarves wrapped around their necks. No one was moving too quickly that day! On the other hand, imagine when you are in the same routine day in and day out. Your body adjusts to the routine, so when you are performing the same show, or in class executing the same or similar exercises, certain muscles are not getting any attention, and therefore may not be getting strengthened or even maintained. I personally believe from my own experience that strength training is a great way to develop muscle groups that may not get adequate work in your dance training. Years ago, I was that dancer who wouldn't dare enter a gym or take an aerobics class; today I could not imagine my life without my workouts. As a dancer, strength training helped to improve my physical strength overall, and it especially helped me to rehabilitate when I was injured and brought me back even stronger.

ENCORE:

Strength training is a great way to develop muscle groups that may not get adequate work in your dance training.

EXERCISE DO'S AND DON'TS

I asked Dr. Baron which exercises, if any, he would not advocate for dancers. "I will sum it up this way: you want to stay away from the activities that are first and foremost pounding. As I mentioned earlier, like jogging or running on a treadmill, this is the last thing you want to do. The upper body bicycle known as an ergometer would be an excellent exercise for dancers to do; this is the only activity where you can gain a sensational amount of activity without using your legs. So no pounding activities, and most importantly for the dancer would be no one-sided sports. I hate to say it, but activities like golf, tennis, or pitching are not good for you. If you spent all summer at tennis camp, then you could be doomed. Think about it—balance is crucial to a dancer. The last thing you want is one-sided activities that could create any imbalances and possibly interfere in any way with the symmetry necessary for your dancer physique and for the execution of your dance."

SOCIAL AND PEER PRESSURE DO'S AND DON'TS

Unfortunately, in the entertainment industry, there is sometimes a natural association with drinking, smoking, and social drugs. Aside from the fact that drugs are illegal, the physical complications that can occur are absolutely detrimental to your health and career. I am a huge advocate of health and nutrition and the tremendous role that they play in keeping you fit and on top of your game. Social drugs simply do not have any place in your life, and I can't say this strongly enough. No curiosity or peer pressure is worth losing yourself to or compromising your integrity for. I have witnessed some extremely talented artists lose themselves to social drugs and serious drinking problems. In the end, it cost some of them their jobs, while it costs others their careers. This is a small business and word gets around. When it comes to your reputation, you want it clean and untarnished. There are a few things that will get you fired with immediate dismissal, and drugs are certainly at the top of the list. Although having a couple of drinks may not get you fired, an addiction to alcohol is a problem that will often interfere with your work and could eventually cost you your job. Do not compromise yourself or your integrity ever, not to any addiction, especially drugs or alcohol. Just stay away from them, period! Choose a healthy path for all the wonderful reasons we're talking about in this chapter. After all, you are an athlete, so why not be a fine-tuned athlete, in mind, body, and spirit. Trust yourself—you know what's best, and making the right choices makes for a much better experience and overall performance. You haven't spent your life preparing for and dreaming about this career only to throw it all away.

Here's what Dr. Baron has to say: "With alcohol, moderation is everything. Now you may have those days where you put the pedal to the metal and party a little too much; inevitably, you will have to pay. When you overindulge, whether it is drugs or alcohol, you are depleting something in your system, so if you understand this maybe you'll make better choices. Don't think that you can overindulge then simply fortify yourself with all the proper nutrients; this is not how it works. You don't simply get to replenish with some supplements and make all the damage disappear. No, you must understand that what you've done has taken away from your system, and this oftentimes produces injuries. As an example, alcohol is a dehydrator; that being the case, consider how you have depleted your system of its essential nutrients."

Dehydration is the loss of water and salts that are essential for normal body function.

"Here's what is really important. I am not just talking about the immediate pain that you may feel from a hangover. I am talking about the depletion and potential for injury you have caused your body. Once the damage is done, you had better take extra care of yourself because you don't want to, and you can't afford to, end up injured. In other words, you play, you pay, and no, you don't just get to suffer quietly through your hangover. Now you have to be responsible and make sure that you get yourself back in shape with a lot of TLC. This means extra work on your part."

During rehearsals, I will forewarn cast members of the intense demands on them during this period, and I will ask them to be intelligent and keep the use of alcohol to a minimum. I understand that some people like to relax with a glass of wine or beer at the end of a long day, and that's fine with me as long as they are not reckless and it does not interfere with their ability to perform the next day. It is very important to the team that you are responsible and there for each other 100 percent.

As an ex-smoker, someone who speaks from having been there and done that, I would love nothing more than to not see anyone smoke ever again. I always said that I would not be "one of those ex-smokers" who drove others crazy about it. And, therefore, I will try not to go on too much; I will simply point out the obvious. Today we know more and more about the terrible effects of smoking, not to mention that it is far less socially acceptable now than it was in the past. Yet so many continue the habit and still too many pick it up. I smoked for years so I can attest to how addictive it is. I add to that the fact that one who smokes must make the firm decision and have the desire to quit in order to be successful. When I finally decided with a firm conviction that I wanted to be a non-smoker, it was so much easier than I had ever imagined. That's not to say it's easy for everyone, but merely to say that it *can* be done, and possibly, with less difficulty than you might think.

On December 27, 1999, a very dear friend suffered a stroke, and I spent the following week at the hospital. Every four hours or so when the cravings got to be too much, I would slip away to have a cigarette, and as I stood in front of the hospital smoking, I thought to myself, *Something is really wrong with this picture. Here I am slowly throwing away my life while my friend is up there in his hospital bed fighting for his.* As the millennium was approaching, I had been talking about quitting and planned to pick up some nicotine patches on New Year's Eve. My best girlfriend from home flew into Miami to celebrate the New Year with me. The nurses at Mount Sinai Hospital were kind enough to allow us to bring in the millennium with our very dear friend, who was doing much better but, unfortunately, still laid up in bed. That night before going to bed, my friend who was visiting took my cigarettes and flushed them down the toilet even though I had not picked up any patches yet. As far as she was concerned, a deal was a deal. I am thrilled to say that I am still smoke-free all these years later, and that was doing it cold turkey.

I do believe that dancers today are better educated in the area of health, even if only for the simple reason that in general, people are better educated. However, as a reminder, and for those who may not be aware of the dangers associated, I will quote a few facts and statistics. According to the American Cancer Society, "About half of all Americans who continue to smoke will die because of the habit. Each year about 443,600 people die in the United States from illnesses related to cigarette smoking. Cigarettes kill more Americans than alcohol, car accidents, suicide, AIDS, homicide, and illegal drugs combined."

Nicotine is a drug found naturally in tobacco. It is highly addictive—as addictive as heroin or cocaine. Over time, the body becomes both physically and psychologically dependent on nicotine. Nearly everyone knows that smoking can cause lung cancer, but few people realize it is also a risk factor for many other kinds of cancer, including cancer of the mouth, voice box (larynx), throat (pharynx), esophagus, bladder, kidney, pancreas, cervix, stomach, and some forms of leukemia. Smoking increases the risk of lung diseases, such as emphysema and chronic bronchitis, and for the first time, the U.S. Surgeon General has added pneumonia to the list.

Smokers are twice as likely to die from heart attacks as are nonsmokers. According to the American Heart Association, "Cigarette and tobacco smoke is one of six major independent risk factors for coronary heart disease that you can modify or control. Cigarette smoking is so widespread and significant as a risk factor that the Surgeon General has called it 'the leading preventable cause of disease and deaths in the United States.' Cigarette smoking increases the risk of coronary heart disease by itself. When it acts with other factors, it greatly increases risk."

There are over 4,000 chemicals in tobacco smoke and at least sixty-nine of those chemicals are known to cause cancer. As I did promise to be brief, I would like to share one final personal story with you. I lost my father at a young age; I was only twenty. He was relatively young, only sixty-nine when he died after a long struggle with both coronary disease and cancer of the lungs and throat. As you can imagine, his final years were not as pleasant and peaceful as they should have been. He was in an out of hospitals and underwent radiation therapy that left him each time feeling and looking much worse for it. If you've ever been through such a loss, you know how difficult and heartbreaking it is to watch someone you love suffer. God bless my mother, who never left his side and took care of him until his last breath. My father, of course, always wanted me to quit smoking. As a matter of fact, when he first found out that I was smoking, he asked me to promise him that I would quit. My mother, who never smoked a day in her life, could not understand how I could continue smoking after watching what my father went through. I, being young and foolish, thought I was invincible; but lucky for me, I eventually smartened up. It might have taken me a while, but I did it, and it means a lot to me that I did keep my promise to my dad.

140

Getting back to alcohol and drugs, as I mentioned earlier, I have seen a few unfortunate situations where both alcohol and drugs have cost people their jobs and careers. I want to be extremely clear and help you understand the severity of such actions. So, in an effort to drive this home, I asked Dr. Baron to point out some of the physical complications you can suffer from a few bad choices.

"Here's the thing," he said. "I hate to keep dwelling on the nutrition issue, but I want you to realize and recognize what not taking care of yourself from the onslaught does to you. There is a whole cascade of things that can go on and that you subject yourself to as a liability for the way in which you think and the way you feel. I will give you an example. Let's say that you did not eat well [the way we've suggested in this chapter] and you are exhausted, having given an exerting and dynamite performance. After the show, your friends want to go for a drink. You would like to join them, but you know that you shouldn't because you need to rest. Due to the fact that you are so tired and depleted from your day, you lose your sense of rational thinking and your discrimination as to what would be the right thing to do or not. Since you did not give your body the proper fuel that it needs to function optimally, you have depleted your system of all nutrients and neurochemicals—those required for proper nerve transmission and thought. Hence, you make poor decisions.

"Our decision making is handicapped when we're tired or exhausted, even when there is just a remote shift in our state of mind; this is the worst time to make a decision. The best time is when we are fresh and sharp; this is when things fire off properly. You cannot push yourself physically and expect to give a pinpoint performance when your body is depleted of its nutrients and basic needs. This is why I cannot emphasize enough as a preventative measure that you absolutely need a good, sound nutritional orientation and meal plan for each day."

The bottom line is, it all comes down to how you take care of yourself, and nutrition is an extremely important factor. Over the years, I have had the opportunity to work with dancers and artists of various backgrounds, and it is the conscientious dancer—"the new athlete or dancer," as Dr. Baron refers to them, who has the edge. Dr. Baron and I discussed the fact that we have both seen in our respective lines of work the differences between those athletes and dancers who are much more conscientious and those who are not. Those who choose to lead a healthier lifestyle sustain much greater longevity in their careers. They avoid cigarettes and drugs completely and moderate their alcohol intake. They ensure optimum health by eating a nutritious and balanced diet, by keeping their fitness at the best possible level, and by working at keeping emotionally balanced. Those who unfortunately are not as conscientious and do not take care of themselves generally pay for it; they are often the ones who end up injured. In the end, it often costs them in time off, which can result in the loss of their job or can sometimes interfere with them getting the next one.

Commit to yourself and your career by opting to make healthier, wiser, more informed choices. Let me remind you that it is never too late to get started on the road to a healthier lifestyle. If you are quite young and first starting out, you shouldn't have acquired many bad habits yet, thus it should be very easy for you to implement some good ones from the get-go. As Dr. Baron says, "You are to be commended on your interest in taking this preventive approach. When we are young, we tend to have the illusion that we are invincible; unfortunately, we don't learn how untrue that is until it is sometimes too late." And so I say it again: It is so absolutely important to be aware.

Dr. Baron gives the example of the new young professional athletes. "They don't take advantage of all that is available to them, not like the senior guys do. The new young ones often have that invincible attitude, and it's usually not until after their second or third year that they start succumbing to the thought that maybe they should be taking better care of themselves. As they start to get hit pretty hard, they begin to realize what is being demanded and expected of them. When the realization of all those long practices and having to be at peak performance all the time sets in, that's when they start to wonder, 'How do I duplicate this every day?' When you're young, you can get away with a lot, but it almost certainly catches up with you."

Once more, I will remind you of the analogy of our health pyramid and the importance of homeostasis—the perfect balance of our mental, nutritional, and physical health. From the mixed examples that we gave, you can see the intimacy of all three areas. You see how easily our emotional state can be affected by stress, or a lack of proper nutrition, or proper rest. Or, how our physical strength can be affected, often weakened or depleted from the same things: stress, no rest, or a bad diet. Last, but certainly not least, our nutritional plan can be interrupted when we are emotionally stressed, physically exhausted, injured, or ill. No matter which way you look at it, it's all the same, and the bottom line is that your nutritional, physical, and mental health must all be in proper balance.

ENCORE:
When we are young we tend to have the illusion that we are invincible; unfortunately, we don't learn how untrue that is until it is sometimes too late.

DR. BARON SHARES A FAVORITE MEMORY

I asked Dr. Baron, with all the various cast members from different Broadway shows, dance companies, and musical revues that he has treated, if there was any one favorite story that stood out. Here is what he shared with me.

"The story that I cherish the most was during *Cats*. It was funny because I had treated several of the actors before they put their costumes on. Then, during the show, this cat came running up to me. 'Doc, Doc, you need to check me. My throat is closing up on me and I can't reach my note.' I had no idea who this was under the costume. I asked her if I had already treated her and she said yes. Even though I was unable to diagnose as aggressively as I normally would, I went ahead and used what expertise I could. Meanwhile she was saying, 'I have to get on stage; I have to sing. This is my main number.' I went ahead and adjusted her, and made sure that the mechanics of the spine were all adequate. I adjusted her further here and there to help loosen up some muscles. I worked on the lymph nodes of the neck and I made sure that all her ranges of motion were free. Once I was done she said, 'Thanks, Doc. Thanks, I'm feeling better already. Are you going to come out and watch me?' I said, 'I'd like to,' so she runs me over to the stage manager and asks him if he can get me out to watch her number. He was on the phone and quickly said no, so I walked back to the green room with my tail between my legs. She darted off saying, 'I'm so sorry but I have to go. I'm on.' Next, I feel a tap on my shoulder and it's the stage manager and he says, 'I'm sorry. I was on the phone with the bigwigs; I didn't mean to do that to you. Follow me,' and he takes off in a sprint. I'm running after him, and we're up and down stairs, through corridors and finally we busted through the front doors. Next thing I know, I find myself at the very back of the house and I see the stage. With my wonderful vision, I see little tiny people on the stage, and all of a sudden I recognize the cat that I just treated and would you believe she goes on to sing '*the*' song: 'Memories!' I actually had tears in my eyes. Because I helped her, these people were able to have this beautiful emotional experience. It was absolutely breathtaking for me. I sat there quietly at the back of the house and a tear rolled down my face. I said to myself, 'This is what it's all about.' Afterwards, when I saw her and congratulated her on her performance, she was so thrilled she gave me a great big hug and said, 'Thank you so much.' I had no clue whom I was treating at the time."

> ENCORE:
> *Recognition and prevention are keys to your longevity as a dancer or an athlete.*

In sync. Dancers perform bolero in *Batucada* production
revue

Chapter Eleven
In Perfect Balance—Mind Over Matter

"The single most effective relaxation technique I know is conscious regulation of breath. Breath is the key to health and wellness, a function we can learn to regulate and develop in order to improve our physical, mental, and spiritual well-being."
~ **Dr. Andrew Weil**

Much of the topic of mental/emotional health has been addressed in the previous two chapters, through the intimate role that it plays with both our nutritional and physical areas. In this next section, I will address how stress affects our daily lives and what we can do to help reduce it. In this incredibly fast-paced world that we live in, where the demands of everyday life seem to continuously become more and more kinetic, it is no wonder that stress is so prevalent. There is good stress and bad stress. The truth is that what makes one tick and absolutely thrive could be the exact thing that drives another over the edge. Some people cannot exist without a certain amount of chaos in their lives; in fact, they can even thrive on it. What could be a thrill for one person could be an absolutely terrifying experience for another. For example, even something like a roller coaster ride, which, of course is intended to be fun, can be total exhilaration for one and complete terror for another. How about the stress of an audition? Absolute excitement or physical illness from the anticipation?

If you weren't already, I am sure that by now you are well aware that our mental and emotional health plays a huge role in our overall well-being. There-fore, it is obvious that stress can be a huge contributing factor. Since everyone handles stress so differently, there is no one set way to control it. A great starting point is as simple as having a positive attitude over a negative one. Sometimes all the best intentions cannot help us from feeling the negative effects of stress. If this is the case, then it will be important for you to find ways in which to reduce your stress. The following are twelve simple suggestions for natural alternatives to relaxation and stress reduction.

EXERCISE

Whether you want to burn some serious calories or do a long slow relaxing stretch, exercise is an excellent stress buster. From high energy and more intense aerobic-style workouts and gym sessions to the more relaxing Pilates, yoga, or tai chi, it is simply a matter of taste and what works most effectively in helping you to relax and take a load off your mind.

MEDITATION AND BREATHING

Meditation has been around for thousands of years, and more recent scientific research in the United States has proven it to have many health benefits. It is a wonderful way to quiet and calm your mind. Properly done, it produces a deep state of relaxation. There are many forms of meditation; one should consider learning the practice from a professional. However, there are many simple ways to get started and reap the benefits of this state of mind, from focusing on a body part to focusing on your breath or a specific sound. It may not be easy initially to quiet your mind for long periods, but as with anything, practice makes perfect, or in this case, practice makes *peace*. If you find your mind wandering, go back to your focus and do this as many times as necessary.

TAKE A WALK

Sometimes all you need is a little fresh air and a change of scenery. Take your pet for a walk through the neighborhood or go exploring some new territory. If you live by the ocean or near a beach, this can be a lovely and peaceful walk when not too crowded. Invite a friend along, or go it alone if you prefer to just get lost in your own thoughts. This could be an opportune time to practice quieting that busy mind.

LAUGHTER

Watch some reruns of your favorite sitcom, rent a great funny movie, or find a comedy club. Laughter is one of the best forms of therapy! It has even been known to heal serious illness in some.

146

SPA DAY

You can create your own home spa or head off to your favorite retreat for a day of complete pampering. If you prefer the idea of the home spa, there's nothing quite like a hot bubble bath. Light some scented candles, add a few drops of your favorite aromatherapy oil, turn down the lights, close the door for a little privacy, and simply relax. You may want to get out the nail files, buffers, and polish, and add a manicure and pedicure. If you opt for heading off to the spa, then you should have a long list of treatments to choose from. How about a massage, a facial, or a body wrap? Set a budget, choose your favorites, and lavish in the indulgence.

PLAY WITH YOUR PET

There is no greater way to de-stress than sitting and stroking a pet. Stroking a pet can actually help lower blood pressure. Playtime can be relaxing for you and fun for your pet. Therapy pets, or visiting pets, as they are sometimes referred to, are used for visiting patients in health care facilities. These visits can help people feel less lonely and can heighten their spirits.

HOBBIES

Hobbies are a great way to escape, and sometimes all we need is that distraction long enough to turn off our busy minds. Some people prefer quiet hobbies like painting or gardening or sorting through old photo albums, others might prefer more exciting and challenging hobbies such as video games, while others will prefer active hobbies like sports or the physical Wii-type video games. The idea here is to unwind, so any activity that helps you accomplish this is perfect.

LISTEN TO MUSIC

Why not make an evening of it? Choose some of your favorite music and kick back and chill to some cool tunes. You might want to check out some new artists or some already familiar ones to add to your iPod collection. If getting out sounds better, head over to one of your favorite music stores (that's if there are any left; unfortunately, they are a dying breed) or check out the music department at your local library. Either way you can get lost in the endless selections, guaranteed for a few hours of entertainment.

WRITE IN A JOURNAL

Writing can be extremely therapeutic and relaxing, so how about setting aside a quiet hour, either weekly or several times a week if you can, to put some thoughts down on paper? There is no set way to keep a journal. You can keep a diary, you can use it for creative writing—poetry, songwriting, or storytelling—or you might want to use it as a way of simply airing some thoughts that you want to get off your chest.

READ A GREAT BOOK

Try setting aside an entire afternoon or evening to escape with a good book. Chances are there's one that you've wanted to read. You may have some magazines piling up; why not settle in with a few of your favorites? Once again, if the idea of getting out is more appealing, head to your favorite bookstore or library.

DINNER AND A MOVIE

Head off to your local video store or choose a few movies from home and make it a movie marathon. Invite a few friends if you like or relax on your own. Either way, you can serve some popcorn and your favorite drinks, or create a full-on menu if you want to get lost in the kitchen for a while. Some people love to cook and use it as a wonderful way to just get away from it all. And if you have that someone special in your life, bring out the gourmet in you and prepare a romantic candlelight dinner for two, then snuggle up for that movie.

RETAIL THERAPY

I'm not sure how this one ended up last on my list, because it is by far one of my very favorite things to do and ways to relax. Now I am not suggesting that you should break the bank or anything; what I am suggesting, however, is that if you like to shop this can be a great way to truly forget about all your problems and get a natural high. The best news of all is that window-shopping can be just as effective. If you can afford to give yourself a budget for a purchase or two that's great, but it's not necessary. Studies have shown that shopping activates key areas of the brain and releases a chemical known as dopamine that boosts our mood and makes us feel better. Just remember, you can have as much enjoyment from browsing and window-shopping. No need to break the bank. After all, it's suggested for pleasure; we don't want any buyer's remorse when the high wears off.

ENCORE:

In order for us to have stability and balance in our health, we need all three areas—nutritional, physical, and mental—to be in balance.

NOTES

Nothing's a stretch! IBM corporate event, Miami Beach, Florida

Chapter Twelve

No More Starving Artist—The Business of Being in "the Biz"

"Opportunity dances with those already on the dance floor."
~ H. Jackson Brown Jr.

I'm sure you've heard the age old question, "What happens when you can't dance anymore?" Or how about those notorious opinions: "Dancers are a dime a dozen," "That's not a real career—you can't make a living at it," or "Why don't you get a real job?" It's been said that there is a little truth in everything, so I'd like to take a moment and evaluate these "words of supposed wisdom."

1) Of course, there could come a day when you may not be able to dance anymore; this may be by choice or by necessity. However, whatever preparation you have done to plan your future will be a huge determining factor in where you find yourself at that time. Then would be a good time to put your other talents, education, or big savings account to work for you. 2) Dancers may not necessarily be a dime a dozen, but there certainly isn't a shortage; at least not a shortage of female dancers. Male dancers will almost always find work. 3) Contrary to popular belief, this is a real career with oftentimes many more years of study than the average profession. It's not the easiest of professions, as we already know, but yes, you *can* make a living at it; you can even make a very good living at it. You may not necessarily make millions, but then again, you could be the next Madonna. Although a legendary recording artist, Madonna started out like so many of you, as a dancer. She attended the University of Michigan on a dance scholarship for two years. She then moved to New York City to

become a dancer, where she continued her studies with the world famous Alvin Ailey American Dance Theater. One simply never knows what the future may hold!

ENCORE:
Dancing isn't the easiest of professions, as we already know, but yes, you can make a living at it; you can even make a very good living at it.

THE "BUSINESS" OF BEING IN SHOW BUSINESS

I'm sure that the concept of "starving artist" is not one that you aspire to. So let's get right down to business—the business of being in *show business*. I personally have never bought into that whole "starving artist" concept. Don't get me wrong—we have already established that you may not make a ton of money at it, and we've established that it is greatly about passion, and without passion, one shouldn't bother.

Are those not the perfect ingredients for the so-called "starving artist" role? Maybe, but not necessarily so. "For the love of the art" is huge in my books (I don't know of any other way); however, there is no reason why it can't be for the love of the art while earning a decent living at it. I made a decision when I was a young dancer first starting out that I was not going to live like a starving artist. I love the business, always have, and I have been very fortunate to have a great career doing what I love. But let's face it—at the end of the day if you really couldn't earn a living at it, wouldn't you get another job or create a secondary means to earn a living, thereby negating the whole "starving artist" syndrome?

After all, wouldn't you be better equipped to truly do it for the love of the art if you created some financial stability? The truth is there are different approaches one can take to do what they love. Is it really possible to have the best of both worlds: to work at what you love and create financial stability? Yes! By simply planning ahead, being intelligent about your business choices, and *dotting your I's and crossing your T's*, you can do just that regardless of how much you earn. Just because you might not make huge amounts of money doesn't mean that you can't be financially savvy and create financial stability. And for the record, just because you love and enjoy what you do doesn't mean it's not a real job. If anything, this is the most envied position of all, and in my opinion, the only way to work. The most successful entrepreneurs of all, business moguls like Bill Gates (Microsoft Corp.) and Richard Branson (founder of Virgin) will tell you that first and foremost, you have to do something you love. Unfortunately, those who are not always supportive are often people who are not doing what they love and don't have the belief that it is even possible.

ENCORE:
I made a decision when I was a young dancer first starting out that I was not going to live like a starving artist.

YOU AS A BUSINESS!

Your talent and the work that you get from having this talent are essentially your business. Just as you would when opening any new business, set yourself up with all that you need to properly operate your business. A good first consideration would be to have two separate bank accounts. Now I do understand that this may sound a bit over the top to you, but don't panic; it's simple and this will save you a lot of headaches later on. One bank account should be for your earnings (income from your business). From this account, you could pay yourself a salary and pay for your business expenses, such as marketing and training, etc.; your second account would be for personal expenses. If you learn to keep things separate early on you will save yourself a great deal of stress in general, but especially come income tax time. Getting advice from a good certified public accountant who deals with entertainers or independent contractors predominantly can be of great value to you. In the meantime, a simple filing system can help keep you organized with your deductible expenses and save you the embarrassment of turning up at an accountant's office with shoe boxes or grocery bags full of receipts.

Although tax laws do change (hence the need for an accountant), certain expenses that you incur for your business are allowable deductions against your earnings. For example: show makeup, rehearsal wear, training and education, transportation to and from classes and auditions, as well as memberships in industry-related organizations and show business or dance periodicals are just a few of the deductions that may be available to you when earning a living as a performer. So make it a first rule of business to find out all of the various deductions available to you. Just a little groundwork and organization can go a long way.

ENCORE:
Your talent and the work that you get from having this talent are essentially your business.

BE ORGANIZED IN ALL AREAS

Why stop at receipts and tax deductions? A simple filing system for all important documents will help keep you prepared for just about any situation or question that could come up. This system can be as simple as an accordion folder, a small filing cabinet, or file box with individual folders in alphabetical order; no need to get complicated. Take into consideration all important documents that you might need to refer back to at a later date. Very important will be your bank account statements and artist engagement contracts, any union or association information, and, of course, all legal documents and any insurance policies.

Some monthly bills will fall into your tax deductible items and, therefore, should be filed under business expenses. Some accountants may even suggest a specific filing system that will simplify their process; thereby saving you money on those year-end accountant fees. If you like to keep a record of all your monthly expenses, even those non-deductible bills, I would suggest that you keep them separate, with other personal documents; this, of course, is entirely a matter of preference. Once again, these are merely suggestions to help you get organized; the sooner you start to create good habits the easier it will be to stick to them and subsequently implement them in all aspects of your business.

In a survey conducted with twenty working performers, I asked what area of show business they would like to have known more about prior to getting into the business. Eighty percent said they would like to have known more about the *business* of *being in the business*. Unfortunately this is an area that is not usually taught in school or at dance classes. Although this material may not be quite as much fun or interesting, or for that matter even seem necessary to you, I assure you that if you read through it all and take in even just a few suggestions, you will be grateful later on. One of the biggest mistakes performers make is not to treat their careers as a business. Even worse, because we believe we are indestructible when we are young and retirement seems a lifetime away, we tend to not worry about the future. The latter applies to the general public, not just performers. In order to be successful at what you do, you absolutely must treat your talent and yourself as a business. I hate to sound cheesy but bottom line is this: If you don't take care of business, your business won't take care of you.

Aside from that file box, you will want a day planner/organizer so that you can keep track of all appointments, phone calls, auditions, classes, and any notes on contacts or upcoming events. Within your day planner you should have a contact database, which can either be on your computer or in good old reliable written form. When soliciting agents or work, it's always a good idea to keep notes on every phone call you make. A quick note in the memo section of the individual's contact details, on the back of a Rolodex card, or in your day planner will help remind you of whom you spoke to on what date and any requests they may have made for promotional material. When sending out promotional material, keep a simple note as well with the date sent out and to whose attention. The next call you make to that person or company, you will be able to remind them of your last conversation and of any promotional material that you sent out.

ENCORE:
The bottom line is this: If you don't take care of business, your business won't take care of you.

SELF-PROMOTION: A NECESSARY EVIL

As for promotional materials, here are a few ideas to implement in addition to the standard photo and resume.

PROMO DVDS

As mentioned in "Chapter Six: Markets and Venues," some production companies and choreographers today will preview talent from a promotional DVD. In the event that you do not already have a promo DVD of yourself or your work, the following are a few tips to assist you in creating one.

Promo videos should be kept short, somewhere between three to five minutes in length, and should show off your talent with the best possible footage. The quality of the footage is most important; you want it to be clear and you want to be easily identified. When it comes to hiring talent, everyone has different needs and specifics they are looking for. On rare occasions you may be asked for something very definite—i.e., a particular style or technique—at which point you would send in only that which they are asking for. However, in general, it is a good idea to have a well-rounded compilation of your talent. Try to show as much versatility as well as any special talents you may have, i.e., tumbling, ethnic dance, etc. Some performers find themselves in that frustrating situation of not being able to get good-quality footage of their performances. If this is the case, request permission from the producers and the choreographer to videotape small sections of your performance for editing and promotional purposes; otherwise, go into a studio and videotape yourself doing some of your own choreography. Keep in mind that you want to keep these pieces short, offer variety, and show off your versatility and any of those special talents. This should be easy to accomplish. There is no need for it to be an extremely expensive ordeal. A good personal video camera can give you first-rate, clear-quality footage, which is what you need, plus a good editor.

Do your preparation in advance so that you know exactly what sections you want edited and save some time and money on the hours you spend in the studio with the professional editor. Ask around—you may have a friend with videography and editing abilities who is willing to help you out. Like many young talented people first starting out, you may have great footage of your recital or competition pieces. This is an excellent starting point. Simply have these pieces edited down so as to show your ability in a condensed presentation. Don't forget to ask your dance teacher or choreographer's permission, especially if this footage was from your personal recording and not sold to you by the studio. Many studios today make copies of year-end presentations available to their students; however, you should still obtain permission to use the footage for your own promotional use.

If you are a seasoned professional with a full library of videos to choose from, these same rules apply. Keep in mind that no one wants to receive or has time to view a half-hour or more of footage, and if they have to fast forward and rewind, you can be almost certain they will lose interest or not bother at all. Some companies, due to copyright laws, will not accept full pieces; they will only accept edited versions. FYI, simply put, a choreographer owns the copyright to his or her work unless the work was created for another party as a work-for-hire. A work-for-hire means that the employer is paying for and intends to own all rights to the material created and the choreographer consents to give up his or her rights and ownership of the choreography. If a work is commissioned as a work-for-hire, it will be clearly stated in the contract. Otherwise, the choreographer owns all rights to their creation. Having said that, the copyright to the work will belong to someone (whether the choreographer or the producer), so make sure to get the proper permission to use it for your purposes.

THANK YOU NOTES, POSTCARDS, AND ANNOUNCEMENTS

Simple yet memorable ways to keep yourself in the auditioner's thoughts is to send out thank you notes after an audition or meeting, a simple email, or even better yet, a thank you card via snail mail with a brief personalized note will do the trick. If you want to show a bit more "flash," you can have thank you cards or postcards printed with your photo to have handy for such occasions. Postcards can be multi-purpose: you can use them for thank you notes or for reminders or announcements of a special performance or showcase. Don't forget to include the name of the production, venue, date, and time. You may want to go the extra mile and print up special announcements that you can send out as a mass mailing for a specific event. These announcements could be for the purpose of publicizing a new gig, a special feature, or an ongoing engagement. These are all relatively inexpensive ways to promote yourself and keep reminding people of who you are.

Once again, I wish to remind you that if you want to have a long and prosperous career, you must treat this as a business. If *you're* not going to promote yourself, who is? As you already know, yes, all of this can be done via email; and although some people may prefer to receive promotional materials this way, I think it just never hurts to add that personal touch with a short handwritten greeting. Due to the overwhelming amount of spam people receive, more and more people are filtering and many have strong controls against unknown email addresses, so you really have no guarantee that your material will get to them. Good old snail mail is a sure way to make it to their desk. Getting a little creative with your mailer could also help you stand out. Remember, your potential employer probably receives a great deal of solicitation every day. Something different and eye-catching can keep you from ending up on the bottom of a pile.

PHOTO AND RESUME UPDATES

Of course, this one should go without saying, but it never ceases to amaze me how many people send out or turn up at auditions with old photos and resumes that have not been updated. With so many people today having access to personal computers and printers, there is no excuse at all for resumes not to be updated as needed. Yet another opportunity to initiate a great and easy habit; just that little organization can make the difference in presenting yourself in a professional manner. As for photos, make sure to keep them current; if you change your look then you should change your photos. Turning up at an audition with short, dark, curly hair and a photo that shows a blonde with long straight hair wouldn't be very wise. A photo that looks nothing like you can be a mark against you. First of all, it can put someone off when they can't even recognize you by your photo, and secondly, it could give someone the impression that you don't care enough to stay on top of your business.

THE INTERNET

The World Wide Web is without a doubt the number one resource for so many people today. I will not go into specific details as this is an ever-changing environment, but it's clear to see that it is a very important means of communication and marketing. In fact, according to Internet World Stats (www.Internetworldstats.com), as of March 2011, 2.1 billion people were using the Internet, up 500 million in just two years.

Although we've talked about the Internet sporadically throughout the book, at this point I want to emphasize a few new ways in which you can use it, as well as reiterate some of what we've already discussed. The Internet may be an old familiar friend or you may first be getting to know each other. Either way, you must not allow its overwhelming options to intimidate you in any way. You may want to consider taking an Internet course to help you along. Just take it one step at a time and remember that when it comes to self-promotion, all of the standard rules apply. Take in all that we have discussed throughout the book on presentation and professionalism and apply it to how you promote yourself online.

One of the beauties of the Internet is the ability to get yourself out there and reach a much greater audience in a quicker period of time. Here are a few ideas to help you promote yourself. Get to know your way around the Internet, and as with everything, check things out thoroughly. There are plenty of industry sites offering different resources so determine what your main objectives are and who your audience is; then start researching the various sites and what they have to offer you. You will want to check out the many casting and audition websites. Some offer free basic memberships, with the opportunity to upgrade for a fee, while others are only available for a monthly or yearly fee. Some will allow you to post your resume and photo and video, others will post auditions and events, and some will do both. There are many dance organizations and publications that have been around for countless numbers of years that are now providing much of their information and services online. Every day there are new dance-related websites and blogs being created and many of them are very reputable.

What's hot today may not be the trend in a year's time, so as with everything, keep current, stay on top of what is happening, and what is available to you on the Web, just as you would in the dance industry. When it comes to social networks such as Facebook, Twitter, and Myspace, be intelligent about what you post. You may be surprised to hear that potential employers will reference these pages. You may want to consider having a separate site or a separate page for business purposes. Facebook, which is rapidly approaching one billion users worldwide, also offers you the opportunity to create a business page and invite people to like your page. LinkedIn is the preferred website for *professional* social networking and is growing at a very steady pace. As of November 2011 it had more than 135 million members in more than 200 countries and territories, and was gaining roughly one million new members per week. These are both great ways to reach a large audience and connect with other professionals both in your industry and in other industries that might influence and/or support the arts and what you do. You've undoubtedly heard of the many success stories and artists who have been discovered through YouTube. This is a perfect showcase for your talent and a way to introduce yourself to the world. As I suggested earlier, when making a demo DVD, take those same considerations into account. This along with a well-thought-out plan for how you want to present yourself to your viewing audience will assist you greatly in creating both engaging and entertaining footage and interesting content for your YouTube channel. There are many books written on the topic of social media and how to get the most out of your experience, and the various websites mentioned also offer a great deal of help through tutorials and articles. Be certain to also take the time to educate yourself about ways to best protect your privacy. There are many applications on these social networking sites that once you engage in, your information becomes public access. So be aware and adjust your settings accordingly.

Aside from promoting yourself on some of these established sites, you also have the opportunity to create a website of your own. Although this can be a costly endeavor, it doesn't need to be; again, know whom you are dealing with. Ask around to get some recommendations, and then make sure that you have a contract that clearly states what you are getting for your money. A simple website with a few well-designed pages is all you need. Focus on your objective, which should be to promote your talent in the most professional presentation. Your head shot, resume, and biography should be standard pages. In addition, you should consider having a page for your promotional DVD, and if you have a good collection of performance and or portfolio photos, you can create a photo gallery. Regardless of whether you create your own website or simply a few promo pieces to send out, put on your public relations hat and use your imagination. The key here is to market and sell yourself, so get creative and have some fun. It's never been easier!

One final reminder—follow-up is very important, so whether emailing a link to your website or attaching promotional pieces, it's always a good idea to follow up to make sure that they received your material. Today, we live in a much faster-paced world, and many business people are much more prone to email or text over telephone calls. However, some may still favor the old-fashioned way of doing things and prefer to speak to a live person. Either way, keep this in mind when making contact and respect their preferred form of communication.

If you choose to make a phone call and if the person is not available, you can always leave a message. Just don't necessarily expect a return call. Although I will touch on agents a little later, I will mention that when dealing with agencies specifically they will most likely have submission instructions on their website and will often state if they do not take phone calls. If so, please respect their instructions. You don't want to get off on the wrong foot (definitely not a smart move for a dancer) or be perceived as annoying.

ENCORE:
You are your own best promotion. Promote yourself in a good light!

CONTRACTS AND AGREEMENTS

I have on many occasions sat down with entire casts and read through their contracts as a group. Believe it or not, for some this was the first time they were actually reading what they had signed. I remember years ago when opening my first bank account in Los Angeles, the bank manager was shocked that I had read the paperwork before signing it. He commented that in all his many years in the banking industry, he often witnessed people sign their name without reading a single word. Okay, now that might be a bit extreme, but the point that I want to make is simple. If you don't read what you sign, you don't have a clue as to what is in the document, so what recourse could you possibly have after the fact? I'm sure you've heard "read the fine print." To begin with, read the entire document thoroughly and make a note of anything you do not understand. You will want to question and have these points clarified for you. It is always an excellent idea to have someone well-versed in legal jargon read through it with you, or for you. This could be a parent, your agent, a mentor, a family friend, or business acquaintance. Of course the best case scenario would be if you had access to a lawyer.

If there is anything at all that needs clarifying by the producers or employers, make sure to have your list ready and go over it with them. As I've said throughout this book, always be respectful and courteous; any legitimate businessperson should respect you for your attention to detail and desire to understand fully what you are signing. Never sign a contract that you do not understand fully. Once you are clear on all the clauses you must then decide, if you haven't already, whether this contract is right for you. If there is anything that you are absolutely not willing to accept or live by, you must give this serious thought and consideration prior to agreeing. Some situations have room for negotiation while others don't. Be intelligent and diplomatic about your approach and you will quickly be able to determine whether you are on friendly ground. If there is no negotiation to be had, then once again I reiterate: Determine what you will or will not accept and either sign on the dotted line and uphold your end of the agreement or graciously decline.

Don't get caught up in the excitement of landing the gig and lose sight of the details of the contract. Don't waste a potential employer's time. The worst thing you can do is walk into what you feel to be a compromising situation and then not fulfill your end of the deal. You will not only upset a few people and possibly leave yourself labeled, you could cause a great deal of expense for your producers and an enormous amount of work for your entire cast and production team if you were to leave your contract early. I stand behind integrity. If you are not going to be happy, be honest with yourself up-front. Don't compromise yourself, the show, or make someone else's experience less than ideal. Once you have signed, you're in for the long haul. Your main objective should be to fulfill your end of the deal with an outstanding performance and a great attitude, and most importantly, to be that talent that your producers would want to hire again. It should go without saying that the same goes for the hiring party; the employer must also hold up their end of the deal.

My number one reason for ensuring that all my cast members have read through and understand their contracts fully is simple: it is to both of our benefits. When I am hiring talent, I expect that if you sign your name to something you will stand by your word. I want to ensure that you know what you are getting yourself into, and you know what will be expected of you. This way, I have the comfort of knowing that we are all on the same page, and I can expect great things from you.

BERNE, BABY, BERNE

The Berne Convention for the Protection of Literary and Artistic Works is the law that governs copyright protection for the author or creator of an artistic work. And yes, this does include choreographers. Earlier in this chapter, I referred to copyright in my discussion of assembling promotional material, specifically when creating a demo reel and using video footage of your performances. I recommend that you obtain permission to use any footage of choreography that you may have performed but did not create, for the mere fact that the choreographer of that work is the owner of the copyright to that work, unless he or she gave the rights to another.

I'd like to share a few incidents with you, which, unfortunately, are not on my list of favorite memories yet are very important lessons that may help protect you or another person in the future. These can be hard lessons if you were to find yourself in a similar situation. So heads up!

I was in my fourth or fifth season of working with this company (whose name will remain anonymous) when there was a sudden change of upper management. I had been working as director/choreographer in charge of several productions for them, and I had a small production team that worked with me and relied on these contracts from season to season. As can often happen when there is a new sheriff in town, the new head honcho decided that he wanted to change how the old team did things. He decided that he was no longer going to use my services or the services of my company and, unfortunately for us, gave us little notice, leaving us without much time to recoup the damage of a lost season. Regardless, he did however decide that he still wanted to use my choreography; he just didn't want to pay for it. And so he hired a couple of dancers to come in and learn all of my work so that they could then teach the new cast members from season to season. This way, he could have the benefit of all my work, which they obviously liked enough to want to continue using in their various shows, and he wouldn't have to pay the fees of a choreographer. Instead, he would pay some lesser amount: a salary to a dancer who would basically go along with the idea of plagiarizing my creative work and using it as theirs.

When I questioned the company's intention and sent a letter informing them of my copyright ownership and requesting that they cease and desist using my work, this new entertainment director further showed his ignorance and arrogance by claiming to be in the business for twenty-five years and had never heard of such a thing as a choreographer owning the rights to his or her work. This man claimed to be so knowledgeable and experienced in the entertainment industry, and even had the audacity to mention having worked at the Lido in Paris as a lead, yet he didn't know about simple copyright laws, which protected my rights as a choreographer. In return, my copyright lawyer followed up with a letter giving him and the company the facts about copyright and copyright usage. We never heard back from them, and in the end I chose not to pursue it further, as it would have been a very costly endeavor and a lot of wasted time and negative energy. What I did instead was simply ensure my copyright protection in all future contracts by clearly adding a copyright clause. Several years later, an assistant choreographer of mine happened to see shows produced by this same company in a new venue and called to tell me that my choreography (or some semblance of), however mutilated, was still being used. Although infuriating, someone told me I should be flattered that they liked my work so much!

The bottom line is that it is not uncommon in our industry for people to either not know or understand the laws governing copyright or to plead ignorance about the matter when convenient. Furthermore, when hiring choreographers, producers and/or production companies will often want to own the copyright to the work being created for them. This is perfectly fine, if, in fact, it is addressed, discussed up front, and mutually agreed upon by both the company doing the hiring and the choreographer. In this event, an agreement will be drawn up to reflect what is known as a "work-for-hire," or a copyright clause with a clear definition of their agreement will be added to the contract being signed. If you are or aspire to become a professional choreographer, you will want to be fully aware of your rights so that you can protect yourself and understand the laws when giving others the rights to your work or when working with a work-for-hire contract.

And that brings me to yet another similar story. This one has a slightly different ending. Once again, I will not disclose the names of the parties involved. In this particular situation, I had also worked with this company for several years and had now moved on. I received a phone call from a performer warning me of a situation where once again my choreography was being used in this show long after I was no longer working with them. A videotape of the show was then sent on to me. So I immediately called the company and addressed the situation with the producer. I explained that the material was copyrighted and they did not have the authorization to use it. That very afternoon, I received a phone call from the choreographer who was now working with them. We knew of each other, had met briefly in the past, and displayed a mutual respect. She expressed to me how sorry she was for any injustice or damage that might have been done to me. She also explained that she had no knowledge of copyright laws. She had worked with this same company for many, many years, and as far as she was concerned, they owned all the rights to the work she had created for them, and assumed the same of mine. She had always worked under a "work-for-hire" contract. We had a very pleasant conversation and ended it on a nice note. I was assured that they would cease and desist from using my choreography in the future, and I was very grateful to her for her professionalism in addressing the situation with me. I believe that when people have mutual respect for each other and their work, and they handle matters between them rather than allowing them to become greater than necessary, things can be resolved in a professional manner.

On several occasions, I have been that choreographer who was called upon to re-choreograph an existing show. Whenever there was material from other choreographers leftover in a show or venue, I always did my best to ensure that they received proper credit in a show program for whatever part of the work was theirs. I would only hope that someone would do the same for me.

If you are interested in reading more about the Berne Convention, you can visit the World Intellectual Property Organization's website at www.wipo.int. You can also learn more about copyright in general by visiting the United States Copyright Office's website at www.copyright.gov.

ENCORE:
I stand behind integrity. If you are not going to be happy, be honest with yourself up-front.

THAT'S ENTERTAINMENT

You may have concluded by now that not only am I passionate about dance, but I am extremely passionate about the "business" of show business. In an effort to proficiently cover the topic of contracts and agreements section of my book I went on a search to find an expert in entertainment law who could support me in my endeavor and deliver to you sound advice. I was very fortunate and had the pleasure of being referred to and then meeting with Mr. David Bercuson, an entertainment lawyer and legal representation for some of the world's most-loved recording artists and television personalities.

As I sat in the waiting room of Mr. Bercuson's Miami office, I was thoroughly entertained by perusing the numerous gold and platinum albums covering the walls. Albums by some of the biggest names in show business and the recording industry all hung beautifully framed and signed to Mr. Bercuson as tokens of their appreciation to him. Among them were Gloria Estefan and the Miami Sound Machine, Julio Iglesias, KC and the Sunshine Band, Flo Rida, Luis Fonsi, The Rock, Trick Daddy, and The Black Eyed Peas and Fergie to name a smattering. Mr. Bercuson represents people of all different levels and in all areas of entertainment, recording artists, entertainment industry executives and managers, and many U.S. and international record labels.

His reputation as lawyer of choice precedes him. His integrity and extensive background in all facets of entertainment law, coupled with his tremendous success record, have earned him distinctions from industry peers such as: "Highest Rated Lawyer" through Martindale-Hubbel Peer Review Ratings for the past fifteen consecutive years, "Top Lawyer" in South Florida's Legal Guide for twelve consecutive years as well as *The Wall Street Journal's* Lawyer of the Year award. Adjunct professor at the University of Miami School of Law, instructor at Florida International University, and guest lecturer at Harvard University Law School are only a few from his long list of credits.

I had the opportunity to meet with Mr. Bercuson on two different occasions and spoke with him at length on the subject of contracts and agreements. The following section is based on those two meetings and all that we discussed.

IT'S CALLED SHOW BUSINESS

When I asked Mr. Bercuson if he had a favorite quote or words of wisdom that he would say best described his philosophy about show business, here's what he said. "What I say in my office all the time is, 'This is called show *business*, it's not called show playtime and if you don't take care of your *show business* you are going to be *out of show business* before you realize it!' You have to be able to realize that this is a business, whether it's a theme park or a cruise line or a major or local record company, this is a multi-billion dollar business. Now you might just be a small part of it, but it is a business and you have to treat it as such.

"If you are going to open up a restaurant you have to buy tables and chairs, cutlery, and napkins. You must have recipes, and pots and pans, and you have to be prepared to run your business. If you are going to be a dancer or a performer you need to prepare yourself to go into that business, whether it's physical training and diet and wardrobe or whatever is necessary to become a success. Your body is your tool and you have to take care of it just like a singer has to take care of his or her voice. You really have to understand that this is a business. It may be something you've always wanted to do and you were always in classes as a kid and then you were in college performances, but when you get out into the real world *it's people's livelihood*. It's how you're going to pay your rent if you don't want to stay living at home with Mom and Dad, and *you've got to prepare*. One of the first and most important aspects of your business are the contracts that you are going to sign to become part of the business. You don't want to get blindsided by not reading and preparing because then you will be miserable."

FIRST THINGS FIRST

Throughout our conversations this one most prevalent piece of advice came up time and time again. "First of all *make sure you read and understand your contract before you sign it*." Mr. Bercuson couldn't drive this point home strongly enough and went on to say, "If you do not understand it, call someone, get a lawyer. People often say that it's too expensive, but the problem is if you sign a contract without getting representation and then you have a serious problem, it's going to be more expensive to get out of the contract or fix the problem. The critical thing is to understand what you are signing. If you go see a lawyer, you can go see him for just one hour. You don't need them to negotiate for you. If you are a member of an ensemble there isn't usually much room to negotiate; however, once again, you must understand what is in that contract."

Mr. Bercuson suggests that with a little preparedness you can go a long way. He suggests that you can make an appointment to see a lawyer and email your contract ahead so they can review it for you, then go in with your questions ready. This way you will limit your cost and in a short time hopefully get all of your questions answered.

"The artist usually cares about three things," he said. "What do I have to do, how long is it going to last, and how much money am I going to earn? These are three very important things," said Mr. Bercuson, "Beyond those three things there may be twenty or thirty more pages that you have to get into, and once again, you must understand it." We also discussed the fact that contracts can often be one-sided and here's what he had to say: "Yes, of course they are one-sided, and they are not in favor of the artist. You are taking a company's contract, which has been worked on by lawyers, often over and over again, and they cover everything." He told me that some of the best contracts he's ever read were professional wrestling contracts. They did not leave one single thing to question and had been worked over and over again. As he put it, "They are beautiful works of legal art."

"Most of my work is in music and television, and, one problem that I face is that you never know who's going to offer clients a contract. You don't know what kind of document (contract) is going to be offered; it can be a beautiful work of legal drafting or it can be a piece of garbage. Furthermore, the contract can be fair or completely unconscionable. For example, I often review contracts for clients and conclude that the client should not sign the document because it was grievously unfair. I often write the client what's known in the law as an exculpatory letter, which is: 'I'm telling you not to sign the contract, and if you sign the contract don't come back to me and tell me that I told you that is was okay to do this. *I am telling you not to sign the contract.*' Unfortunately, it often happens that everything I told the client comes true. The hardest thing for the client to do is to turn down a contract, especially if it's the only offer they have. It's hard to say no, and it's very rare that a client will say no."

Sometimes you have to make tough decisions in order to benefit in the long run, and no good usually comes from desperate situations. Although it might feel like you just can't say no, sometimes it is to your benefit to do so. Sometimes you have to take a step back and have a lawyer, someone with a completely unbiased opinion, look it over and advise you accordingly. In the end, *forewarned is forearmed*. As dancers, you sometimes have to make decisions that may cost you up-front but will cost you much less in the long run. For example, imagine you've just moved to the city to pursue your career and you take a job as a server to help pay the bills, but if you got to the point where you were always working your regular job and not available to attend class or auditions you might have to rethink your situation. This would, in effect, be defeating your entire purpose for being there in the first place. So although you have to work to pay the bills, you also have to be able to balance your time and money efficiently in order to benefit your professional career goals and work toward your big-picture plan. "Sometimes you have to spend a nickel to make a dime. And those can be tough decisions," Mr. Bercuson said, "whether it's about what work to take on or hiring a lawyer." He went on to tell me about a very famous client that "couldn't sell tickets in their hometown because they constantly played locally at bat mitzvahs, quinceañeras, all types of social events and people were not buying tickets because they knew they would see them for free at the next social event. And although they were making very good money doing these extra gigs, they had to make the decision to change direction, and once they did they sold out at their next local performance."

ENCORE:
Sometimes you have to spend a nickel to make a dime.

HE WHO SPEAKS FIRST

I must preface these next few paragraphs with some advice (although it has already been mentioned and probably will be several more times). As a dancer you are often a member of an ensemble and not always in a position to seriously negotiate; however, the following advice is invaluable to you from a learning standpoint, so take it all in, trust me—I know it will come in very handy one day.

When it comes to the art of negotiation, Mr. Bercuson says he never likes to speak first. He doesn't like to be the one to first come up with a number. "Don't be afraid to just sit back and have them make the first offer, if you can get them to, because if you say, 'Well, I'd really like $100 for this gig,' and meanwhile they were willing to pay $125, they will naturally say, 'Fine. You got it!' You want the other side to set the monetary level so hopefully you can push it up from there. Try to get your manager, your agent, or your lawyer to do the negotiation for you. I know in the beginning it might be difficult because of economics but it really is better. It is hard to negotiate for yourself and one should try to avoid it at all costs. It is not so easy for you, the artist, to tell the talent buyer or producer that you are the best; *It is, however, very easy* for a manager or a lawyer to do so. That person can elevate your status when it may be uncomfortable for you to say these things. Additionally, you must think of everything included in the contract and not just money. For example: How are issues interrelated? What are you giving up? What will you be able to do in the business outside of the contract? The truth of it is, as already stated, you may not have the negotiation power as a member of an ensemble or when first starting out. However, there may come a time when things are more in your favor, when you might be in a stronger negotiating position. At that time this advice will prove to be invaluable, so please take notes or file it in your memory for a later point in time when you will want to draw upon this knowledge.

Do not negotiate out of sheer ignorance or haste. Take the proper steps to protect yourself by speaking to a lawyer first. This brings me to my next question to Mr. Bercuson: Is there anything that an artist should never sign or try to avoid at all costs? In the case of the creators of a work, for example, the songwriter, the choreographer, the costume designer, the writer, or graphic designer, there is in fact one other very important area to consider: copyright. I have already touched on the topic of copyright in the Berne, Baby, Berne section of this chapter, but I wanted to simply reinforce the importance of it. Mr. Bercuson clearly states that, "If you are a creative type and can derive a copyright from your work, number one you should do so and secondly do all that you can to maintain those rights. Try not to give them up; copyright can put your grandchildren through college."

If you are going to sign a work-for-hire (allow me to reiterate—this means the producer or person hiring you will own the piece that you create), then you must consider what that is worth to you. Is the contract they are offering enough? There has to be some gain for you to give up all your rights. As Mr. Bercuson said, "Everything has a price, and it becomes a bit of a balancing act. If you are going to create something—whether it's choreography, some fabulous scenic design, or a costume design—you have to anticipate that someone is going to say that they want to own it, and if you want to do the gig that is the price of admission. Then you must make sure that the price of admission is something you want to pay to get the work. There are different ways to work these deals out. If you are going to give something away then you want to get back as much benefit as you can. And it might not just be money; it might be credit and notoriety or future opportunities. If you want to be on the red carpet as the creator of the work, that credit alone may be worth more to you in future gigs." So once again it really is a balancing act and one that you must consider and weigh out carefully.

> **ENCORE:**
> *It is not so easy for you, the artist, to tell the talent buyer or producer that you are the best; it is, however, very easy for a manager or a lawyer to do so.*

LUCKY STREAK

In certain circles of the business it may not be uncommon for a performer to be offered contracts simultaneously, let's say in the example of cruise ship work. Because there are specific seasons and therefore audition times, often auditions can be back-to-back or all within the same few weeks or monthlong period. Now in the case where you may be lucky enough to be offered two different contracts at the same time, what should be the deciding factor? Mr. Bercuson says simply, "I don't know." This is, after all, a very subjective decision for the individual to make. He went on to say, "If the money was the same then you have to delve further. What are the conditions, how long is it going to last, where do you have to go, how much time off do you have, how are the facilities—one might be the Taj Mahal while the other could be a dump—who will you be working with? The money might be better somewhere else but you might have greater opportunity with one choreographer over another." The same thing goes for scholarships. Should you be in a position where you have applied to various dance companies you could very well be offered multiple scholarships, so the above facts are some of the many things that you should consider if, in fact, you are lucky enough to find yourself in one of these situations.

Here is an example that Mr. Bercuson shared with me, not of one artist receiving two contracts but rather the story of two young artists being offered similar contracts. "One male and one female artist both offered music publishing/songwriter contracts with equivalent money, not a huge amount but for a kid it was nice. The girl was insulted and said, 'I'm going to be so big that in a year from now they will be offering me ten times that amount,' and since she didn't really need the money at the time, she turned the offer down. The young man said, 'Where do I sign—my wife is pregnant, I've got to pay the doctor, my car is broken down, I have to get her to the hospital—where do I sign?' Bottom line is *he became famous, she didn't*. But here's the thing, you can't look at things with 20/20 hindsight because you don't know what's going to happen.

Consequently, you must consider all opportunities very carefully. Talk to a lawyer, review it with your parents or maybe a friend of the family who is a lawyer or a good businessman that you have respect for or a teacher. Gather as much information as you possibly can and put it all in that big computer between your ears, and then make the most intelligent decision and the best decision you can, *for you* at that time. Mom and Dad might think that you should take the contract offering more money, but you may prefer to live somewhere other than where that contract must be performed. Or you may take a contract because you want to work with a particular choreographer or director and you feel you will gain more experience and better possible future opportunities from it. It may simply come down to *been there, done that* and you prefer to take the gig that is touring Europe because you've never been there before."

Whatever the reasons are it is your decision to make, and you must feel 100 percent confident in your decision. As I mentioned earlier you must be prepared to take this on fully; once you've made a commitment to the contract many people will be relying on you to perform. Don't forget how truly lucky you are to even be in the position of weighing out your options and having a contract to consider. Count yourself lucky, consider intelligently, make your decision, and do the right thing.

DIVA IN THE HOUSE

As you already know, Mr. Bercuson deals predominantly in television and the recording industry, and he deals with some very big names in the business. I asked him, putting talent aside, what he felt separated the cream of the crop from the rest. Were there any similar qualities in attitude, likeability, and business acumen from them? He said, "How they deal with people. Don't be a diva, especially if you have not earned the right to be a diva! You can't demand things from people before you have the right to, before you've earned it. If the choreography stinks and you just don't like it, understand that this is your first gig, you do the choreography and you do it the best you can and you stand out, excel and as you keep on going then maybe you can give your input. But they are not going to take criticism from some young punk just because she put on some ballet shoes and got accepted to this company. *Don't be a diva.* Learn, pay your dues and grow, and earn peoples' respect. To me, the bigger the person is, most of the time, the nicer they are and the lesser, least-important people are often the ones that demand the most."

Mr. Bercuson spoke so fondly of many of his mega-superstar clients that he says personify just what it really means to be a superstar in the true sense;

stars that have all the right to be divas but are the nicest people you could ever meet. He talked about the first lesson he ever learned backstage. It was with one of his first big clients from Spanish-language television. "The artist was a girl that grew up in South Florida and had been very successful here and then went off to L.A. only to return home again to work with Telemundo, one of the top Spanish-language television networks.

"The artist was hired for a major daytime Spanish television show. I would often go to the studio with her, and from the moment she walked into the building, not just the studio but the building, she had a smile and a kiss for everybody. If it took you five minutes to walk from point A to point B it took her twenty because she had to stop and say hello to everyone, from the receptionist to the guy holding the cables to the director and camera crew, and she was loved by everyone. She was never too big to say hello to somebody, she was always there with a smile and a kiss on the cheek, and again she was loved by everyone! And, that's what I would tell people to do," he said. "It doesn't cost you anything to be nice. And if you're nice people are going to be nice in return."

ENCORE:
Don't be a diva. Learn, pay your dues, and grow, and earn people's respect.

PROPER REPRESENTATION

What should you look for when looking for representation? "First of all you have to feel comfortable and be unafraid to ask questions. You have to have a rapport with someone. Hopefully you won't have to see your lawyer too often once your contract is done as long as there are no problems, but a manager is a day-to-day babysitter, that's who you're going to call if you have any problems and you will spend loads of time with them. The kiss of death oftentimes is when an artist chooses their mother or father or husband or wife as a manager, who has no experience and often does not know anything about the business. If someone is interested in representing you it's not a bad thing to ask who else they represent. Don't be afraid to ask questions and check people out. You have to do an in-depth investigation of who this person is. Most important, there has to be mutual respect. This business is full of sharks. I'm sure every business has plenty and although I don't like to generalize, there may be more in the entertainment business. Many people are attracted to the glamour of show business and so you have to be careful. As careful as you are when you read your contract, you have to be equally as careful when putting your team together. Nobody—whether you are a dancer or choreographer or singer—nobody gets younger. Everyone gets older, especially dancers; they're like pro football players. You just can't do it forever. You have a shorter life expectancy in that profession so you can't take the risk of hooking up with people who are going to take up your time and not to do anything for you. You have to be very careful who you associate with; as a talent you can choose who you want in your team. You may sign contracts with a manager or a business manager and you may be tied to those people for a long time, and you don't want to have to sit it out and lose valuable time. Find people you are comfortable with, who you have confidence in and who can and are willing to help you at all stages of your career."

CONTRACT REVIEW

The most common mistake that Mr. Bercuson sees time and time again with entertainers is simply the fact that they don't read their contracts. "Again, you must read and ask questions before you sign it! *If you don't read it then you won't know what is expected and required of you.*" In order to give you a better idea of what questions to ask and what to look for, *Mr. Bercuson and I went over two different contracts together.* One was an independent contractor agreement while the other was an employee contract. Mr. Bercuson was kind enough to take the time to explain the good and the bad, and to give us a heads-up on what you should look for, what you should make sure is in the contract, and how to better understand what some of this legal jargon means. If you haven't already you may want to get out your highlighter or pad and pencil to take some notes.

- Independent contractor or employee – Make sure that your contract defines whether you are an employee or independent contractor. You have to know what you are signing because if it's an independent contractor agreement versus an employee agreement then you are required to pay your own taxes and, depending on the jurisdiction, there may not be any workman's compensation, health insurance, or other benefits. If it is an employer/employee relationship then the taxes will be taken out and there may or may not be any benefits.
- Position and provisions – What are the exact duties that the artist is being hired for? Are you a dancer, a singer, or both? Make sure all duties and responsibilities are set forth. When is the show scheduled to open?

172

- Performance schedule – Be certain the contract clearly states the number of performances per day and a maximum per week. What clean-up rehearsals or maintenance technical run-throughs will be required of you beyond opening?
- Duration of contract and options – How long is the initial contract for? If there is an option to extend the term, how are the options exercised?
- Compensation – Are performance weeks and rehearsal weeks paid at the same rate, or are rehearsals and any preproduction weeks paid at a different rate? What is the rate of pay?
- Rehearsals – Are rehearsals held locally or will there be travel involved? If there is no rehearsal pay, is there a per diem or cost of living allowance? And if you have to travel, how are you going to get to the rehearsals or show venue? Are you responsible, or will producer be paying for travel?
- Per diem – If there is a per diem it should state if it is for food or food and lodging.
- Travel – If the show is not local or if rehearsals are in a different city, who is paying for travel costs? If the producer is paying for travel, will they be making all arrangements or are you meant to get yourself there and then be reimbursed? Again make sure it is clearly laid out, including what type of travel, whether you'll be flying or driving, etc.
- Accommodations – If accommodations are provided will they be single or shared, and if shared, with how many people, and what type of accommodation will be provided, hotels or apartment-style? If you are responsible for any upkeep to any paid-for accommodations you have to know up-front what those costs will be. Also ensure that you do a full walk-through of the accommodations with someone from the company in charge of the facility—for example, if there is a rental agency or management company—do this to determine the condition in which you are accepting the accommodations. Make sure you receive acknowledgment in writing for the condition of the accommodations and some form of agreement that outlines your responsibility in reference to it. Have someone sign and date your copy and maintain this copy for your records. This may seem nitpicky, but if it's not signed they could claim that you added to the list.
- Publicity and promotion clause – This is usually where the producer will state that you as a performer must be available for photo shoots and other promotional and publicity events. This oftentimes can be subject to abuse so there should be a limit to the time involved and this should

be delineated. Even with the word *reasonable* in a contract you can have a problem, as everyone has a different opinion of what is reasonable.

- Rider or attachment – If there is a clause stating that there is a rider or attachment—often referred to as Exhibit A, for example—make sure the rider is attached and that your review the rider. Otherwise you are agreeing to something that you haven't seen. It must be attached or the clause must be removed.

- Rules and regulations – On the same token, if there is mention of an employee guide or book of rules and regulations or venue or ship guide of rules and regulations, then make sure that you have been given a copy and be sure to read it.

- Cancellation clause – If the producer has the right to cancel at their option with a certain notice period, then this clause shall be reciprocal for the artist; what's fair for one should be fair for the other. And of course, depending on who you are and what your status is in the show, you may or may not have any bargaining power.

- Costumes – What will you be supplied, and what is expected of you from a maintenance standpoint? Are there any charges to you for any costumes, shoes, or tights, as an example? There is often a stipulation about costume maintenance in an attachment or rider, which will define how costumes should be handled and cleaned—whether you are responsible for the cleaning or for turning costumes in for cleaning.

- Conduct and appearance – Often these clauses will state that one can be dismissed for unruly conduct or embarrassing activity, as an example. Make sure that the wording is not vague or can be subject to someone's opinion or interpretation. Something that is in violation of the law or a public scandal is to be expected and is fine, but try not to sign anything that is too subjective and could leave room for abuse.

- Early termination – In the event of early termination, who pays for your travel home if you are out of town?

- Nonperformance, injury, or illness – What if you sustain an injury or are sick? In case of injury how much time are you given before you will be replaced? Are you responsible for your own rehab costs or are there provisions for such in the contract?

- Safety rules – When working at sea or when dealing with magic shows, per se, there will be safety regulations that you must adhere to. Again, be informed. Is there a separate guide and or additional training that you will have to undergo? You could be dealing with heights, animals, fire, etc.

- Confidentiality agreement – You will most likely be asked to sign a confidentiality agreement or take an oath of secrecy when dealing with specialty productions such as magic.
- Medical information – If artist has to provide medical information or has to perform a physical examination, then that information should be kept confidential, and your contract should require confidentiality of your medical records.
- Warranties and indemnities – Again, this is somewhat standard for the producer, however, there should be a reciprocal indemnification for the artist in the event the producer causes harm or damages to artist. When being hired as a group or when an artist comes with a team, one person should not be responsible for the actions of all team members. Each member should sign accordingly.
- Legal fees – Artist will be responsible for any legal fees associated with harm brought on by the artist. Fine if it's your fault, but not if it's your fault because of something brought on by the show or what has been requested of you by the producer or director.
- Force majeure or act of God – This is a pretty standard clause that you will most often see in any contract you read or sign. It basically protects the producer from events outside of human control, such as sudden floods or other natural disasters for which no one can be held responsible. So if a show were to close early due to an act of God (hurricane) the contract may be terminated.
- Jurisdiction – This is a very important provision. This determines what state and therefore what courts shall have jurisdiction over the contract and what state law will be utilized. Make sure that it is written in and you know where the jurisdiction is.
- Totality of contract – The written document constitutes the entire understanding between the parties and no other promises, understandings, or discussions not contained in the written contract are valid. Furthermore, the written contract can only be changed by another written document signed by all parties to the contract. Consequently, if the parties agree to make changes in the contract, those changes must be in writing and signed by all the parties to be bound by the change. This clause is in every contract; in fact, Mr. Berucson says that it is so pervasive that it even has a name: It's called an *integration clause*. And, it's very, very important because if someone tells you something and you rely on that but it's not in the contract, then it doesn't exist. So if someone is

making promises to you and it's not in the contact, you are not going to get it and you can't hold them to it. So if you've been told something *get it in writing* and have the writing signed by all of the parties!

ENCORE:
Again you must read and ask questions before you sign it! If you don't read then you won't know what is expected and required of you.

As we wrapped up our conversation on contracts and agreements, Mr. Bercuson rounded it up by saying the following: "Now all these things that we've talked about are all good, however, if you are a rookie or in the corps de ballet, you are not going to have a lot of bargaining power, consequently, the thing that you *absolutely* have to do is *make sure you read everything and ask questions.* Certainly you can ask for things to be changed in the contract. Whether or not they will be changed is unknown, but chances are you are not going to have the bargaining power. So you *must, must* read everything, you must know what it says, know what your obligations are, know what is required of you. Because, as we've said before, it's called show 'business' and *it's a business.* Yes, it may be glamorous for however long you are on the stage, but it's still work, and it's still a business and you have to conduct yourself as such or you won't be in business for very long. I tell clients who are signed to contracts, 'If you think you worked hard before, you are just getting started.' There are a lot of people that want your job and if you don't do what you are supposed to do and if you don't perform as required, you will be replaced. The threshold to get fed up with a superstar is a lot higher than it is with a rookie. A producer can and will put up with a lot more aggravation from a superstar or someone that is critically important to their production than somebody who's not, so don't become consumed with your own self-importance. Remember, there is always someone waiting in the wings to do whatever is needed to take your job. Look at the auditions for *American Idol* or *So You Think You Can Dance.* There are thousands of kids out there that want to be a star, but at the end of the day there is only one winner. No matter what the field everyone wants to be the star, whether it's a dancer or a singer or an actor or a boxer or an athlete or a chef. You have to understand that nothing is handed to you. You must earn your success. And even then, don't be a diva."

THERE'S NO BUSINESS LIKE SHOW BUSINESS!

As Ethel Merman said, "There's no business like show business, like no business I know."

I hope that the information I've shared with you to this point has inspired you and will help to guide you, and I hope that the stories have entertained you. Some of them will reinforce the lessons I am teaching. Lessons like, when opportunity strikes, never give up, don't let anyone take your dreams from you, and look out for number one. You never know where things come from or what is waiting just around the corner, and last, but not least, there are plenty of highs and lows. I believe that there is good to be found in all situations, which I have shared several times over. However, in an effort to always find the good, we mustn't be foolish or ignore what is real. This business also comes with a certain amount of jealousy and a whole lot of ego. Someone often wants what you have, or the very thing you are going after, so here's one last bit of advice. I want you to stay positive and keep your focus, keep your eyes wide open and squarely on the prize, but don't forget to also watch your back. I've been working in this business in one capacity or another since I was a young girl, either as a performer or later on as a director/choreographer and producer, and that can make for a whole lot of storytelling, but I won't go on and on. I will however, leave you with this.

There may very well be as many difficult moments as there are great ones, if not more, but the bottom line is if you always maintain the utmost integrity in all that you do, keep your chin up, and never give up, you can survive the trials and tribulations and revel in the highs along the way. If you see that a door is slightly ajar, go ahead and open it. You just never know what is waiting on the other side.

ENCORE:
If you see that a door is slightly ajar, go ahead and open it. You just never know what is waiting on the other side.

REPRESENTATION—AGENTS AND MANAGERS

Artist representation, talent agents, and managers have been around forever. "Dance agents," however, really came onto the dance scene back in the mid '80s and have been growing in popularity ever since. Today's dancers most likely don't even know of pre-agent days. Having an agent can introduce you to an area of the market and producers that you may otherwise never get to know. Many production companies like the ease and efficiency of going through dance agents for their casting calls as the agents can prescreen and take all the guesswork out of who might turn up at such auditions. This is a real comfort for a production company and can also be a huge savings in time, money, and frustration. The cost to the producer is a simple 10 percent or 15 percent commission added on to the dancer's salary. There may be certain occasions where the commission could come directly from you, if the producer and agent do not have a special agreement or working relationship.

There are many benefits to having such representation working on your behalf. As previously mentioned, many auditions and castings will be closed to agents' lists only. Short of successfully crashing an audition, if you are not on an agent's list you will not get past the sign-in. Agents prescreen so you will get called for parts for which you are the right look and fit. Agents can be very instrumental in helping to groom you for the business as they can point out your strengths and weaknesses. They often offer advice on how to best prepare for auditions as well as your career in general. Agents negotiate your contracts, ensure you get paid, and stay on top of working conditions.

There are, of course, some production companies that still prefer to go it alone, preferring the old-fashioned way of handling their auditions and casting needs. These companies will post their notices and hold their own open calls, as I discussed earlier in "Chapter Six: Markets and Venues." So although you may have greater exposure with an agent, don't fret if you haven't landed one yet. While you do not have representation, you will still have plenty of resources for finding work. I outlined earlier the many ways in which you can find work. Now I will discuss how to find an agent.

Not unlike finding work, dancers seeking representation should submit photos and resumes with a cover letter, and demo reels when requested, to the various agents. Agencies hold auditions on a scheduled and regular basis. Talent having submitted their photo and resume might get an invitation to a set audition being held by the agency or to a class where their agents will be scouting. There may or may not be a callback, and you could be signed on the spot or called at a later date. Either way, once approved you will be called in for orientation. Most important, I reiterate to you be courteous, respectful, and professional. Just as an employer doesn't want to deal with a diva or "problem child," nor does an agent. Ultimately, they need to know how you will perform for their client. You want to put your best foot forward and be viewed as a positive addition to the agency and any production company they introduce you to.

Los Angeles, and more recently New York City, are home to the majority of dance agents. You will find that some are bicoastal and some have offices in other major cities in the United States. Following is a list of such agents that you may want to investigate further and consider when you are ready to submit. Most agencies prefer submissions by mail or email and many will clearly state "no telephone calls." Most have websites where you can go to learn more about their requirements for submissions. They will give detailed information, sometimes with a specific contact; pay close attention to their requirements. If there is no contact name listed, write on your package "Attention: Dance Dept." and you may want to add "New Talent Submission." You want to ensure that your package gets into the right hands. Other major cities that are not necessarily known for their dance agencies will still have a long list of talent agencies that you can investigate. You will want to determine if these agencies have a performing arts or theatrical division that handles dancers. If so, as with all the above recommendations, make sure to submit a cover letter with your photo and resume. It seems redundant to say, but make sure that all your contact details are on your cover letter, your resume, and on your photo. In the event that your photo was to get separated from your resume, it is a good idea to have a label on the back of your photo with contact details. Below is a list of some of the most well-known agencies.

AGENCY CHECKLIST AND RECAP

Locate agents you are interested in contacting.

Check agency websites for submission requirements or audition requirements.

Respect their online instructions.

Submit photo and resume with a cover letter and demo reel if specified.

If interested, agencies will contact you for audition or interview.

Again, double check their instructions, can't stress this enough.

Be prepared, do your research: Know who they are and what they expect from you.

If you are not familiar with the audition location, map out your route and know where you are going ahead of time.

Be early, be courteous, be respectful, be pleasant, and be professional.

Just as with all auditions, dance your ass off and sell yourself!

Don't forget to thank them on the way out.

Very important, once you have an agent, be sure to let them do their job—that of representing you—and always treat them with the utmost respect.

LOS ANGELES

BBA Talent
www.bbatalent.com
4116 W. Magnolia Blvd., Suite 205
Burbank, CA 91505
Tel: (818) 506-8188

Bloc
www.blocagency.com
5651 Wilshire Blvd., Ste. C
Los Angeles, CA 90036
Tel: (323) 954-7730
Fax: (323) 954-7731

CESD Talent Agency
www.cesdtalent.com
10635 Santa Monica Blvd., Ste. 130
Los Angeles, CA 90025
Tel: (310) 475-2111

Clear Talent Group
www.cleartalentgroup.com
10950 Ventura Blvd.
Studio City, CA 91604
Tel: (818) 509-0121
Fax: (818) 509-7729

DDO Artists Agency
www.ddoagency.com
Attn: Dance/Choreography Dept.
6725 Sunset Blvd., Ste. 230
Los Angeles, CA 90028
Tel: (323) 462-8000
Fax: (323) 462-0100

Kazarian/Spencer/Ruskin & Associates
www.ksrtalent.com
11969 Ventura Blvd, 3rd floor
Box 7409
Studio City, CA 91604
Tel: (818) 769-9111
Fax: (818) 769-9840

McDonald/Selznick Associates Inc. (MSA)
www.msaagency.com
MSA Los Angeles
953 Cole Ave.
Hollywood, CA 90038
Tel: (323) 957-6680
Dance Fax: (323) 957-5694
Choreography Fax: (323) 957-6688

Schiowitz Connor Ankrum Wolf Inc.
Theatrical Dept.
1680 N. Vine St., Ste. 1016
Hollywood, CA 90028
Tel: (323) 463-8355

NEW YORK
Bloc NYC
www.blocnyc.com
Attn: NEW TALENT
630 Ninth Ave. Ste. #702
New York, NY 10036
Tel: (212) 924-6200
Fax: (212) 924-6280

CESD Talent Agency
www.cesdtalent.com
257 Park Ave. S., Ste. 900
New York, NY 10010
Tel: (212) 477-1666

Clear Talent Group NYC
www.cleartalentgroup.com
325 W. Thirty-Eighth St., Ste. 1203
New York, NY 10018
Tel: (212) 840-4100
Fax: (212) 967-4567

DDO Artists Agency NYC
www.ddoagency.com
224 W. Fourth St., Ste. 200
New York, NY 10014
Tel: (212) 379-6314
Fax: (646) 519-4279

Kazarian/Spencer/Ruskin & Associates
www.ksrtalent.com
Media Arts Building
311 W. Forty-Third St., Ste. 1107
New York, NY 10036
Tel: (212) 582-7572
Fax: (212) 582-7448

McDonald/Selznick Associates Inc. (MSA)
www.msaagency.com
MSA New York
140 Broadway, 46th floor
New York, NY 10005
Tel: (212) 858-7549
Fax: (212) 858-7750

Schiowitz Connor Ankrum Wolf Inc.
Theatrical Dept.
165 W. Forty-Sixth St., Ste. 1104
New York, NY 10036
Tel: (212) 840-6787

SOUTHEAST

Bloc South
www.blocsouth.com
Attn: NEW TALENT
475 Moreland Ave. SE
Atlanta, GA 30316
Tel: (404) 622-4116
Fax: (404) 622-4118

XCEL Talent Agency: Atlanta
www.xceltalent.com
P.O. Box 191731
Atlanta, GA 31119
Tel: (404) 514-4258

ENCORE:

You want to put your best foot forward and be viewed as a positive addition to the agency and any production company they introduce you to.

Picture perfect! Cast of *Swing Train*, Celebrity Cruises' *Mercury*

Chapter Thirteen
United We Stand—Union or Non-Union?

I grew up with six brothers. That's how I learned to dance—waiting for the bathroom.
~ **Bob Hope**

One's career can often begin with non-union work. Undeniably, there is a lot to be said for our hometown training ground—the many dance recitals, showcases, fashion shows, local cabarets, nightclub performances, or dinner theatre. Where you are living, and what entertainment markets are strongest in that area, can determine the type of work you do. Some dancers will make entire careers out of non-union work, while others will never know what it means to work non-union. I believe that becoming "union" is an ultimate goal of most aspiring professional dancers. Much of the best work is union. Broadway, film and television, many trade shows, industrials and conventions, as well as many community and regional theatres fall under union jurisdiction. Even some theme parks and specific cruise contracts may fall under union jurisdiction. Now that's not to say that there isn't any great non-union work out there. There is plenty, much of which I spoke about in "Chapter Six: Markets and Venues." There are many great producers and production companies whose work happens to be mostly in non-union circles and venues.

It really comes down to where you ultimately want to work, and in what capacity. When I say *in what capacity*, I mean that some of you may choose careers in different areas of the industry, such as stage management, costume or scenic design, makeup artists, stylists, etc. There are unions and associations for performers, directors, writers, stagehands, and designers alike.

Answering two questions—1) Where do you want to work? and 2) What capacity do you want to work in?—will help you determine your ultimate goal, and, therefore, will help you determine the smaller goals necessary along the way.

Following are unions in the United States as well as the Canadian and British Actors' Equity. First, I will list unions that pertain to you as a performing artist—dancer, actor, and singer. Next, I will list unions that relate to other career paths within the entertainment industry; i.e., the technical, production and/or creative areas. I suggest that you visit their websites and learn more about them. Even if these are not your chosen career paths you can learn a great deal about the industry, and some of the people you will be working with, and working for. Their websites will teach you about their history, who their members are, what they offer, and so much more. The following descriptive information is information gathered from the unions' respective websites and approved by a representative from each of the unions described below, the information is reprinted with their permission. I have not written about those unions that I was unable to contact directly. However, I have listed them with website addresses to further assist you in your own research.

ENCORE:
Some dancers will make entire careers out of non-union work, while others will never know what it means to work non-union.

ACTORS' EQUITY ASSOCIATION (AEA)

AEA, or Equity, as it is known, was formed in 1913. It is the labor union that represents more than 48,000 actors and stage managers in live theatre in the United States. Equity has offices on the East Coast (in New York City and in Orlando), on the West Coast (in Hollywood), and a central office in Chicago. Equity negotiates wages and working conditions and provides a wide range of benefits, including health and pension plans, for its members. Actors' Equity Association is a member of the AFL-CIO, which is a voluntary federation of 56 national and international labor unions, and is affiliated with the International Federation of Actors, an international organization of performing arts unions. To learn more about Equity or how to become a member, you can visit their website at: www.actorsequity.org.

Actors' Equity Association
National Headquarters
165 W. Forty-Sixth St.
New York, NY 10036
Tel: (212) 869-8530
Fax: (212)719-9815

CANADIAN ACTORS' EQUITY ASSOCIATION

Canadian Actors' Equity Association (Equity) is the professional association of performers, directors, choreographers, fight directors (one who coordinates stage violence, he works directly with the director) and stage managers in English Canada who are engaged in live performance in theatre, opera, and dance. Equity supports the creative efforts of its members by seeking to improve their working conditions and opportunities. The business of Equity is to negotiate and administer collective agreements, provide benefit plans, information and support, and act as an advocate for its membership. To learn more about Equity or how to become a member, visit their website at: www.caea.com.

Canadian Actors' Equity Association
National Office
44 Victoria St., 12th Floor
Toronto, Ontario, Canada
M5C 3C4
Tel: (416) 867-9165
Fax: (416) 867-9246

BRITISH EQUITY

British Equity is the only trade union to represent artists from across the entire spectrum of arts and entertainment. Formed in 1930 by a group of West End of London performers, Equity's membership includes actors, singers, dancers, choreographers, stage managers, theatre directors and designers, variety and circus artists, television and radio presenters, walk-on and supporting artists, stunt performers and directors, and theatre fight directors.

The main function of Equity is to negotiate minimum terms and conditions of employment throughout the entire world of entertainment. Looking to the future, they also negotiate agreements to embrace the new and emerging technologies. Satellite, digital television, new media and so on are all covered, as are the more traditional areas. In addition, they also operate at an international level through the Federation of International Artists, the International Committee for Artistic Freedom, and through agreements with sister unions overseas. To learn more about Equity or how to become a member, visit their website at: www.equity.org.uk.

British Equity
Head Office
Guild House
Upper St. Martins Lane
London, England, UK
WC2H 9EG
Tel: + 020 7379 6000
Email: info@equity.org.uk

THE AMERICAN FEDERATION OF TELEVISION AND RADIO ARTISTS (AFTRA)

The American Federation of Television and Radio Artists (AFTRA) is a national labor union representing over 70,000 performers, including dancers, journalists, and other artists working in the entertainment and news media. AFTRA's membership includes an array of talent—sound recording membership includes artists who bring pop, rock, country, classical, folk, jazz, comedy, Latin, hip hop, rap, and R&B to the world. AFTRA members perform in television and radio advertising, non-broadcast video, audio books, and messaging, and provide their skills for developing technologies such as interactive games and Internet material.

The union negotiates and enforces more than 300 collective bargaining agreements that guarantee minimum (but never maximum) salaries, safe working conditions, and health and retirement benefits. AFTRA was the first industry union to establish employer-paid health and retirement plans for members and their dependents that qualify. With more than 30 local chapters across the country, AFTRA promotes the success and welfare of members in a variety of ways, including contract negotiation and enforcement, advocating on legislative and public policy issues, supporting equal employment opportunities, and sponsoring or supporting health and retirement benefits and programs. For more information, visit www.aftra.com.

AFTRA
New York National Office
260 Madison Ave.

New York, NY 10016
Tel: (212) 532-0800
Fax: (212) 532-2242

AFTRA
Los Angeles National Office
5757 Wilshire Blvd. 9th Floor
Los Angeles, CA 90036
Tel: (323) 634-8100
Fax: (323) 634-8194

AMERICAN GUILD OF MUSICAL ARTISTS (AGMA)

American Guild of Musical Artists, founded in the 1930s, is the labor organization that represents musical artists in opera, concert, and dance. Soloists and
choristers, dancers, choreographers, stage managers, and stage directors are all
part of AGMA.

AGMA is in business to protect performing artists. They negotiate contracts,
called collective bargaining agreements, which provide guaranteed wages,
standardized working conditions, rehearsal and overtime pay, regulated work
hours, vacation and sick pay, resolution of disputes, and protection against discrimination and abuse in any form.

They enforce the contracts and assure that their collective bargaining agreements provide for health insurance, pension coverage, and protection against
unreasonable working conditions and unsafe work places. For more information and to learn how to become a member of AGMA you can visit their website
at: www.musicalartists.org.

AGMA
Head office
1430 Broadway, 14th Floor
New York, NY 10018
Tel: (212) 265-3687
Fax: (212) 262-9088

SCREEN ACTORS GUILD (SAG)

Screen Actors Guild is the nation's largest labor union representing working
actors. Established in 1933, SAG has a rich history in the American labor movement, from standing up to studios to break long-term engagement contracts in

the 1940s, to fighting for artists' rights amid the digital revolution sweeping the entertainment industry in the twenty-first century. The Guild exists to enhance actors' working conditions, compensation and benefits, and to be a powerful, unified voice on behalf of artists' rights.

With 20 branches nationwide, SAG represents nearly 120,000 actors who work in motion pictures, television, commercials, industrials, video games, Internet, and all new media formats. SAG is a proud affiliate of the AFL-CIO. To learn more about SAG or how to become a member, please visit their website at: www.sag.org.

SAG
Hollywood - National Headquarters
5757 Wilshire Blvd., 7th Floor
Los Angeles, CA 90036
Main Switchboard: (323) 954-1600
For SAG Members outside Los Angeles: (800) SAG-0767
For information on the SAG contract involving dancers, please contact: SAG National Dancers Department
Tel: (323) 549-6864

STAGE DIRECTORS AND CHOREOGRAPHERS SOCIETY (SDC)

The Stage Directors and Choreographers Society is a national independent labor union representing members throughout the United States and abroad. SDC has jurisdiction over the employment of directors and choreographers working in the following areas: Broadway and national tours, Off-Broadway, The Association of Non-Profit Theatre Companies, New York City (ANTC), League of Resident Theatres (LORT), Council of Resident Stock Theatres (CORST), Dinner Theatre (DTA), Regional Music Theatre (RMT), Outdoor Musical Stock (OMS) and Non-Equity Tours. For more information on SDC or to learn how to become a member, visit their website at: www.sdcweb.org.

SDC
1501 Broadway, Ste. 1701
New York, NY 10036
Toll free: (800) 541-5204
Tel: (212) 391-1070
Fax: (212)302-6195

190

DIRECTORS GUILD OF AMERICA (DGA)

The Directors Guild of America represents nearly 14,000 members working in U.S. cities and abroad. The DGA represents directors, unit production managers, first assistant directors, second assistant directors, technical coordinators and tape associate directors, stage managers, and production associates working in film, television, commercials, and new media. The Guild seeks to protect directorial teams' legal and artistic rights, contend for their creative freedom, and strengthen their ability to develop meaningful and credible careers. For more information, visit their website at: www.dga.org.

THE NATIONAL WRITERS UNION (NWU)

The National Writers Union is the trade union for freelance and contract writers, journalists, book authors, business and technical writers, web content providers, and poets. It has approximately 1,700 members in sixteen chapters nationwide. The NWU works to defend the rights and improve the economic and working conditions of all writers. For more information, visit their website at: www.nwu.org.

INTERNATIONAL ASSOCIATION OF THEATRICAL STAGE EMPLOYEES, MOVING PICTURE TECHNICIANS, ARTISTS AND ALLIED CRAFTS OF THE UNITED STATES, ITS TERRITORIES AND CANADA (IATSE)

IATSE was originally chartered by the American Federation of Labor as the National Alliance of Theatrical Stage Employes in 1893. (They kept the Old English spelling "Employes" until 1995). Since its birth, it has grown to include not only the original stagehands and projectionists, but a great variety of other crafts persons in the numerous branches of the entertainment industry, including motion picture and television production, product demonstration and industrial shows, conventions, facility maintenance, casinos, audio-visual, and computer graphics. It is the largest labor union in the entertainment and related industries, boasting more than 110,000 members. For more information, visit their website at: www.iatse-intl.org.

IATSE General Office
1430 Broadway, 20th Floor
New York, NY 10018
Tel: (212) 730-1770
Office of the International President

Fax: (212) 730-7809
Office of the General Secretary-Treasurer
Fax: (212) 921-7699

UNITED SCENIC ARTISTS LOCAL USA 829
(AFFILIATED WITH IATSE SINCE 1999)

United Scenic Artists, Local USA 829, is a labor union and professional association of designers, artists and craftspeople, many whom are world famous, organized to protect craft standards, working conditions, and wages for the entertainment and decorative arts industries. The members of Local USA 829 are artists and designers working in film, theatre, opera, ballet, television, industrial shows, commercials, and exhibitions. The current active membership totals more than 3,300. For more information visit their website at: www.usa829.org.

United Scenic Artists Local USA 829
29 West 38th St., 15th Floor
New York, NY 10018
Phone: (212) 581-0300
Fax: (212) 977-2011

Writers Guild of America, East (WGAE)   www.wgaeast.org
Writers Guild of America, West (WGAW)   www.wga.org
Songwriters Guild of America (SGA)   www.songwritersguild.com
American Federation of Musicians (AFM)   www.afm.org

As mentioned previously, not all these unions will be relevant to you specifically; however, there is a wealth of information to be had. I hope that you will take some time to peruse the various websites listed and take advantage of the opportunity to educate yourself further about these different aspects of the entertainment industry. By visiting these websites, you can learn a great deal about the entertainment industry's history and the great strides that have been taken to secure some of the bylaws and standards that we enjoy today.

Artist and talent exploitation has always, and continues to be, an issue. Our industry, like so many others, needs protection—not just from the outside, but sometimes from within—from those who unfortunately lack principles and respect for their profession and their peers. Regrettably, they often make decisions that have an adverse affect on the entire industry. As I just spoke of in the last chapter, "No More Starving Artist," always remember integrity first and foremost. I implore you to consider very carefully every move you make along your career path. You never know how your actions and decisions will affect not only your own outcome, but that of others. If you are going to blaze a trail, let it be the high road!

Thanks to the courage and efforts of those who chose way-back-when to come together and stand united and the many people who have joined the cause along the way. Today we have unions that continue to work on our behalf, making their voices, *our voices*, heard, where it matters most.

ENCORE:
If you are going to blaze a trail, let it be the high road!

Places please. Cast of *Broadway Babies*, Costa Cruise Lines' *Romantica*

Chapter Fourteen

Money Makes the World Go 'Round—You Are Your Business

"Money isn't everything—as long as you have enough of it."
~ **Anonymous**

I will preface this next section by saying, I know that some of what you are about to read in this chapter can all seem a bit over the top, especially if you are first starting out in your career making a pittance of a salary. I'm sure you are thinking, "Why on earth do I want or need to know about all of this finance stuff?" Perhaps you already know about it, in which case you don't need to read this chapter at all. But to those of you who, like most of us, no matter what age, can use some sound advice about money matters, there is much to learn in this chapter.

Although it can be a bit overwhelming, don't panic; this information is for your edification and simply to help you recognize the importance of securing your financial future starting *now*. This is one area you do not want to be clueless in!

THE BIG SCARY F-WORD: FINANCES

"While it's never too late to start financial planning, thinking ahead when you're in your 20s and 30s can pay you very large dividends in your 60s and 70s and probably beyond. The earlier you begin to put money away (even in small amounts), invest it for the long term, and know how to protect it, the more you'll have when you need it, or want it." —Kenneth M. Morris, Virginia B. Morris, and Alan M. Siegel, *The Wall Street Journal Guide to Planning Your Financial Future.*

Terry Fay, a financial strategist with Fay Financial Group in Orlando, Florida, was kind enough to offer his expertise as a financial advisor and allowed me to pick his brain so that I could offer you some sound financial guidance. Terry walked me through a typical meeting with a first-time client. He calls it the three steps for rainy days and opportunities: Protection, savings, and investments.

ENCORE:

The earlier you begin to put money away (even in small amounts), invest it for the long-term, and know how to protect it, the more you'll have when you need it, or want it.

STEP ONE – PROTECTION

Protection is absolutely imperative to each and every one of us.

Terry says, "*Always protect first.*" Let's take a look at some of the ways in which you might protect yourself.

RENTER'S INSURANCE

If somebody is renting, they will want to have renters insurance. Of course, if any of you are homeowners, then you will be familiar with and have a home-owner's insurance policy. You might be thinking that you can't afford this extra insurance or that you don't have anything worth insuring. Often, when some-one is first starting out and may not have that many belongings, they put less importance on their need for such insurance. However, what Terry points out is that in the unfortunate event of a fire or burglary, you could lose everything. He reminds us: "These belongings are possessions that you have collected and ac-cumulated over years—goods that you may have purchased as you could afford them. When we're young and first starting out, we don't always have the luxury of purchasing everything that we need all at once, so you may have purchased these items on sale or maybe even from a garage sale."

Many of us have had family members help us out with a bedroom set from Uncle Lou, a sofa or a dinette from Mom and Dad—you get the idea. The point is very simple: If you were to lose all your belongings in such an unfortunate event, you would have to replace them all right away. You wouldn't have the great luxury of waiting for the "great deals" again. Having such an insurance policy is not only sensible, it should be a priority. First of all, it's very inexpensive and believe me, you will be thrilled that you did it if, God forbid, you ever need to file a claim.

It will be very important for you to have an inventory of your belong-ings; you'll need this proof for your insurance company in the event of such a misfortune. You must have a detailed recording of all of your personal belongings and valuables; this can be in the form of a list on paper and photographs or on DVD/video. Either way, you'll want to ensure its safekeeping by storing it in a safety deposit box or someplace other than your home. If there was a fire at your home, this would be the last place you would want your proof to be.

ASSETS AND LIABILITY

Terry goes on to say, "We want to protect our assets and we want to protect our earnings from liability in the event that you were ever to get sued by someone. You wouldn't want all that you've worked so hard for to be taken away in a lawsuit, and, of course, the more money you make, the bigger the target you could be. So initially, the struggling artist first starting out may not be a very big target if something were to happen. However, as you become more successful and assets are accumulated, then you need to protect yourself with an umbrella policy or some other protection strategy. A financial advisor can help you develop such a plan. Some products are protected completely or in part (depending on what state you live in) from lawsuits. Those include life insurance, annuities, and government retirement plans."

For those of you who are considering owning your own business such as a school, a production company, or an agency, you will want to incorporate. Some specialty performers who book themselves out as individual acts may also prefer to work under a corporate entity. When you are ready to consider taking this step, you should speak to a financial advisor who can assist in devising a strategy that will be most relevant to your situation and for protecting your assets.

I would like to take a moment to address the young artist first starting out. The idea that we want to get across is the importance of sensible habits. Thinking ahead and educating yourself about the value of such protection is all a part of developing and instilling these habits. Let's face it, as an artist, you must have discipline. Just as you must be regimented in your training and performance, it is equally essential to have strong business acumen. Even if at this moment you don't think that you need liability insurance, we simply want you to be aware of it so that when you do need to protect yourself, you will know what to do.

AUTO INSURANCE

Terry gives a great example. He says, "Imagine that you were the cause of a car accident and you're in a courtroom about to be sued for some undetermined amount of money. How much protection against a lawsuit would you want to have from your insurance company? Most people would want the maximum

STARTING YOUR CAREER AS A DANCER

protection available because, unfortunately, you just don't know how much you could be sued for. This is a good guideline to use when purchasing insurance. Often young drivers purchase the very minimum requirements, and the obvious problem with this is that in the unfortunate event of an accident, you could find yourself under-protected. Some required minimums are so low that they don't even cover the cost of replacing a vehicle."

The amount of coverage you choose is certainly up to you in the end. "However, you absolutely should consider more than the state minimums. You will also want to make certain that you have proper protection in the event that the other party does not. For example, if you were hit by someone who did not have proper insurance, you would make a claim against your own insurance company through the uninsured and underinsured motorist coverage. This would replace any damages to you." As the laws can very from state to state in the United States, and certainly from country to country, you will want to seek proper counsel in this area. "A general rule of thumb in property and casualty coverage," says Terry "is one times your assets or twenty times your income. For example, if somebody makes $50,000 per year, twenty times their income would be $1 million. If someone harms another and causes them to lose a job, they can be sued and in some states, their wages can be garnished. What you want to do is to protect yourself and your earnings against such a lawsuit."

DISABILITY INSURANCE

"Disability insurance replaces your income in case you cannot work because of sickness or injury," Terry points out. "All athletes can, and the smart ones do, purchase disability insurance because unfortunately, all it takes is one accident or injury—a twisted ankle—and they are out of the game; a serious injury can cost them their career." As with athletes, disability insurance is equally as important to big-name entertainers. There are companies that specialize in underwriting entertainers. You can be certain that every big name singer has their voice insured, just as every big name dancer should have their legs insured. After all, this is the foundation of their business and without an able body, they have no business, and, therefore, no income.

MEDICAL INSURANCE

There are many different types of policies available. If you are traveling a lot, you may want to consider an international policy where you are covered in any country in which you might be traveling and performing. Otherwise, a standard policy for your country of residence should suffice. Travel insurance may also

198

be a way to cover your medical needs when traveling for a contract. Different countries will offer different policies, and there are many options available. Once again, seeking the correct counsel is always extremely important.

WILLS AND TRUSTS

This is an area that we naturally do not give consideration to when we are young as it is often unfamiliar and may seem unnecessary. I have said throughout the book that when we are young, we have a tendency to believe that we are invincible, and, therefore, why would we even be concerned with such needs?

Terry explains that wills and trusts are vitally important to you, the artist, especially if you have children. It is of equal value and will be very significant to any parents of young artists reading this material on their behalf. Terry is adamant in saying, "It will be extremely important to have the guardianship for your children established." He stresses the importance of ensuring that you have trusts and various other legal devices set up so that in the event that your children do make it big, and in the unforeseeable misfortune that something were to happen to you, the parents, your children would be protected from all of the vultures trying to get at the money. These legal documents are invaluable and must be set up by a good attorney and reviewed on a regular basis.

LIFE INSURANCE

Life insurance is designed to replace lost income. Terry uses the example of a runaway truck causing a fatal accident: "I guarantee that the survivor would look to sue the truck company. The purpose of such a lawsuit is to replace the income that has been taken away from the family. Let's look at a different scenario: If someone has a heart attack in the middle of the night and suddenly dies, the end result is the same for the family, but there's no truck company to sue. This is where life insurance comes into the picture; it should replace the full economic life value of the victim, roughly about twenty times their income. The purpose of life insurance is not to pay off the mortgage, although some people do; its real purpose is to replace lost income and the deceased person's economic value. If the deceased was a stay-at-home parent, there may not be any lost income; however, there is economic value that needs to be replaced. Suddenly, there could be the need to hire a nanny or a housekeeper or both, to carry on the duties of the lost parent; this is an economic value that is often overlooked. To lose a parent or a loved one is a horrible tragedy, and it would be a travesty to also have the children's dreams vanish because of something that was not taken care of; something that is so simple and easy to obtain such as life insurance.

"Oftentimes, young and single people think that because they are not married or don't have children, they do not need life insurance, but the reason a young person needs to consider purchasing life insurance early is to lock in their future insurability. The truth is no one needs life insurance; people want it, but nobody needs it. There may come a day when you decide that you want life insurance, maybe once you are married. However, if somewhere along the way, you were diagnosed with an illness that rendered you uninsurable, you would then find yourself in the unfortunate situation of not being able to purchase this life insurance at a later date. Unfortunately, these are some of the things that we never think of until it's too late."

If you are young and considering life insurance, Terry suggests that you also include a rider to your policy that allows you the option of purchasing more life insurance in the future on a guaranteed basis without the need for medical underwriting (this means without the need for further medical examination). For example, if you were to become ill with cancer, yet survive it, you would now have this illness on your record. Even though you went on to be healthy, without this rider, you would either be uninsurable or unable to get additional coverage, whereas with the rider, you could at certain intervals add more coverage without the need for any evidence of insurability. This is a wonderful feature to have.

Another critical rider to have is called waiver of premium. "Basically, what happens is this," explains Terry. "If the insured were to become disabled and no longer able to work, and therefore not able to pay the insurance premium, then the insurance company would pay the premium for them. Let's use the example of a whole-life insurance policy that builds equity in cash value. If the policy holder suddenly became disabled, the insurance company would make those premium payments on their behalf for the rest of their life. Thirty years down the road, they would have equity built up, the policy would have cash value, and the insured would still have a little bit of savings. Chances are that any retirement plans and savings accounts would probably have come to a screeching halt. And, of course, without working for all that time, their insurance policy with cash value would be their only asset that had continued to grow."

ENCORE:
Always protect first!

200

STEP TWO: SAVINGS

"Once your protection has been analyzed, the next step is savings. You and your family are, in fact, and must be considered, your number one priority and the most important bill you pay. Therefore, you should be trying to allocate 15 percent of your gross income to your own personal savings plan. In the beginning, most of that money should be going into a completely separate savings account for those rainy days and opportunities. This way, should a sudden unforeseen rainy day come along, you will have the money set aside, whatever the emergency. Whether the air conditioner goes or the car breaks down, there is no additional stress and there's no credit card payment at the end of the month with hefty interest to worry about. It is simply taken care of through your savings account."

Let's take a look at the opportunity side of having this savings account. What if the prospect of buying into a business or investing in a great piece of real estate came along? How about an associate who would like to open a theatre or start up a dance company? You just never know what opportunities might be available, and as Terry points out, "Cash is always king in tragedy and opportunity. To have the cash in the bank is huge. How much cash? The ideal plan would be to have 50 percent of your gross income in liquid cash."

Terry says that people often react unfavorably at the thought of setting aside 15 percent or even 10 percent. They just don't see how it's possible. He then asks his clients how they would react if their boss were to come to them suddenly one day and explain that the company was downsizing, but that they could keep their job if they took a 10 percent decrease in salary. (This may not be completely foreign to performers. It has happened on occasion and sometimes with new works first trying to get off the ground, where a producer might ask a cast to help save the production by taking a little less salary and thereby helping to guarantee the longest run possible.) Inevitably, in Terry's example, the clients always reply that they would find a way. They would just have to make it work. So he asks, why wait until there's a downsizing to figure it out? "Why not figure it out now and set aside that 10 percent or 15 percent, if possible, for your own needs? This way, if you ever were hit with a downsize or other emergency, you would be prepared for it."

We understand that to go from never having saved, to 10 percent or 15 percent in your first year of work or first attempt at saving, can seem rather overwhelming, so start small and move incrementally. After all, our ultimate goal here is to instill the habit of saving and be successful at it. So be realistic. What can you commit to and stick to? Terry suggests that "you can start out with as little as 1 percent, and then every six months, add another percent until you reach your ultimate goal. You will be surprised at how well you do and how quickly it adds up. The truth is that when you commit and make it a habit, you don't miss it and you don't spend it. Just keep it very simple. You can have a savings account attached to your checking account and have it automatically programmed to transfer a set amount over on a specific day every month. The key here is making the whole thing systematic, so it's easy and it happens all the time. All you have to do is write it in your checkbook register and you won't even notice it missing."

> ENCORE:
> *Our ultimate goal here is to instill the habit of saving and to be successful at it. So be realistic. What can you commit to and stick to?*

STEP THREE: INVESTMENTS

"After you are in the habit of putting 15 percent into savings, (or whichever percentage you have determined feasible and realistic), and you have successfully set aside at least six months worth of savings, then the next step is investing. Obviously, the more you can save, the better off you'll be and the quicker you will get to your goal of 50 percent liquid cash. Liquid cash means those investments that do not go up and down in value; it means investments that are safe and guaranteed—cash that you can get to and access instantly when an opportunity comes along. As examples, your savings account and any cash values in life insurance policies. These are your more conservative investments; you know that your money will not fluctuate, and it will be there when you need it. Money market accounts are also considered conservative; however, although marginal, it is possible for them to lose value. The next tier of risk would be mutual funds; these may be more attractive to some. The cash is liquid; however, they can lose value.

"If somebody is making $100,000 per year, then 50 percent in liquid cash would mean that fifty thousand should be available in cash." Now, using this same example of a yearly income of $100,000, let's consider how long it could take you to reach your goal. If you were to save the ideal 15 percent per year, it would take you just over three years to have that 50 percent cash available, and that would be just from your savings alone. That wouldn't include any additional investments that you might have made along the way.

"Although the ideal plan is 50 percent, for some that could be more or less. Start by putting your 15 percent into your savings account and allow it to build until you reach your goal of 50 percent liquid cash; from there you can go into long-term investments. You see, tragedies never happen tomorrow or ten years from now; they always happen today and, unfortunately, we're never ready for them. This is why cash and protection are very important. This simple plan allows us to protect against those unexpected things that happen suddenly."

Terry goes on to say, "Most of the time, people have it backwards. They usually start by planning for things that may never happen thirty years from now, all the while leaving their families completely exposed in the present. So first and foremost, protect and save for *today*. Then you can start planning for thirty years from now for your long-term plan and investing strategy. At the point where you have reached a comfortable amount in your savings (remember the ideal goal is 50 percent liquid cash), then your 15 percent savings can start to go into other investments such as mutual funds, individual stocks, bonds, bond funds, and real estate."

> **ENCORE:**
> *Liquid cash—investments that do not go up and down in value. It means investments that are safe and guaranteed—cash that you can get to and access instantly when an opportunity comes along.*

LEARNING AND INSTILLING *GOOD HABITS* IN THREE SIMPLE STEPS

The following information is based on a plan that Terry has laid out in order to help you identify the simplicity of creating good habits with these three easy steps.

Learning this information is not enough. It's putting it all into practice and then owning it (for the rest of your life) that will make the difference.

Knowing what good habits are and making them a part of your life are two completely different things. In order to learn these habits and make them work for you, we are going to suggest you follow these three steps: step one—create a budget; step two—consider your values; and step three—be willing to make changes.

> **ENCORE:**
> *Knowing what good habits are and making them a part of your life are two completely different things.*

STEP ONE: CREATE YOUR BUDGET

First and foremost, identify how much money is coming in; it is essential to know how much you are making. Earlier we addressed how extremely important it is to treat yourself as a business and your earnings as your business income. Next, you should identify how much is going out. Pay yourself a salary to carry you through the ups and downs and live on that set amount of money just as you would if you had a regular job with a regular paycheck every week or two. From this salary you will want to set aside your determined percent for savings. In addition to, or as a part of your overall savings, you may want to include a "splurge fund" and a "long-term savings fund." The splurge fund amount and frequency should be determined in advance, and then you must stick to it. The splurge fund could be for that little something special, while the long-term savings could be for bigger, more extravagant purchases, such as new furniture, a vacation, or even a home.

The additional money, over and above expenses and savings, should remain in the business for those times when you are not earning a steady salary or don't have any business income. As you may have already experienced, or if you are first starting out, you will most likely soon learn that there are financial highs and lows that can come from the lack of steady gigs. In the entertainment business, you are sometimes employed in long-running gigs, while other times, you will find yourself doing "one-off's" or "one-nighters." These could be corporate engagements or television shoots, as an example. Then there could be the most dreaded time of all, when there is no work. Of course, an equally important consideration is the differences in the financial compensation you might be paid; sometimes you are making great amounts of money and sometimes you are earning much less. Because of such inconsistencies, this is all the more reason to get a grip on your spending and savings habits. It will be extremely important to be meticulous in the area of budgeting. If you take this advice, you will have secured a steady availability of cash when a low point comes along. The additional money from your more prosperous jobs will pay your bills during those leaner months. Essentially, what you will be doing is creating a stable situation for yourself from what could otherwise be unstable. Good habits are absolutely critical to securing finances in general, let alone being a performer with sporadic work and pay. Remember, the point to all of this is *no* "starving artist."

TAXES

If you are not working as an employee, you may want to consider putting aside a separate savings for your taxes. In some cases, you'll be considered self-employed and in the United States, you will be issued a 1099 form at the end of the year. This is a tax form that you will receive from any company that pays you over a set amount for work performed within that tax year. This means that you'll be responsible for paying your own taxes. It is always a good idea to have that money set aside in the event that you owe the Internal Revenue Service come April 15th. This way, you are prepared; no surprises. A tax accountant and the IRS may advise you to pay the IRS in quarterly payments so that you do not get hit all in one go. This may or may not be necessary. If this applies to you, your accountant can give you an estimate based on your previous year's tax return. He or she will estimate what you might owe and break it down for you into four quarterly payments.

ROUGH SPOTS

There will be rough spots; there will be hiccups along the way, and it is absolutely to your advantage to be prepared for them and not be surprised by them. You must have a financial back-up plan in place so that when they do come (and trust me, they do come), you're not back to a mattress on the floor and eating macaroni and cheese.

Look ahead to your future. Wouldn't it be great to know that if you wanted to make a change—whether to change careers entirely or to reinvent yourself within the industry—you could be in a strong financial position to do so? Long-term savings can help you by affording you the opportunity to take a hiatus while you decide what it is you want to do. Or it can be the funds that you invest in either retraining or educating yourself in a new field. Last but not least, it might be the capital you need to start your own business. This could be something entirely new and different, or it could be something dance-related, such as a dance company, a school, a theatre, an agency, or maybe a production company. If you decide that it is time for a change, but you are not prepared for that day, you could find yourself at a major and difficult crossroad.

Here are some tips and considerations when writing your budget:

There are four main categories to laying out a budget. Within each of these four categories, you will decide what is discretionary and what is not discretionary.

a.) The first category is *fixed expenses*; these are the ones that don't change from month to month, like your rent, your mortgage payment, or your car insurance. These are your fixed expenses and they are fixed non-discretionary expenses.

b.) The second category is *fixed discretionary expenses*. These are also our expenses that do not change from month to month, like a cable TV bill, or a housekeeper, but they are discretionary expenses you choose to have.

c.) The third category is *variable expenses*. These are the ones that are probably going to be different every month, like the utility bill, gas bill, or groceries.

d.) The fourth category is *savings*. What amount will you allocate to set aside regularly, commit to, and stick to?

BUDGETING TIP. Here's a great tip when it comes to budgeting. Understand this: the goal of retail stores is to have you make a purchase once you are in the store, so advertising is designed to lure you into the store. If you find yourself considering a purchase, and in that very moment, you feel you have to have it, *don't buy it*! Wait forty-eight hours; this will serve as what we have called the cooling-off period. When you find yourself with credit card in hand justifying the purchase, then you know this is a good indication that you probably shouldn't make this purchase in the first place. First ask yourself, "Do I need this for my business? Is it absolutely necessary, or is it just a pride thing?" There's a fine balance between keeping up the image and satisfying your ego. Second, you will want to ask yourself, "Do I need this on a personal level or is it just for fun and something that I merely want, not that I really need?" There's nothing wrong with buying something just for fun or splurging once in a while, but it would just be wiser to do so when you have the *splurge fund* saved up.

Set a goal of a certain dollar amount and when you reach it, you can reward yourself with a special purchase. This could be something you've had your eye on for some time or a special shopping spree. That way, when you walk into the store you know you can afford it and you don't have to question or justify it. Best of all, there is no credit card statement and no interest on top of it. By keeping a splurge account, these purchases become rewards instead of regrets.

ENCORE:
Set a goal of a certain dollar amount and when you reach it, reward yourself.

STEP TWO—CONSIDERING YOUR VALUES

The approach you take to budgeting will be based on your priorities. Some will choose to go at it in baby steps, while others will want to jump in head-first and take a more aggressive position. Terry points out that "It all goes back to a person's values: what is in their heart, what is important to them in their life, and where they ultimately want their life to go." He says, "Identifying those values first is critical, because they define who you are, they motivate your financial goals and, in turn, they will be the catalyst for change." Changing your behaviors will be necessary if the lifestyle you desire is different from the one you are presently living. On the other hand, if it's not broken, don't fix it!

Consider what it is that you desire most and aspire to. Make a list of your values, and then choose the top three that are most important to you. Does the lifestyle you desire align itself with your values? From this, you will be able to determine the necessary changes. Don't be shortsighted! Keep your eyes on the prize.

ENCORE:

The approach you take to budgeting will be based on your priorities. Some will choose to go at it in baby steps, while others will want to jump in head-first and take a more aggressive position.

STEP THREE—MAKE THAT CHANGE

Here are a few examples of how you might make some changes. Terry explains, "For example, if financial security is a value to you, then you may need to rethink your spending habits if they are keeping you from having the emergency fund that would give you the feeling of more security. You might choose not to have cable TV because although it may be fun at the time, it could be keeping you from saving and accomplishing your long-term goals."

Those little extras that you might be able to live without could make the difference between having that safety net or not. Remember those unforeseen situations like a show closing early, or downtime in between gigs. You might want to rethink purchasing a few discretionary items that you might not miss.

You should think of it like having a crystal ball. If you could see into your future, what would you want to see? Where do you want to be in one, ten, or thirty years from now? The answer to that question then becomes the motivating factor for choosing more carefully, creating better habits, and making positive changes.

ENCORE:

Those little extras that you might be able to live without could make the difference between having that safety net or not.

GET A GRIP

At the end of the day, we all know that we can talk ourselves into just about anything we want; we can be experts at the justifying game. And on that note,

Terry says, "Get a grip." The biggest problem is this: "Many people just don't get it! They don't have a handle on how much is going out, so when they get to the end of the month and they have more bills to pay and no money left, they wonder what happened to all the money. So first and foremost, create that budget, know what's coming in, and know what's going out.

"Secondly, identify what your values are. What is important to you and what are the expenses in your budget right now that are keeping you from living the life that you really want?

"Thirdly is change, and that is the hardest part of the whole process. 'Change is scary,' most people would say, but the truth is change can be great! And you must remind yourself that without change, you will not reach your ultimate goal. Ask yourself 'Who am I? Where is it that I want to be?' Then look at how you're spending your money, and if it doesn't match up with your ideal vision, you have to make a change. What if you have children and you want to make sure that they grow up with financial security, no matter what the circumstances are, whether you're here or not? If that is important to you, then you need to have life insurance, plain and simple. So if the movie-of-the-month-club membership is keeping you from paying fifteen dollars a month for a life insurance policy, then you need to ask yourself which is more important, the Movie of the Month Club or life insurance?"

Terry reiterates: "There are only two ways to create financial security. One, you can either reduce your expenses, or two, increase your income." So you need to sharpen your pencil and cut back on a few extras, or if you like the lifestyle you have and do not want to cut back, then you need to work a little harder or smarter and create some additional income.

And so there you have it, the three steps to creating good habits. If you would like to, and think you can implement all the changes that you want to make in one shot, that would be great. However, if you would rather focus on one change per month, go ahead and do just that. For some that's easier. Remember, your goal is success, so implement the necessary change in a schedule and manner that you know you will commit to and stick to.

Sound financial advice is invaluable; talk to friends and family who use financial advisors and can share their experiences. (Securities & Investment Advice offered through G.A. Repple & Company, A Registered Broker/Dealer & Investment Advisor. Member FINRA & SIPC. 101 Normandy Road, Casselberry, FL 32707, 407.339.9090.)

> *"Open your arms to change, but don't let go of your values."*
> ~ **Dalai Lama**

NOTES

In the moment. *FantaSea*, Celebrity Cruises' *Constellation*

Chapter Fifteen
Life after the Stage—Career Transitions

To dance is to be out of yourself. Larger, more beautiful, more powerful.
~ **Agnes de Mille**

Has anyone ever uttered to you those dreaded words, "What will you do when you can't dance anymore"? Surely someone has. Oftentimes it is a concerned parent or a loved one, sometimes it may very well be your own intuition or foresight. Either way, as painfully dreadful as the thought may be to you, it truly is an inevitable and necessary consideration.

What will you do when you can no longer dance professionally? What will you do when it's just plain old time to hang up your dance shoes? Change can be tremendously exciting and it can also be awfully intimidating. The truth of the matter is if you are a professional dancer working as such for a living, a career transition, whether by choice or by force, can be extremely difficult if you are not prepared. The magnitude and the spectrum of emotions that can come up can leave you feeling lost and not knowing which way to turn. If dance has always been your first love and it's all that you've ever done and wanted to do, then what to do next is going to be a huge decision for you. I want you to have not only a fighting chance, but plenty of choice to equip yourself with a great Plan B.

Although I've already mentioned sporadically throughout the book and specifically in "Chapter Six: Markets and Venues—Where and How to Find a Gig" many related professions that can be a very comfortable and natural fit for life after the stage, in this section I will revisit them and add to the list so to encourage

211

you to take a realistic and closer look at what options may be available and best suited to you. Having truly considered your options and all that you love about what you already do—and how those passions can be transferred to a new career—will give you the ability to be as best prepared as possible, thereby laying the foundation for a smoother transition. With a well-thought-out plan you can feel confident in your process and enjoy this new adventure and the excitement that comes from an opportunity to transform yourself.

METAMORPHOSIS

The first options I am going to present for your consideration are familiar and often very comfortable transitions. Of course for some dancers it is still a sad day when he or she realizes that it's time to leave the stage, fearful that it means leaving behind all that they've loved and so enjoyed. The passion that it takes to even pursue a career in dance and the performing arts doesn't suddenly vanish in light of a logical realization that a backup plan is in order. You may consciously understand the need to look at your options, yet your heart may be breaking every step of the way. It is really difficult to walk away from something you love so much, and dance is what you have loved, aspired to, and accomplished. I am not going to say that there is nothing to it. No, this realization that it may be time to hang up your dancing shoes can be one of the toughest, most complex obstacles you ever have to face in your career. You may be absolutely gutted by it all, but the first thing I want you to know is that it is perfectly normal to feel this way and that you are not alone. This is a loss for most, plain and simple, no matter to what degree there will be some feeling of sadness, some form of grieving, and it's all absolutely natural. Knowing this alone doesn't make it any easier, however. At the end of this chapter I will introduce you to a wonderful organization called Career Transitions for Dancers—a group dedicated to assisting dancers through their transitions.

For some of you it will not be so difficult; you may very well be perfectly content with the idea of transition, and you may be well prepared for it and therefore not feel the loss that many do. In the pages that follow I will share with you several very inspiring real-life stories of dancers who have transitioned, reinvented themselves, and transformed their careers both within the industry and outside the industry. You will see through their individual stories opportunity and experience, options to possibly consider and ways in which to help you be prepared for some of the emotional hurdles and how to avoid a few pitfalls. Together we will share with you words of wisdom gathered along the way through our journeys and personal experiences within this industry. I hope that you will take this advice onboard because the bottom line is if you are well prepared with a strong career plan you truly can have the best of both worlds. You can be financially stable and creatively fulfilled by following your passion and simply looking ahead and planning accordingly. As we've already covered in "Chapter Twelve: No More Starving Artist—The Business of Being in 'the Biz'" and "Chapter Fourteen: Money Makes the World Go Round—You Are Your Business," it is extremely important to take care of your business in order to have success in this business. The same goes for transitioning. Both of these chapters are full of important information coupled with expert opinion about entertainment law and financial planning. Just honest straightforward advice and great insight for you to carry with you in all that you do!

The good news is, the sooner you consider all of your needs and give some serious thought to the various options available to you, and make some firm decisions about what direction you want to take, the smoother the overall transition will be and the greater the outcome. There are so many wonderful avenues to take within the business that there may be no need to completely hang up your dance shoes. Some of these options we touched on earlier in Chapter Six, merely to introduce them as career options for those readers who may aspire to be in the business but not necessarily perform. Whereas here we will elaborate a little more as the same applies to those of you who are performers or aspiring to become performers, perhaps not at this moment, but certainly at some point later in your career when the need for transition comes into play. As I look back on my own career I have transitioned throughout, from dancer/performer and choreographer simultaneously, to choreographer/director and choosing at that point to no longer perform, then adding to that producer and writer. As I mentioned previously, although I loved to perform it was easy for me to come off the stage for I was equally as in love with the production side of it all. At twenty-nine I did my last two contracts back-to-back in Atlantic City. I left my last contract early due to a fracture in my metatarsal. I went back home to Los Angeles at the time and once rehabbed I continued working as a choreographer/director and performance director. Two years later I made the permanent move to Miami Beach when I was brought in to open *An Evening at La Cage*. I continued working with them as resident director/choreographer and, as I had decided to make this home, I opened my own production company where I produced entertainment for corporate events, hotels, casinos and resorts, and various cruise lines.

I think of the many dancers I have met along the way, those with whom I performed and those who have worked for me, and I am fascinated by the diversity of professions and the versatility of the dramatis personae. Which of them are still in the business and what are they doing today? And which of them are no longer in the business and what entirely different career paths might they have chosen? Within this eclectic group of men and women who all at one time or another graced the stage, we have doctors, lawyers, real-estate moguls, project managers, producers, dance studio owners, dance teachers, choreographers, lighting designers and set designers, costume designers, and the list is endless. Again I repeat, with foresight and good solid planning you can enjoy the journey fully from your process to your end result, both on- and offstage!

ENCORE:
There are so many wonderful avenues to take within the business that there may be no need to completely hang up your dance shoes.

IF THE SHOE FITS

There are many careers that are just that, a perfect fit, a natural progression for one transitioning from a performing career. Dance teacher, dance studio owner, choreographer, artistic director, rehearsal director, performance director, and producer or production company owner, casting director, casting agent, and dance or talent agent all fit the bill. In any of these positions you are working directly with the talent and in many cases hands-on, teaching, mentoring, helping to mold and develop talent. Mostly you are now able to utilize your own creative talents and have a huge impact on the end production or result. This can be very fulfilling for you as a performer and as a creator.

Dance company manager, theatre manager, production manager, dance critic, dance writer, and press agent—with these careers you get to enjoy the benefits of being around and working within the industry. In any of these positions, again you are working with and surrounded by performers. Depending on what choice you make you may be working within or writing about the very performance aspects or venues that you once performed in. So essentially you can still get the exhilaration that you might be worried about missing. Considering the diverse education that a dancer can gain from the exposure to so many facets of the business, the possible career transitions can be endless. Production support work can range from costume design and wardrobe stylist to makeup artist, scenic design or lighting design to sound and audio. All right-brainers are somehow closely entwined with similar characteristics and qualities, so it may be easier than you think to develop a secondary talent within the business. Often we don't try our hand at something new unless there is a need. Creative people must have an outlet for their creativity and, depending on your exposure to specific markets—i.e., stage versus film and television per se—this in itself can open up a whole slew of possibilities. Film and television director, writer, producer, concert promoter, tour manager, booking agent, special events coordinator, meeting planner, corporate events producer, account executive, production manager, and stage manager, the list goes on and on. The position of entertainment director is an excellent career but somewhat rare as there will most often be only one post at any given cruise line, hotel, vacation resort, or theme park. This position is not unlike other directorial positions in that the perfect candidate must possess not only creativity and passion but also the organization skills, leadership qualities, and vision to be able to achieve the overall results and bring the company or corporation to new heights.

Another area that is an absolute natural is a fitness career. Not surprisingly, many dancers cross over into the world of fitness when they stop dancing, often in an effort to stay in shape when no longer under the rigorous demands of a dancer's life and schedule. Fitness studios and gyms are popping up everywhere and they are infiltrated with dancers both still performing and already transitioned. Certification for fitness trainers and group instructors are available through several organizations: the American Council on Exercise and the Aerobics and Fitness Association of America are two of the largest and most reputable. Yoga and Pilates are two areas that dancers can identify with and ease into most naturally. The array of fitness classes offered is infinite and although dance has always been popular, today it has an even stronger presence in fitness establishments worldwide. Zumba Fitness is the latest dance-fitness craze and has been steadily climbing and dramatically sweeping the fitness and dance industry since its inception in 2001. Zumba, if you haven't already been exposed to it, is a fun and invigorating Latin-inspired dance-fitness program that blends international music and contagious steps to form a fitness party that is downright addictive. Millions of dancers around the world are becoming licensed to teach. Talk about a perfect fit! (No pun intended.) People love to dance, it is a feel-good activity and excellent for one's emotional and physical well-being, so as the Zumba slogan goes, "Ditch the workout and join the party."

A college degree in dance, theatre, musical theatre, or performing arts can help you to prepare for many of the careers mentioned above as well as several other areas, depending on which type of program and degree you decide to go with. Some areas not yet mentioned might be advertising specialist, public relations specialist, publicist, sales and marketing representative, community relations director, director of an arts council, and/or editor. It goes without saying that when considering your future, a college degree not only gives you something to fall back on but can be the determining factor as to which avenue you will pursue. Transitioning into certain areas of the industry may very well require a degree, something that your experience alone may not afford you. However, there are many areas within the industry where although you might benefit from a college degree it will not necessarily be a determining factor. It really all boils down to what your chosen path will be, and this alone is why it is so important to look ahead and have a bigger-picture plan. Dancers who have transitioned careers most smoothly and without much heartache are those who were realistic about their future and took action, hence they were well prepared. It is always best to remain flexible and open to opportunity yet be in control!

For those of you die-hard performers there are areas of dance where performance longevity is greater than others. For example, a ballroom dancer or Latin dancer can have a much longer life expectancy on stage than a ballerina or concert dancer per se. Robin Ray, a beautiful dancer who worked with me on several contracts, transitioned into ballroom dance at a young age. She did so initially when she was recommended to a male dancer who was looking for a partner to compete with him. Today she is the manager of a ballroom studio in Nashville, Tennessee, and absolutely loves it! She teaches, performs, and competes with her students and fellow professional teachers.

Here's Robin telling me about her transition: "At first, it did feel like I was leaving the performance world, but now I feel like I have actually found a career that will allow me to dance much longer than the performing world ever would have. Plus I have the stability and ability to make a living and a life. At thirty, it is hard to compete with the young, fresh eighteen-year-old girls straight off the competition circuit. In ballroom you get better as you get older." Although ballroom was completely new to her when she first transitioned into it, and what perhaps at the time appeared to be just another gig has since led her down an entirely new path within her dance career. Robin says that ballroom dancing was an amazing career transition for her and she highly recommends it to any dancer past the age of twenty-five who is starting to consider his or her options and would like to continue dancing.

As I have mentioned on numerous occasions throughout the book, longevity is certainly possible and plenty of dancers have defied gravity and had lifelong careers as performers. Of course this still requires some transition, for as we get older things change, our abilities change, and the roles naturally begin to change. As a triple threat you will certainly be better equipped and therefore better able to move through different areas of the business, from stage to film and television to print work. The more you do, (act, sing, dance, model, etc.) the more options you give yourself and hence the longer you can continue to perform. We talked about many dancers who have gone on to have fantastic careers as actors in both film and stage and these are just the few who have gained celebrity status. What about the millions of dancers around the world working in theatre and film and television at all ages? Many dancers who are triple threats, and have honed their other talents, have evolved into more acting roles or singing roles and have thereby made themselves somewhat ageless. As you get older you may find that the roles are fewer and more infrequent, and if this is the case, then the art of reinvention comes into play.

Allow me to explain. "The art of reinvention" is just as it sounds and something that many older dancers understand very well. It is not only an additional talent; it is a necessary talent. Often as creative types we inherently possess this quality but may not hone in on it early on. We may spend our lifetime refining it and eventually becoming masters at it by osmosis. This being the culmination of a lifetime devoted to doing what we love and making a successful career at it! As I have prefaced so many times throughout the book the goal here is to have success and longevity, none of that starving artist attitude! Bottom line, success can be defined in various ways and by each individual; what is success to one may not necessarily be to another. I believe success and longevity is created by the combination of all that we've talked about throughout this book. It's about being smart, it's about being proactive, being intuitive, and going for it. Learning to reinvent one's self is a strong survival tactic to possess in this industry. It is only one of many necessary, not only to pursue a career in dance but to have a successful career in dance, both onstage and offstage, during our performance years and beyond.

> ENCORE:
> *Dancers who have transitioned careers most smoothly and without much heartache are those who were realistic about their future and took action; hence they were well prepared.*

ALLOW ME TO INTRODUCE YOU TO

In this next section I am going to introduce you to several dancers, men and women, who have transitioned their careers, once or twice, some several times over. Their stories are wide-ranging, exciting, poignant, heartwarming, and some even heartbreaking at times. They are, each and every one of them, inspiring in their own way, and they all have one common thread—that of a survivor. Some of them have remained in the dance world, in show business, and the entertainment industry while others have taken a complete 180-degree turn. All of them have shared their stories with me through interviews so that I may in turn share them with you. I hope that they will lend inspiration and in some cases caution, while opening your eyes to the many realities of our business and yet the endless possibilities that are available to you!

MARYANN DELANY – ENTERTAINMENT DIRECTOR, ROYAL CARIBBEAN PRODUCTIONS, ROYAL CARIBBEAN INTERNATIONAL, HOLLYWOOD, FLORIDA

COME SAIL AWAY. First up I'd like to introduce you to a wonderful woman who has inspired many and helped to define dancers' career paths by creating opportunities for numerous dancers after they retired from the stage. MaryAnn Delany has set a new stage for, and written the parts for these passionate die-hards who love the business of show business and want to be involved for years beyond their so-called dancing days.

If you've ever aspired to work for, or have worked for Royal Caribbean International (more commonly known to the general public as Royal Caribbean Cruise Lines), then you might very well be familiar with the name MaryAnn Delany. MaryAnn is the entertainment director of Royal Caribbean Productions. At the time of this interview she is sixty-three years old, originally from Chicago, Illinois, raised in South Bend, Indiana, and now lives in Hollywood, Florida, where she heads up Royal Caribbean Productions. MaryAnn has proudly held this position for the past six years, a third of her eighteen years as an employee of the company. She began with RCCL back in 1992 as assistant manager of their then small in-house team, which she would later take on the role of developing and growing to what we know of today as the incredible in-house production company that is Royal Caribbean Productions.

I am thrilled to be able to share her story with you as she is a magnificent example of how to be successful doing what you love. She has led a full and exciting career in the entertainment industry and has never worked one day outside of her chosen field. Although you may be familiar with MaryAnn, what you may not know about her is that she began her professional career first as a dancer. MaryAnn started studying dance around the age of ten and began her professional career at nineteen. She danced professionally until she was thirty-eight, at which point she began thinking that she was getting to old to be featured with eighteen- and nineteen-year-olds. MaryAnn performed in concerts, musical revues, nightclubs, hotels and resorts, and in the corporate entertainment market. She was a featured dancer with Miller-Reich Productions, one of the leading show producers of their time. And although I unfortunately never had the pleasure of seeing her perform onstage, I have been told by many peers what an absolutely beautiful dancer she was. MaryAnn also performed in her own production company, and when she decided it was time to leave the stage she began producing and choreographing her own small productions. She continued to work with Miller-Reich, and, as she had worked for them in many capacities from featured dancer to dance captain, to company manager and rehearsal choreographer, she was eventually asked to work in the office auditioning, hiring, and contracting the performers. Not long after, the company began producing shows for Carnival and RCCL. When Miller-Reich closed its doors, RCCL asked her to join the company to help bring the entertainment program in-house. In her position as assistant manager she would be handling all casting, hiring, and contracting. At forty-five she was making her third major transition in her career, and this time it would be her first in a corporate environment.

When I asked MaryAnn if she had ever considered the need for or had a plan B for that day when she was no longer able to perform, she explained: "My career just started to evolve; I kept myself open to all possible opportunities. I was happy doing what I was doing and it just evolved. I have never had any job in my entire career that was not entertainment related." As entertainment director of RCCL, MaryAnn has had the wonderful fortune of creating a vehicle by which so many young dancers and singers today have, and for the past two decades have had: the opportunity to follow their passion long after the stage by working in the Royal Caribbean Production offices. To quote MaryAnn further: "We are the only non-entertainment company that has developed an entertainment career path. Our singers and dancers, when growing tired of the high seas, have become our rehearsal choreographers, vocal directors, music arrangers, stage managers, producers, and administrative staff. We hire outside talent to create and develop our shows along with our in-house talent." All of her team comes mostly from the dancer community: 95 percent of them have worked onboard. She finds that dancers are the most disciplined, dedicated, hard-working, loyal, and passionate people that you could ever find anywhere.

MaryAnn and I discussed life after dance and she shared with me her own difficulties in letting go. "How am I going to survive without being on stage? I went through that just like everybody does," MaryAnn said. "In fact when I gave up casting that was, I thought, my very last connection with performing. It was very emotional for me and it was really hard to give it up because I just kept thinking that was my last connection. My boss said to me, 'Until you leave that behind nothing else is going to open up for you.' I thought the fact that I was picking the people to be in these productions was a creative thing to do and nothing else I was doing was creative, but the minute I let that go I built this place! And now we have 150 singers and dancers coming through here monthly, we are open fifty-one weeks out of the year, and I see all of these people grow and develop and move into different directions and how creative is that! It's scary to let go but you have to let go to move on. And when I look back on it I think this is the most creative thing I've ever done."

When MaryAnn first joined RCCL in 1992 there were three people in this new upstart in-house production department. At the time they had six ships, they were doing new shows every couple of months, and had cast changeovers every three or four months. It took them five years to evolve completely into a full in-house production department. Today they have twelve full-time staff members and their production offices consist of three buildings in Hollywood, Florida, fully equipped rehearsal facilities—the envy of any production company—and two costume departments, one for new builds and the other for maintenance. They house approximately 120 to 150 performers, rehearsal choreographers, vocal directors, and producers per month, and they rehearse up to eight casts for eight ships at one time. They have twenty-four ships in total that MaryAnn's department is responsible for, and more than fifty-six production shows, three ninety-minute Broadway productions, three aerial/gymnastic productions, fourteen ice shows, twenty-two parades, and four water shows. This operation is an absolutely incredible production company and complex—I don't know of any other like it in the business.

MaryAnn and RCCL are really very proud of the quality in what they do and for the last eighteen years MaryAnn says she has been trying to dispel the stigma about working on cruise ships. "Ooh, why do you want to work on a cruise ship?" she laughs. "Because the truth is who else is offering performers this many opportunities?" She goes on to tell me about some of the newest prospects they are so excited about and once again are able to share with the many dancers, singers, choreographers, directors, and vocal directors who come through their doors. "We are working with a Broadway casting director for many years now. He does the casting for *Chicago* on Broadway, the revival of *La Cage Aux Folles*, and for the national touring companies of these Broadway shows. And now we've contracted him to cast our lead roles for our three onboard Broadway shows. He's got that door that swings both ways; he hires them for the cruise ships and if he likes them he can cast them for Broadway. As a matter of fact the actor that we had hired for our Billy Flynn and Corny Collins had worked for us ten years prior, and this casting director is now putting him in *Chicago* the musical on Broadway. And there you have it; yet another opportunity for performers through RCCL."

During our interview MaryAnn shared with me that she had just announced her retirement from her position as entertainment director. She stepped down in October of 2011. However, she may very well find herself transitioning once again, not necessarily into retirement but possibly into a whole new field. She is currently overseeing a potential move for their production offices. They are at present in negotiations with a local university and if the deal happens there is the possibility of moving all of the Royal Caribbean Productions offices to the university campus. MaryAnn said: "Everything would go over there including hotel. We would build a hotel and this would now involve all hotel operations. The possibilities are endless and the direction we could go in is limitless." This move would represent more overall growth with adding hotel operations to the mix and an even greater opportunity to develop the in-house production company further by also training their own sound and lighting engineers and then some.

MaryAnn tells me she is excited about her retirement and seeing how things fall into place. She is excited at the thought of possibly transitioning into something new and she is planning to stay with the project at least until the contracts are done. She's already drawn up the space plan based on what they think they are going to need and as always she remains open to all possibilities. As we were finishing up our interview I asked her what she loved most about her job and these were her closing words to me: "I just love what I do and I am so lucky and so fortunate to have done what I've done. To have done what I love, for my entire life."

MaryAnn Delany has been positively influential in building Royal Caribbean Productions and from it has created tremendous opportunities for dancers around the world. In one of the most difficult and sometimes brutal industries to be in, that of entertainment, cruise lines are certainly offering more than their share of possibilities for performers. There are much greater options here than in many areas of the business, and as I've already discussed at great length in the "Chapter Six: Markets and Venues—Where and How to Find a Gig" there are in fact many fabulous reasons to choose a performance career on the high Seas. To learn more about Royal Caribbean Productions please visit their website at www.royalcaribbeanproductions.com.

*STACEY ENYART – FOUNDER AND ARTISTIC DIRECTOR OF
SUNCOAST DANCE THEATRE, TAMPA BAY AREA, FLORIDA*

BORN TO INSPIRE. Stacey Enyart is a force to be reckoned with. She is a
highly talented, beautiful dancer and performer, and beyond the stage she has
a special gift and she knows just how to use it. Stacey epitomizes the meaning
of inspiration; she is a natural-born teacher and choreographer and she touches
the lives of her students in a way that is truly special. At only twenty-four years
old, when Stacey certainly had many great years left in her as a performer, she
chose to leave the stage early because of an internal calling to teach.

I remember one day while sitting at lunch in Key West with our cast from
the Celebrity Constellation, my husband Alex and I had lunch with them all as
we would be leaving them the next day. It had been a long few weeks of rehearsals and we had just opened two brand new shows. This was the first day off and
an opportunity to enjoy being with the cast away from rehearsals. Stacey and I
were chatting and that was when she first mentioned to me her desire to have
her own dance company. And I remember thinking how brilliant she would
be yet feeling sad that I would probably lose her as a dancer. She was such an
incredible asset with all the skills that make a great assistant choreographer and
dance captain. We had enjoyed having her on our team. But my loss was the
dance world's gain and for this I am both thrilled and so proud. I had the chance
to visit her studio and watch her in action, and I was overjoyed at witnessing the
love from her students and the tremendous impact she has made in their lives.

Stacey is twenty-nine years old and a native of Florida. She started dancing
at five years old—ballet, tap, jazz, and tumbling, she later added modern to her
studies. Stacey received cum laude honors with a bachelor of arts in dance from
Point Park Conservatory in Pittsburgh, Pennsylvania, in 2004, having taken one
year off to perform on the high seas. Stacey had the wonderful experience of traveling from British Columbia, down the West Coast, through the Panama Canal,
across the seas, and throughout the Mediterranean while working as a dancer
onboard Celebrity Cruises – Mercury Ship and the Constellation (the newest
and largest of the fleet at that time). Professionally she also did concert company
work for five years, worked at Busch Gardens, and did film and television sporadically throughout her performance career. Stacey is a very bright woman and
to me the kind of young girl that just always had her head on straight. She told
me that she was always looking ahead to a "bigger picture" plan.

"Honestly, I started thinking about my future beyond performing when I
was in high school. Seeing artists get injured and not being able to fulfill their
performance contracts thus making it impossible to support themselves was an

eye-opener. I knew then and there that having an education background would 'save' me should I ever become injured to the point where I couldn't do anything in the realm of dance."

Stacey's transition from performer to teacher and now owner and artistic director of Suncoast Dance Theatre is one of the most seamless and natural transitions a dancer could ever make. And of course, there is a lot to be said about knowing in your heart what you want and what you were made for. Stacey has that beautiful gift of inspiration and of being a great mentor to others, and knew as she said that this was her calling.

"I knew from the high school age I wanted to teach and be behind the scenes as I feel my heart is most fulfilled when I can see how I inspire others. But starting my own company came from working in various fields of dance and seeing many different philosophies taught. I wanted to make a place that molded many great concepts together to make my own mission statement. Don't get me wrong, I loved performing and I felt as if it was necessary for me to experience that because as a teacher you want to have background knowledge and experiences to share with your students. It lends itself to yet again another way for your children to be inspired. If they see you have done it and experienced it then they know *they* can. Besides knowing that I always wanted to teach, ownership was always in the back of my mind as a 'when I get older' idea. I never thought that at twenty-five I'd be opening my own space. The sudden shock of my father's passing really made me realize that if it was something I wanted to do, I should do it now. So one year after his passing I opened my doors and felt as if the dream that my parents always supported and wanted for me finally came to fruition."

And the wonderful support of her parents is something that Stacey always had. Apparently her father was always encouraging her to get into business and her mother, "Miss Terry," as she is affectionately called by all the students, is right there by her side running the studio with her.

When I asked Stacey whether she had had any fears or emotional difficulties in making the decision to stop performing she said, "I think the difficulty in not performing is finding creative ways to stay moving. When you are teaching or directing your plate is full with not only your wants but all your clients' as well, so continually being re-inspired and making it a point to dance yourself is what I find difficult." As for what she has taken from her years of training and performing and how she applies it to her career as an artistic director and studio owner, Stacey tells me that it's all encompassing, and that she feels she has so much more to offer as a teacher, choreographer, and director because of the richness of her experiences. "Again this goes with

223

directorship," she said. "Students look to you as someone who is knowledge-able and experienced in many fields of dance, and they hope that the fields you are not so experienced in you have other teachers that are available to them. If I didn't give myself the opportunity to experience performing I couldn't imagine what our shows would look like at the end of the year. I think it would be pure chaos. Performing not only taught me what things should look like on-stage but more so what should be happening offstage to make everything look flawless."

Stacey is highly motivated, free thinking, and a self-starter. Aside from oper-ating her full-time business, Stacey is the founding director of the entire dance department at Wesley Chapel High School, where she spends the early part of her days teaching. She also recently held the post of jazz director at New Tampa Dance Theatre as well as residential jazz teacher and choreographer for Ruth Eckerd Hall's Marcia P. Hoffman Institute in St. Petersburg, Florida. As they say, if you want something done ask a busy person. Stacey is a wealth of knowl-edge, talent, and experience and the dance world needs such positive influences. Make sure to visit Stacey and Miss Terry online at www.suncoastdancetheatre. com, and for any of you dancers out on the West coast of Florida looking for expert training in dance and a well-rounded education in entertainment, be sure to put Suncoast Dance Theatre on your list.

SUSAN SALGADO – CASTING DIRECTOR/OWNER, TRIPLE THREAT CASTING, LOS ANGELES, CALIFORNIA

WHEN OPPORTUNITY STRIKES. You've seen her work, or the result thereof, you just may not know it. Susan Salgado lives the exciting life of a Hollywood casting director; she works both as a freelance casting director and under her company name of *Triple Threat Casting.* At forty-seven years old, Su-san has spent the greater part of her career surrounded by talent: dancers, cho-reographers, musicians, singers, and recording artists, some famous, others first being discovered. And that is the beauty of what Susan does for a living in an industry that she fell in love with at a young age as a dancer herself. Susan has the ability to make careers happen or at the very least help them get a break, and sometimes it's that first all-important break into the business. She has an incredible eye for talent and this she owes in part to having been a performer herself. When I asked Susan how she thought her time as a performer may have helped her in her career as a casting director and agent, here's what she had to say: "Having been a performer has helped me tremendously when cast-ing dance and music projects. I have seen so many different talents around the country and you just know when they have it! Being around the dance world for so long has made it is easy to spot the special ones."

Susan began dancing at twelve years old and studied jazz, ballet, and hip hop. She was also a summer scholarship recipient at the Joe Tremaine Studio in Los Angeles in 1981 where she was then scouted by a dance agent. She was obviously a naturally gifted dancer, for no sooner had she been scouted she went on to tour with various recording artists and performed in live shows, music videos, feature films, and TV shows. She danced professionally for only a short period of time, roughly a couple of years. She stopped dancing professionally at twenty-five, not because she had to but merely because she found an equivalent love—that of working behind the scenes. Although Susan had a short-lived career as a dancer, it was an exciting career and one that so many young dancers aspire to: Hollywood and all its glamour.

Her first career transition, the position of dance agent's assistant at the Bobby Ball Talent Agency back in 1990, had been recommended to her by her boyfriend at the time. Having just signed up for representation with the dance agent himself, he had noticed that the office was very busy and seemed to be short-staffed. This, her first transition from the stage to behind the scenes, was the very momentum that gave the start to the tremendous career that followed. These were in fact the very early days of dance agents, which I speak of in the "Representation—Agents and Managers" section of "Chapter Twelve: No More Starving Artist—The Business of Being in 'the Biz.'" To quote Susan: "I never even knew that dance agents existed at that time. I only wanted to dance, perform and travel." For Susan the opportunity to work and train at Tremaine's Dance Studio was a real learning experience; it took her knowledge about the dance industry to an entirely different level. When I asked Susan about her early career transitions here's what she had to say: "I quickly learned the types of dancers that were most marketable at the time. I accepted this and made it my focus as I moved up into a junior dance agent position. And after three years I became a senior dance agent. After five years in the dance department, I was given the opportunity to develop the music department, representing some of L.A.'s top vocalists and musicians, etc. Within a short period of two years I was offered to run both the dance and music departments."

Susan's decision to take this position was a great move and, combined with the stars aligning so perfectly, a very lucky one. As I mentioned above these really were the early days and Susan was fortunate enough to get in on the ground floor. Not only was she instrumental in helping the development of the dance and music departments at the Bobby Ball Agency, but she was privy to and sat in on negotiations that helped shape some of the industry standards for dancers that we enjoy today. There were only two dance agencies in Los Angeles at the time when she got started. Julie MacDonald and Tony Selznick had started the first dance agency at KSA – Kazarian, Spencer and Associates. (They later left and started MSA in 2000.) And so, KSA and the Bobby Ball Agency were the only games in town when it came to dance agents. The time frame in which Susan got started was a very favorable one, as dance agents were first being defined in the entertainment industry. When I asked her what that experience was like, here's what she had to say: "If you were a professional dancer at this time, you were either with us or the other agency. We sat through endless hours of negotiations and meetings with SAG and AFTRA to put dancers in union contracts for film and television jobs. We helped create the organization known as Dancer's Alliance." This group, by definition, was formed to unite all dancers together with their agents in order to pledge that they would not accept employment for less than what the agents had in fact implemented on non-union jobs, i.e., music videos, tours, live events, and rehearsals. "We compiled a list of additional fees for hazardous conditions (smoke on the set, wet environment, scaffoldings, etc.), basically considering anything that could cause harm to dancers while working on these non-union projects.

These new standards were also enforced in union jobs. We made sure that there was a cap on hours worked in a day and also ensured that dancers could not be hired at a flat rate for a full day of work. Prior to this standardization dancers use to work as extras in most jobs for film and television." By justifying that professional dancers go through extensive training to hone their craft they were also able to change the status by which dancers were contracted. According to the new standards, dancers would then be contracted under union feature rates and be allowed to receive residuals for their work. This was an incredible opportunity to help make a difference. Dancers throughout history have been and often still are at the low end of the totem pole, and it's thanks to the hard work of all those who gave their time and were so passionate about making a difference that today we have far greater benefits in many areas of the business.

After ten wonderful years as a dance and music agent at the Bobby Ball Talent Agency, Susan chose to move into casting, making yet another very natural and seamless transition. She first started casting music videos and live shows then quickly moved into casting reality TV shows. Once again, talk about timing and being in the right place at the right time. As Susan explained: "It was back in early 2000 when the SAG union strike happened and paved the way for reality TV shows. I just happened to be right in the start of it all and here I am

226

still going strong eleven years later." Her first love, dance, still plays a big role in her career; Susan tells me that her biggest satisfaction in what she does is when casting shows that involve dance- and music-related talent. She's cast three seasons of MTV's *Making the Band*, NBC's *Nashville Star* and recently, choreographer to the stars Laurieann Gibson's new dance competition show for BET titled *Born to Dance*. She also cast several recording projects when seeking new talent for their groups and she cast the band (musicians and background vocalists) for Lady Gaga's recent world tour.

A combination of talent, timing, and being *open* (once again always a key point) to new opportunities that come along has proved again to be a winning recipe for success. As for advice she would have most wanted to know as a young dancer starting out Susan says: "I would have liked to have known the importance of supporting your agent! Your agent is there to help you and is on your side. Let them do what they are there for and that's to work for you. Oftentimes, dancers are so desperate to take a job that they will take whatever is out there. Unfortunately, they will only contact their agent when they are having issues like not getting paid or issues with the environment such as dancing on a wet surface or smoky set, etc."

Because Susan chose these options, she did not experience the fear and insecurities that many dancers do. She even says: "As much as I loved to dance, travel, and perform, I prefer what I do now!" Susan believes that the transition from dancer to dance agent and then into casting was about as smooth and natural of a transition as possible; she genuinely loves what she does and loves the life she lives. And to all aspiring dancers out there she offers this advice, "Always have a plan B. You never know when your career will end unexpectedly; it could be an injury or a show shutting down without notice. Save your money so that you can be prepared in the unfortunate case that you have to make an unexpected career change. If and when that time should come, just go for it! I never planned on becoming an agent or a casting director but I have loved every moment of it. If you always dreamed of doing something, you have to try, or you will always be wondering, 'What if?'"

CHRISTOPHER DIETRICH – PARTNER/EXECUTIVE DIRECTOR OF ACTOR'S CONNECTION NYC AND LA

BACK IN LOVE AGAIN. It was the opening night of *La Cage Aux Folles*. Christopher had just moved to New York City with twelve years of a successful career as a dancer and musical theatre performer under his belt. Having danced in numerous productions of *West Side Story*, *A Chorus Line*, *Sweet Charity*, and

The Best Little Whorehouse in Texas, several national and European tours of *42nd Street* and over a year at sea, Christopher had never been out of work. And here he was at last in his first New York production. There he stood on stage and as the overture began he suddenly had an epiphany; he heard his own voice loud and clear. In that very moment he came to the realization that he did not want to be there and he knew in his heart that there were hundreds of dancers who would love to be in his shoes. That was it, he was done.

At roughly twenty-eight years old, Christopher Dietrich—a strong, beautiful dancer with great versatility—decided in that very moment that he was hanging up his dance shoes. As a choreographer I can honestly tell you I felt a huge loss for the dance world and the entertainment industry. Christopher was an exceptional talent and the kind of male dancer that any choreographer would have loved to work with. We first met when he came to work with me at Costa Cruises. Already in rehearsals I was short one boy and a friend of Christopher's who was also working with me at the time recommended I contact him as he was just finishing a European tour of *42nd Street.* With the six-hour time difference and his show having just closed that night, (we laughed when he reminded me that) I managed to reach him by landline in Berlin somewhere around midnight. That was back in 1996, when although we did have cell phones not everyone carried them and you certainly wouldn't be calling Europe on one. Today, of course, he would have received a text message, a Facebook message, or an email and we would have been communicating instantaneously regardless of the time difference or the miles between us. Ah, the wonders of technology!

Christopher's career transition is about falling out of love and back again. It's about discovering that the one and only thing you ever knew and loved your entire young adult life is no longer your passion or your desire. It's about facing the fear of what that means and the guilt of letting down a supportive and loving family who've been there for you every step of the way. Parents who not only encouraged you to follow your dream but who also made your dream of Broadway their own. Christopher told me that this was the most difficult emotional aspect for him in deciding he no longer wanted to perform. Although the decision was his, he felt a tremendous amount of guilt over all the money his parents had spent helping him to further develop his passion and his talent, the years studying for and the degree that he thought he might never now use. All of that hard work only to stand there in the end and face the realization that the passion was gone and that the dream of being on Broadway was no longer his.

Christopher was a graduate of Webster University, where he received a BFA with a double major in musical theatre and dance. He was originally set to go to Southern Methodist University with an opera scholarship, but after a successful audition he was told that he had to choose between the music department and the theatre department as they didn't have a musical theatre department at SMU. And although SMU had one of the most respected theatre departments, Christopher's true passion was in musical theatre. Webster University, on the other hand, had a brilliant musical theatre department and so off he went leaving behind the opera scholarship at SMU. As he had been singing and acting forever, Christopher felt that dance was his weakest talent, so he decided to take a hiatus from the conservatory and joined the dance department, becoming a double major. He joined the Webster Dance Theatre and was with them for 3½ years. In his graduating year, Christopher was scouted by a guest director and offered a contract with PCPA Theaterfest based in Santa Maria, California, to do *Joseph and the Amazing Technicolor Dreamcoat*. The contract was to start in June and he would graduate in May. This was his first professional gig out of school and only the first of many to come.

He worked predominantly in musical theatre and performed with many civic light operas, and after a second production of *Joseph* he was cast for his first national tour of *42nd Street* beginning a stint of thirteen different productions of the show. He was on hold for *Showboat* with Susan Stroman and decided to take the European tour of *42nd Street*. Already successful in his performing career, opening night of *La Cage Aux Folles* would prove to be a turning point, but not the one you might expect. Christopher was about to set out on an entirely new journey; he just didn't know yet how it was going to unfold. Here he was having made the decision to hang up his dance shoes but didn't know what was next; he spent the next four months "putting it all on" as he says, to finish out his contract. "I was still toying with it all because it's all I've known. 'What am I going to do next?'" he thought. "There I was in a contract in New York but it certainly wasn't paying enough to live in Manhattan so I started temping," Christopher worked for a temp agency "temping by day and *La Cageing* by night." One night while performing he sustained an injury that dislocated his leg and as he told me during our conversation, "I was already out of love and now I'd injured myself. It was time."

This was Christopher's first career transition and although he did it merely to survive—not with a specific plan in place—it paid off big-time when he was offered a full-time position that came with a financial security and comfort that Christopher had yet to know as a dancer. The company was Capital Company

America, a commercial real estate company owned by Nomura Securities. He started out as a receptionist and was quickly promoted to executive assistant and overtime to a junior financial assistant, and as he put it "I was making $125,000 a year with no degree in business or finance versus my BFA and $25,000 a year." He was pretty comfortable in his new life and worked with them until October 2000 when the Japanese bond market crashed and the company started closing all their regional offices except New York. He was contracted through March of 2001 and as they were already downsizing, in October it was his turn. He was called into a meeting and they announced to him that they were buying out his contract for $55,000.

As a dancer Christopher says he was pretty amazed; first the difference in the money he was making and now they were just handing him a check for $55,000, and so off he went. He travelled for six months before settling into his next job with yet another commercial real estate company, this time SGI. Not long after a friend of his told him of an opportunity to possibly reenter the entertainment business. "One of the guys that I had worked with at *La Cage* had a friend who was looking for someone to run her company. She wanted someone with West Coast and East Coast experience in the arts who also had a business background." This was both timely and a perfect fit for Christopher as he had been missing the heartstrings of his dance community. "So when the opportunity came along for me to go back into the business and on the other side of the table where I am now able to contribute to the development of other performers, it was really exciting."

Christopher has now been with Actors Connection since November 2001. He is a partner and the executive director of the New York City and Los Angeles offices. This transition could not be a better fit had he planned it, and developed it himself, the business and the role he plays in it suits him to a "T." Today Christopher has the opportunity to share all of his talent and experience from both sides of the business. As he told me in our interview: "I am in a relationship with the majority of the industry on both coasts and I know what they are looking for and for me to be able to pass this on is huge." Christopher spoke about his own time at the musical theatre conservatory and how he wished that he had been better prepared for the reality of "the business side" of the business and how thrilled he is to now be able to pass this information on to actors of all ages "to be able to let them know that it's not solely based on talent," he said. "Here's the thing, if you go to New York or Los Angeles you're in Broadway territory, you're in Hollywood territory, everyone migrates generally to those two markets to become a feature film star or a television star or a Broadway star. How are *you* going to be that one that pops? It's through the networking. It's not only who you know but who knows you. It's great that you have this talent, now, where can we really target that talent. Where do you want to work, are you just going to send out your resume and take the first gig? No, if you know where your specialty lies then you target the market for your specialty. And that's what's really exciting to me, this is the stuff that I was never taught."

Christopher has had the opportunity to develop this company along with his partners over the past ten years and he has been instrumental in its growth. He is very excited about all that they offer. The premise of Actors Connection is just as the title suggests, connecting actors to the industry, networking them with different casting directors, agents, and managers in all aspects of all media: film, television, commercial, theatre, musical theatre, hosting and industrials, voice-over, and print. The idea is to introduce them to the industry in the hopes of furthering their networking and their education. The plethora of paid workshops, special events, and classes offers a wide variety from one night meet-and-greets (where you participate in a half-hour Q & A with an industry guest then get four to eight minutes of one-on-one time with that guest to showcase your talent) to ongoing classes for furthering one's education. These classes can range from mini workshops to individual classes and intensives, and vary from evening sessions to full-day or weeklong sessions covering all aspects of the business. Everything is a la carte and you can craft a package that suits your budget monthly. And most importantly, as the industry is always changing Actors Connection is always offering a wide variety of workshops with a wide variety of industry guests. One of Christopher's many programs that he is very passionate about is a weeklong workshop aimed at preparing actors for the transition between cities. They offer *The LA Connection* for the actor wanting to make the leap from New York to Los Angeles, and *The Broadway Connection and NY Connection* when making the move from Los Angeles to New York City. Even if you are not based in L.A. or N.Y., but are thinking about launching your career in either major market, these are both amazing opportunities to hit the ground running with a huge number of contacts upon your arrival!

As our visit was coming to an end I asked Christopher as someone who deals with the industry of preparing talent on a daily basis if he had any advice that he would like to share with all of you and here's how we left off. "Be proactive. Don't expect anything to come your way, create your path and be smart. Be a smart actor; agents and casting directors want to work with smart actors. The smart actors do their homework, they utilize all that is available to them, and know who is who in the industry, who is casting what, and therefore is prepared to take advantage of the products that are available to them. People move around the industry and it is always changing so a casting director that you had previously met may now be with a new upcoming series and you can take advantage of that, and possibly even attend a seminar that they may be a guest at by simply being on top of your game. As opposed to just throwing stuff up against the wall and seeing what sticks, do your homework and know who you are appropriate for. If you fine-tune and narrow down to twenty or ten people and target those people then your "hit ratio" is going to be much bigger because you are much more appropriate for those specific offices. If you are not ready for Gersh don't waste your money and go see someone from Gersh. Save your money on postage, re-productions of head shots, envelopes, etc. and find a small boutique agency and have them start developing your career. Find out do they freelance or do they sign? Freelancing allows you to work with various agents. In Los Angeles, the equivalent of freelancing is termed hip-pocketing. Signing is when you become exclusive. Do your homework before you sign up or start submitting to different offices on your own. There are often multiple agents within the agency, so research who at the agency represents your age range, type, and specialty. The information is out there and we hope that you take the time to prepare yourself." And last but not least, "As trite as it may seem, follow your heart and don't listen to 'No you can't.' Having been the dancer, the performer, I speak from experience when I say we all deal with rejection and yes, you can work through it, but taking that leap of faith is so hard especially when you've been told no your whole life.

"One of the things that I always tell my actors when I am working with them on the transition from N.Y. to L.A. or London to L.A. or whatever, is if it's not right, New York will always be here, if the transition to L.A. doesn't feel right after six months or after a year or so, you can always get on a plane and be back in N.Y. in four-and-a-half hours." Essentially what Christopher is saying is that nothing is irrevocable and you have to take that initial step and find out for yourself. "Actors are constantly told things like you can't move to L.A. until you have an agent or unless you have this on your resume. 'Well, why can't I?'" Christopher says. And this is where Christopher does some of his most important work today; his mission in that transition is being the support system, the hand-holder, and the voice that says, "It's OK, take the leap of faith. I'm coming with you. Let's do it! I'll be in the back of the room cheering you on." Be sure to visit Christopher at the Actors Connection website at www.actorsconnection.com.

LILIANA MORALES - CLASSICAL SPANISH AND FLAMENCO DANCER, NEW YORK, NEW YORK

ONCE A GYPSY ALWAYS A GYPSY. A great flamenco dancer is the complete embodiment of passion, becoming one with the dance, almost as though some extraordinary spirit takes over. Often referred to as "duende," *tener duende* in Spanish means "to have soul," and is often used to describe a great flamenco performance. And, as I said in the very beginning "Chapter One: Born to Dance"—A dance void of passion is like a life without purpose.

Liliana Morales is both a classical Spanish dancer and a Flamenco dancer, and, at sixty-seven years of age, she is still performing. She is 5'6", thin, beautiful, and in great shape! She lives in Manhattan in the Upper East Side in the same apartment she moved into forty-one years ago. "Flamenco is more than a dance done by gypsies in ruffled skirts; it is a means to propel a dancer into a fruitful career," she says. "Girls, when you are hanging up your pointe shoes you can slip on your castanets," she tells her students. Liliana encourages dancers to study flamenco for longevity in their careers, and she knows a thing or two about a lifelong career as a dancer.

She goes on to explain that classical Spanish dance and flamenco are two very different things. Classical Spanish dance uses castanets and classical orchestrations while flamenco is exclusively done a cappella or with guitar and/or guitar and lyrics. And, although most flamenco dancers are not classical Spanish dancers, Liliana was a natural. She had sixteen years of classical ballet training (as well as tap and jazz), and her first teacher was a classical Spanish dancer. Liliana later joined companies in New York City before going on to Spain, and through these various dance companies she was introduced to flamenco. She says she always knew she would be a dancer, actually she corrected herself and added, "My mother always knew I was going to be a dancer. She took me to dancing school and she knew it!"

From the moment that Liliana decided she wanted to pursue the life of a dancer, she also made the decision that she would do whatever it took. So as far as she is concerned, although she always had a plan as to how she would survive in this business, she never really had a plan B because it was always just part of the deal from the get-go. Liliana had a chemistry scholarship to go to university and her mother wanted her to go to a four-year program; however, as she wanted to dance more than anything, she made an agreement with her mother. She convinced her to let her go to New York City Community College, a two-year program where she would study to become a legal secretary. She thought this was pretty intelligent as she would be able to come and go from such jobs whenever she landed a dancing gig. And although she loved chemistry she knew this would not be the case in the chemistry field. And so, Liliana's story is not about transitioning out of performing, hers is about longevity as a performer and the choices she made in order to survive in the business and live her life as a professional dancer. And since that came with no guarantees, she would work at a regular job to support her passion, whether it was full-time days while dancing at night or full-time in between her dance gigs. She never had any fears or insecurities, she said very simply, "I loved it, I did it, and did what I had to in order to keep on doing it and, I'm still doing it!"

Liliana worked as a legal secretary, she worked as a court interpreter, and she even ran a law firm, then later she worked as a hostess in a restaurant, and most recently as a receptionist at a beauty salon. She did however tell me that she didn't really like any of it, but she pulled from her talents as a performer and turned it on, she says. "We're people-pleasing people, we know how to deal with an audience and so in a sense we're always onstage. Not that we do it consciously, it's just that we're natural at it, we make people feel comfortable, we enjoy them, and we appreciate them because we get so much positive feedback as performers from our audiences, so we naturally like people." Liliana went on to say, "I was only really happy when I was dancing, whether performing or in the studio. I am one of those dancers who love to rehearse, I just love the studio." With all that said, Liliana still thought her plan was a brilliant one for it allowed her to pursue her passion; she would, however, advise young dancers when choosing either a simultaneous secondary career or a plan B to make sure and choose something you love.

As a performer, Liliana's career has spanned thirty-five years, ten of which were spent studying and performing with various dance companies in Spain. She has graced many stages here in the United States and abroad: Lincoln Center, Carnegie Hall, the Royal Albert Hall in London, and the Sydney Opera House to name a few. In 1965 she auditioned for the legendary flamenco dancer Jose Greco. She turned up in her business suit as she was on a lunch break from her job as a legal secretary. Without changing she performed a few dance steps for the renowned dancer, and next thing she knew she was performing as a guest artist in his upcoming show. When she speaks of her mentors, she speaks tenderly of Carmen Mora, expressing that she was one of the most important people in her life. She first met her in Los Angeles and went on to dance with her company in Spain. Carmen's husband Mario Maya was an innovator of male dance and one of Spain's most influential flamenco dancers and choreographers. Another fortuitous occasion was when Liliana met her idol, Maria

Alba. Both Maria and Carmen were very influential in her career and she had the pleasure of dancing with both their companies. She has worked as a solo artist, a freelance choreographer, and a guest teacher at Stephen's College in Columbia, Missouri, danced with various opera companies, been a guest artist with numerous Spanish companies, and danced in film, television, and music videos. This year Liliana will be joining the teaching faculty at Ballet Hispanico in New York City.

When I asked Liliana what she would have liked to have known most when she was first starting out, she said, "The importance of self-confidence and taking risks. I didn't have much confidence in myself and I didn't take risks and that was to the detriment of having other work. Because you don't have to take risks if you're never pushed up against the wall and you always have something to fall back on." Essentially I believe what Liliana is saying was that she had created a safety net for herself and therefore held herself back to a certain degree. Although she has had a full life and exciting career as a dancer, she maybe never pushed past her comfort zone or felt the need to expand it and therefore never knew what other magnificent opportunities might have awaited her. So as I've said repeatedly, never hold back. Just go for it all; what do you really have to lose?

As for work today, Liliana says, "The work itself has not changed that much there just isn't enough of it. Before the jobs in the clubs were six days a week, now they're only on weekends. When I worked at Chateau Madrid (in Manhattan on East 48th street) we did eighteen shows a week, three shows a day, and four on weekends. A lot of the clubs and restaurants where we use to work regularly have all closed down. Today it's more the one-nighters, themed parties, and corporate events."

Liliana is in the studio a couple of times a week to work through choreography and routines, and is still studying to this day. She grew bored of always doing her own choreography and decided to begin studying with a student of hers from Ballet Hispanico, Nelida Tirado, a magnificent dancer and featured dancer in *Riverdance* on Broadway. Liliana added to that, "as a result of the knee injuries and my feet always hurting I can't just go in and do a ballet class or anything like that; I have to do what's within my capacity. I can't just go take a class with a guest teacher today, because the competition is very heavy in class, and I have to really take care of my knees and my feet. I know how to work with the limitations of my body; I know what I can and cannot do. And, that's why I'm still dancing at my age!"

As our conversation was coming to an end, Liliana told me a story about her brother who had volunteered her services to perform at his college for a

STARTING YOUR CAREER AS A DANCER

Columbus Day celebration, and she was very upset with him for offering her services. "The only thing I remembered other than how pissed I was at him was that one of the students said something to me that I'll never forget. He said, 'You must never stop dancing because when you dance you make people happy.'" She thought "how amazing," and went on to tie this into one of her philosophies about talent. She told me, "My mother wanted me to be a dancer because she saw, when I got to dancing, *I got to dancing*. But the talent I didn't ask for, the talent is a gift from God and as a teacher and as a performer I am giving that gift back. Here's what I tell my girls: Some days you dance better than others and this is why you have to rely on technique. Because there are days when you just don't feel in the mood and then there are days when it is so magical. I tell them, 'Girls, you have to know your choreography like you're a machine; when you know your choreography you leave room for the dance angels to take over.' That's when I really feel the talent, and when you have a really great performance you're outside of yourself, for some reason, or something outside of you comes in, and I have no idea what that is, but I call that the dance angels. We didn't ask for the talent, it was a gift, so that's what I tell my girls, and that's what helps them to learn the choreography and be serious."

DEE FUJII – RIGGER AT CIRQUE DU SOLEIL'S LOVE,
LAS VEGAS, NEVADA
KIMBERLEY FUJII – PERFORMER AT LE RÊVE, WYNN HOTEL AND
CASINO, LAS VEGAS, NEVADA

ALL YOU NEED IS LOVE. You may remember that I said earlier, "One thing is certain—dancers know about passion and burning desire, and if they don't, they shouldn't be in the business." That was in "Chapter One: Born to Dance—Turning Dreams into Goals into Commitments." The story I am about to tell you defines passion. Dee Fujii's story is full of passion and love. It's about his passion for dance and for the stage, and it's about love for family and all that we do for love!

I first met Dee when he worked with me at Opryland Productions, that was roughly twelve years ago, and he worked with me on several contracts after that. Dee was the perfect cast member, a great performer and a strong male dancer who also did partnering. He was a hard worker, he would put the time in; if there was something that he didn't get straight away you could always rely on his work ethic and passion for what he was doing to pull it all together. He just had a great, great attitude and was an absolute pleasure to work with. I asked Dee if I could share his story as I think it is a beautiful love story.

236

Dee is thirty-eight years old now and lives in Las Vegas, with his lovely wife Kimberley (whom you will meet shortly) and two gorgeous sons, Kai and Teo. Originally from Oklahoma City, Dee started dancing at twenty. He studied at Northeastern State University in Tahlequah, Oklahoma, for five years. He studied modern, jazz, hip hop/funk, a lot of partnering with lifts, some jive and swing, and as he says, "a lil ballet and a smidgen of tap!" Dee danced professionally for seven consecutive years from the spring of 1996 until April 2003. He performed in film and television, variety musical revues, casino hotels and resorts, cruise ships, theme parks, and large-scale magic shows.

Dee was doing fantastic, enjoying his life and work as a dancer, travelling the world and never out of work. At twenty-nine just about to turn thirty, Dee was working on a cruise ship when he sadly received an emergency phone call, one that we all dread. His father had taken severely ill falling into a coma-like state. Dee immediately disembarked at the next port so that he could get home and be by his parents' side. What he couldn't foresee at the time was this, he said: "When I got off, I did so not realizing I would stop dancing professionally." I asked Dee if he was prepared, did he have a back-up plan for this day when he might no longer be able to, or choose to, not dance professionally anymore. "No. I had no official back-up plan. We, me and other dancers, had discussed our post-dance plans and one of mine had been to work backstage." Today, Dee works as a rigger for the Beatle's show *LOVE* produced by Cirque du Soleil at the Mirage Hotel in Las Vegas, Nevada.

When I asked Dee about his transition he told me to get comfy. "I'm going to babble," he said. "My transition was emotionally difficult. I had gone back to Oklahoma to help with Dad. My wife, who was my girlfriend at the time, came out for a week and then returned to finish her contract out on the ship. From there, we went back to Las Vegas where we lived with a fellow dancer who we had worked with. As I said, I left the ship never thinking that I would not dance professionally again. Kim and I went to class and began the whole audition process that we are all so familiar with. I got a job to keep money coming in as Kim (being from England) did not have a green card or work visa at the time." Dee's initial transition off the stage was not planned as he mentioned above but he did have an idea as to where he ultimately saw himself working. If not on stage then it would be backstage, still encircled by all that he loved. In the short-term Dee took on a few different jobs, he bartended, worked as a receiving manager for Barnes and Noble, worked as a barback, and finally worked as a stage hand at a hotel in downtown Las Vegas. Dee told me that it was during this period of time that he made two very big decisions. "First I decided I was going to ask Kim to marry me, and two, I was going to give up the idea of dancing professionally. There were a few factors in deciding this," he said. "I was not a spring chicken anymore. I was a male in a town where women had an easier time getting dance jobs, and the traditional shows that once used dancers were falling to the wayside as Cirque du Soleil took over. In making these decisions I wanted us to not have to struggle, so I thought I could get a steady job and my wife could continue to perform."

Aside from the emotional loss of no longer being on stage Dee felt the transition itself was not difficult. He had a friend who was able to help him get his first backstage job as a stage-hand and although he says it wasn't glamorous, it paid better than anything he had done to date. He went on to say: "A guy I worked with was talking about rigging. It sounded interesting and paid well so I looked into taking a class. There were, and still to this day are, no official rigging classes but there were two gentlemen—who are looked at as some of the best in the entertainment-rigging-field—who did seminars. No certifications but you can say you took their course. The hotel wouldn't pay for me to go as I was on-call at the time, so I shelled out the $900 to take the course. I had finally found a job in the entertainment industry that I really liked!"

The same gentleman who first introduced Dee to the idea of rigging was also the one who recommended him when his own boss was making a move over to Cirque to open the Beatles' *LOVE* show. This friend's recommendation coupled with the fact that Dee had paid to take the rigging seminar on his own aided him in getting hired by Cirque du Soleil.

When I first asked Dee if there had been any fears, insecurities, or emotional difficulties as a result of him leaving performance and the stage, he said, "Yes." And he really emphasized it. "Not so much insecurities, nor fears," he said. "I knew I could get a job or two to support Kim and I. It was more emotional, like losing part of yourself. There was a point where I was pretty depressed about it. While I was still performing, I had written a poem about the fear of not performing anymore and I kept thinking about that. I kept thinking am I really done? I kept trying to attend class now and then to lessen the blow, but between getting married, getting a new house, working, dealing with family back home, dance was put on the back burner. Very slowly the pain of accepting that I was not going to perform anymore turned to a dull ache and was replaced by the joy I found in being a husband and now a father."

Kimberley, Dee's wife, is a wonderfully talented dancer, gymnast, and aerialist who is currently working in *Le Rêve* at Wynn Hotel and Casino in Las Vegas. She has been working in the show for five years now as a generalist—generalists do a bit of everything in the show, dancing, swimming, and aerial work. By the way did I mention she did all that through two pregnancies as well!

I have had the pleasure of having both Dee and Kimberley as cast members on more than one contract. And recently while on a trip out to Las Vegas with a group of women whom I had danced with in my first professional long-running contract, we went to see Kimberley perform at *Le Rêve*. She was fantastic as I already knew she would be and the show was tremendous—all the girls had such a fabulous night. We got to visit backstage after the show and as we were leaving Kim was getting out the ice packs. She was nursing a back injury. Of course you would never have known it from the spectacular performance we had all just witnessed. Watching her fly what seemed like hundreds of feet above our heads, spinning and dropping and all the while looking so graceful with such an ease about her, it would have been impossible to fathom that she might be in even the slightest bit of discomfort.

The back injury she suffered was unfortunately as a result of a solo position that she used to cover, the "red girl" solo, for any of you who may have seen the show. The injury was that of bulging discs in her thoracic spine and really put her back and neck muscles into complete spasm. Kimberley has not gone back into that role since having the kids, and she tells me that if she ever does go back into it she would have to alter the end choreography in order to keep her from any possibility of re-injury. Here's what Kim shared with me: "*Le Rêve* is a huge strain on my body at ten shows a week. After the injury I took about six weeks off and did lots of physical rehab to recover. Luckily we have a health services department to help us recover from injuries and retrain and condition our bodies to prevent more injuries. I work out with them pretty much every day to try to preserve my body. I get massages and do Pilates as much as possible and also use a lot of ice!" I hope you dancers are taking notes. "Aerial work puts an added strain on your body—particularly your shoulders and neck and lower back if you do a lot of harness stuff. Ice, ice, ice—I hate it—it sucks, but if you want your body to work for you, you have to take care of it!"

Of course at twenty-nine, Kimberley still has a few good years in her as a performer; however, the wear-and-tear that her still-young body endures on an ongoing basis is quite brutal. It was bad enough that being a gymnast there was already a certain amount of concern for longevity, but now adding to that the concerns of additional risk, Kimberley herself is already thinking ahead to what might be next for her. She says she has signed her contract through to September 2012 and she will see what happens then. "I would love to get into the artistic side of things—choreographing, producing, or just being on the artistic coaching side of a show, but who knows what the future holds."

And although there isn't a specific plan in place, both Dee and Kim love the idea of working together again and possibly creating something in their future that will give them that opportunity. They tell me they've discussed a number of things that they might be able to do together in the entertainment industry, including opening a studio or putting up a dance show. They hope that maybe in the future the right opportunity will arise for them.

In the meantime they are enjoying their lives and simultaneous careers in the entertainment industry in a fabulous city for just that! Juggling their careers while raising their family is just part of a performer's life and they do it beautifully! And to quote Dee one last time, I think this says it all: "My yearning to dance on stage will never go away, and maybe when the kids are old enough I'll find a way back onstage, whether it be community theatre or simply getting back in class again. But for now, I am happy and content to be a family man!"

PAM KILLINGER – FORMER CHOREOGRAPHY SPECIALIST AT DISNEY WORLD, ORLANDO, FLORIDA

A BITTERSWEET MAGICAL JOURNEY. Pam Killinger is a name that has been indistinguishable with dance at Disney World. Pam's story is all about timing. I had the pleasure of meeting with Pam on a couple of different occasions at Disney when she held the position of choreography specialist. She was so lovely, so upbeat and positive, she always made you feel so welcome and right at home. I always thought her story was great and when I decided that I wanted to write about these "real-life stories" for this chapter on career transitions I immediately thought of hers.

Pam's first dance lesson was at the age of four and as she says she hasn't stopped yet. "I'm still a student. If you love dance, you never stop learning about it. I studied Cecchetti ballet, jazz, tap—even toe tap (what a hoot!), acrobatics, and snippets of Hawaiian and flamenco while growing up in Pocatello, Idaho." After high school graduation Pam moved to San Francisco and continued studying dance. Although not her first paying job, she went to work as a dancer at Bimbo's 365 Club in San Francisco; this is where celebrities went to polish their acts before going to Vegas. After touring the United States and Canada for three years with a mini-Vegas revue, *Pardon My Can-Can*, Pam was tired of living out of a suitcase and decided to drop out in Florida just as Disney was opening in Orlando. And this is where it all began, her magical journey through the wonderful world of Disney. She auditioned for and was hired as one of the four full-time dancers at the Diamond Horseshoe Revue in Magic Kingdom. She earned her undergraduate degree from the University of Central Florida while still performing at Disney. She then stopped performing to travel and study in Italy for six months before returning to Florida, this time to pursue her masters of fine arts degree in dance from Florida State University in Tallahassee. And that was her first transition off the stage.

When I asked Pam about her tremendous career working at Disney World and how she evolved with and through the company, here's how she described it: "Timing is everything! When I returned from FSU to Orlando, Disney was preparing for the opening of Epcot. I was brought on board as a contract choreographer to work with George Koller on the grand openings for each of the pavilions. George and I had a blast creating the numbers for the all World Showcase pavilions. Each one was more grand and elaborate than the next with the pavilion being the set piece. For example, the opening of the French pavilion incorporated three grand pianos going up on lifts, 100 dancing waiters coming from the shops with champagne bottles, and of course can-can dancers bursting forth for the finale. Dancers were staged in the windows of all the buildings and the entire street was filled with themed vignettes."

What a great period in time and what timing this was; not only did Pam just happen to be in Orlando when Disney World was first opening its doors, but then to also return, after graduating from FSU, to the opening of Epcot. Although Pam was no longer performing she had transitioned into a dream gig. Disney World is such a huge part of our popular culture that we sometimes forget that it wasn't always the world-famous attraction that the Disney parks are today. Magic Kingdom had opened in 1971 and Epcot opened in 1982; Disney was still in its infancy stages and Pam was a part of history in the making. To be actively involved in the grandeur and the opening of Epcot, to get in on the ground floor and be a part of the growth and spectacle that we know today was a magnificent opportunity on so many levels. Pam, through her work, also had the wonderful experience of working with some fabulous talent whom she proudly speaks of: "The group, named the World Dancers, lasted for a decade. There were so many wonderful dancers who came through this group and with whom I was privileged to work. Just this year, (2011) two of them were associate choreographers to Tony-nominated Broadway shows, Joey Pizzi (*Catch Me If You Can*) and Vince Pesce (*Anything Goes* with Kathleen Marshall). And, Robby Mackey directed the big fifth anniversary celebration at Hong Kong Disney. We fed a lot of dancers to Broadway and beyond from that group and watching them perform on Broadway has been enormously gratifying."

Pam went on to share with me how exciting it was to be involved with Walt Disney World in the '80s and early '90s. "The entertainment division was flourishing and driving many of the events, shows, and parades. We had on property 132 Equity dancers—I was told more than were performing on Broadway at one point. We produced nationally televised Fourth of July spectacles on the Magic Kingdom Castle stage for several years featuring Carol Channing, Tommy Tune, and Rita Moreno. At first I was intimidated to stage 'name' stars, but I quickly came to treasure the experience as I found them to be not only consummate professionals, but genuinely nice people." Her time and work at Disney went on to include an enviable list of celebrities. She told me a story about Ben Vereen that depicts the consummate professional he is. "What an example he set for our dancers. We were filming his finale gospel number for the show in front of the Riverboat at the Magic Kingdom. It was a 4 AM call for a 5 AM shoot and it was cold and damp. Everyone was complaining about the weather and the chill until they turned around and saw Ben doing a Martha Graham warm-up on the asphalt road. Nothing needed to be said."

Pam's second career transition within Disney was when she was given her first directing opportunity for the *Holiday Splendor* show. And although this eventually transitioned her away from dance she found it to be extremely gratifying. "I was surprised by the satisfaction that came from guiding the choreography instead of being responsible for every count. I directed *Mickey's Starland*, a cute character show for four to five years as well as all the dance numbers and nightly New Year's Eve shows at the Pleasure Island nighttime entertainment area.

"One of my most enjoyable assignments was to direct the *Here Come the Muppets* show at the MGM Studios. Ironically, this happy fantasy was interrupted by Jim Henson's untimely death. The cast and crew were devastated." Up to this time Pam was still working on contract, she was not yet an official cast member (Disney's term for employee). It was at this point that she was officially brought on board as an employee and appointed the position of choreography specialist for the creative entertainment division. Yet another transition, Pam explained that her assignment was to create and groom a pool of local choreographers. She said, "I didn't think about it when I accepted, but that pretty much ended my choreography and dancing days. At first there were some pangs of 'I wish I were working on that show,' but the regrets lessened as I grew to appreciate the administrative and mentoring tasks and got to meet some talented choreographers."

As many of us in the entertainment field have witnessed, and you most likely will at some point or another in your own career, corporate downsizing and change is often inevitable. Unfortunately, that doesn't usually make it more palatable, and it can be very difficult and painful. Pam shares with us how the Michael Eisner years brought major changes throughout Disney, and how it of course affected her directly. Michael Eisner was the chairman (1984 to 2004) and chief executive officer (1984 to 2005) of The Walt Disney Company. When you are creative and so passionate about what you do, it is difficult to witness what is or can oftentimes lead to the destruction of creativity. For example, she told me: "Rather than the entertainment division, it was the marketing division which now began to make the ultimate decisions on shows. Artistically, this proved very frustrating. The bottom line became most important, and non income-generating shows like the Easter Parade and Fourth of July spectaculars went away. Sadly, musicians lost their jobs and most shows were now supported by music taped in London or other locations that did not have the restrictions of the American Federation of Music. The World Dancers were disbanded because of the costs of costumes and rehearsals and replaced with "atmospheric" entertainment. A single actor could now entertain people on the streets for a fraction of the costs of a musical stage show."

The next blow that was about to go down was not one that Pam could have ever been prepared for. In 1997 Walt Disney World went through yet another corporate reorganization and in the process Pam's position was eliminated. Shocked and at a loss for what to do, Pam was given six months to find another job within the company. She said, "Nothing appealed to me, because the positions had nothing to do with dance. Since my joy had always been in the active, artistic side of the company, I wasn't interested in producing shows or moving to the business area of entertainment. Months passed. Shortly before what was scheduled to be my final day with the company, my boss, Don Staples, was reassigned to be the director of entertainment for the Magic Kingdom, and he asked me to follow."

Pam was moving back to the Magic Kingdom where her journey had begun back in 1971, but this time it wouldn't be the glamour and the magic that she had once known. As she put it, she wouldn't be picking up her wig and heading over to the Diamond Horseshoe to dance five shows; no, instead she would be heading to an office where she would begin her new work as a manager of atmosphere entertainment. She told me, "I now supported the talent, which frequently involved such mundane tasks as arranging keys for lockers and scheduling custodial services. At first, the situation was very depressing for me, because I felt so far removed from the process of putting on a show. I

243

considered quitting and returning to teaching dance or doing research in dance history, but I stuck it out long enough to have an attitude adjustment.

"As I adjusted, I came to better understand what I had heard my whole dance life—the show-behind-the-show is as important as the show itself. As I focused on their needs my respect for those performers helped lighten the blow of losing the job I loved. It also helped that I started managing the staging specialists in addition to the talent. The staging specialists are the dedicated dancers who rehearse new people into their roles, give show notes, and keep the shows and parades accurate, looking as good nine months after the opening as on day one.

"Looking back, I guess you can say that I transitioned from doing the show myself to gaining great satisfaction in knowing I was helping others put on the show. It was hard. However, it did help that I had always stayed active in the dance community outside Disney. I would spend part of my vacations and days off adjudicating dance competitions and teaching master classes. One lesson that I brought away from this challenging transition is this: It is important to stay connected with the larger dance community, to stay in touch with current trends, and to stay interested in all aspects of the field."

Pam retired from Walt Disney World in November of 2008 after more than a thirty-year run. Today she continues to live in Orlando and spends her summers at an Idaho mountain cabin. As she shared with us there were certain emotional difficulties—specifically towards the end. And when I asked Pam what traits as a dancer she possessed that most helped her along her career path, here's what she had to say: "Dancers learn at an early age how to focus and concentrate. We learn determination and perseverance. We learn how to observe and we learn the importance of paying attention to detail. We learn about working with others, and the importance of not having our own way. (The dancer who insists on showing off the height of her extension at another's expense will never be a Rockette!) Through auditions we learn to be resilient to rejection. We develop awareness to the subtleties and nuances of gesture which are invaluable to acting and understanding others."

Pam's journey depicts much of what a life and career in the industry can offer. Her story is about right timing, living your true passion, being open to the experience, being flexible enough to go with the flow even when it's not how you like to roll, and it's about acceptance and moving on. Lastly when I asked Pam what advice she might offer to aspiring or working dancers in reference to career transitions, here's what she had to say: "I think having a broad liberal arts background is important to anyone pursuing work and life in an artistic field. It is especially critical for anyone in the dance field given the physical limitations that dancers inevitably face. You can still paint when you're in your nineties, but you can't execute gorgeous grand jetés! My studies in the humanities opened up travel opportunities in Italy where I was able to see and experience dance in another culture. Taking ballet classes in a frescoed Renaissance palazzo in Florence gave me a greater sense of the timelessness of the art. The MFA dance program at Florida State University exposed me to all the modern dance techniques, to dance history and criticism, and thus expanded my horizons to see dance beyond the immediacy of doing steps. Having this broad educational experience aroused my curiosity and interest in a number of areas beyond performing and that broader experience kept dance in perspective and made transitioning easier."

RACHEL SPECK – FORMER MIAMI CITY BALLET APPRENTICE, MIAMI BEACH, FLORIDA

EVERYTHING WAS BEAUTIFUL AT THE BALLET. Rachel Speck, formerly a ballerina with the Miami City Ballet, was a child prodigy with all the promise of a tremendous career as a professional ballerina. She began studying dance at the age of three as so many little girls do and at the age of five she told her mother there would be no need to save for college for she wouldn't be going, she already had her sights set—she was going to be a professional ballerina. A combination of her natural talent, advanced level, and the exceptional training that she obtained from the Central Pennsylvania Youth Ballet made her the perfect candidate for a ballet company's summer school intensive. At thirteen, eager to set out on her career path, she auditioned for the Miami City Ballet Summer School program and was offered a full scholarship. Attending students are normally placed in levels by their age, and at thirteen, Rachel should have been placed in level one, but rather was placed in level eight, the highest level obtainable. Not only did she have the usual demands of a summer intensive but now she was working alongside the older and most advanced students in the program. To say that Rachel held her own would be too little; in fact she not only held her own she gave them all a good run for their money. At thirteen in her first summer intensive she was cast in the female lead role in Balanchine's *Diamonds.* The following two years she was invited back again on full scholarships. At fifteen and in her third summer program Rachel was invited to become a member of the Miami City Ballet Company as apprentice.

Tragically this little girl's dream would be put to the test and unfortunately eventually come to an end. At fourteen Rachel was in a debilitating car accident that nearly ended her career before it even got started. She suffered damage to her entire spine including several herniated discs and complete loss of range of motion. She was unable to dance for almost a full year and underwent extreme therapy to fully regain her strength and range of motion. Rachel experimented with a variety of healing alternatives and found her greatest success with integrative manual therapy (IMT). IMT is a new approach to health care and was developed to address the needs of complex patients. It identifies and addresses the underlying causes of dysfunction using a comprehensive and holistic approach. Although predominantly hands-on, IMT also uses a wide range of treatment technologies including nutritional programs and psychotherapeutic approaches. Fully aware of the accident and her newfound challenges, the Miami City Ballet still chose to not only have her back on scholarship for the third summer in a row but to then offer her this contract with the company. They obviously had a lot of confidence in her, and this was some testament by them of her character and exceptional abilities.

A beautiful young lady of fifteen years old living on her own in South Beach, Florida, this certainly could have been a recipe for disaster, but this was no usual fifteen-year-old. Rachel was both very mature and focused; she was determined and had her goals in sight. Rachel's parents and the Miami City Ballet agreed that she could stay on providing she would have a host family, and so arrangements were made and Rachel went ahead and relocated. Unfortunately, the distance between her host family and the MCB studios was too great for her to travel daily. No sooner had she arrived in Miami Beach she was pounding the pavement looking for a new accommodation, and in the end she settled into an apartment right smack in the heart of SoBe on Lincoln Road. At fifteen she was already well on her way to fulfilling her greatest dream; in fact she was already living her dream. However, her life was somewhat of a dichotomy; there she was on one hand living her dream and on the other it was a bit like skating on thin ice or balancing on a high wire—at any moment the dream could be shattered. The debilitating injuries she had suffered and the constant reminder of the long slow road back to recovery, (although she was almost fully recovered when she joined the company) along with the discomfort she still endured on a daily basis continuously haunted her and threatened whether or not the dream would last. Rachel's biggest fear and worst nightmare was the loss of her technique and all that she had worked so hard for. Not being able to dance for almost a full year after the accident had made it difficult to get back to where she had previously been. "My biggest frustration came from having always been so ahead of the game and now finding I was on even level with everyone else." Knowing the level she had previously attained and all that she had been capable of, having been this child prodigy at thirteen, and now the realization and the fear that she may never be there again or that she may never surpass her own high expectations was a devastating truth and one that began her gradual downward spiral.

Unfortunately this accident impacted her far beyond the physical aspect. Although it didn't stop her from eventually dancing again, it was the beginning of her ballet career's demise and an emotionally tumultuous journey into her forced career transition. Her dream of being a prima ballerina was sadly halted, throwing her off course and forcing her to make decisions about career transitions at far too young of an age. Rachel felt that this was all she knew and although it was painfully and emotionally difficult by now to remain at it, it appeared far more difficult to figure out what else to do. It seemed like all doors were closing for her, almost as though she was being guided or re-directed away from the ballet. At the time the Miami City Ballet was suffering some financial problems and she considered going elsewhere, she said: "I didn't have a plan B and so I felt like I had to keep doing it because I didn't know what else to do." She auditioned for and was offered contracts with several other companies. Unfortunately the reality was that with a new company she would have to start all over again as an apprentice and since ballet companies don't pay very well and she had no additional financial assistance from her family, she didn't see it possible to support herself and start over in a new city. Rachel said, "It was like God was really showing me, 'You know what, this is over,' because he really closed every door. I almost didn't have any other option because anywhere I would have moved for ballet I couldn't have supported myself. It just wasn't going to work and so I had to accept that it was time to figure something else out and move on."

At eighteen Rachel left the Miami City Ballet and now had to consider what would be her next move. She had to ask herself why she was still living in South Beach when her entire family was in Pennsylvania. She felt as though maybe she should move back home, but she worried what she would do once she got there, work at Wal-Mart? She felt a longing to remain here in Miami Beach; she felt like it was now her new home. She was so emotionally beat up by it all, the rise, the fall, the constant uncertainty that was now facing her on a daily basis: what to do next, what else did she know, what could ever compare to the dream that she had been living? She had realized her dream of becoming a professional ballerina and was very proud of it. She loved the reaction she would get when people asked her what she did for a living and she told them "I'm a professional ballet dancer with the Miami City Ballet." To have had all that, she now questioned, what next?

Needing a break from it all Rachel headed home to regroup; she spent three weeks deliberating over what was to come of her newfound fate. During the time that she had lived in South Beach she had had many offers to do various modeling jobs and so she decided she would come back and give this a try. Once back in South Beach she signed on with a few agencies and got to work putting together her portfolio and going out on calls. She landed a few jobs working in television and print, and although she was having fun she knew she needed to pay the rent and therefore still needed a real plan B. Rachel tried her hand at a few things—she did some corporate dance jobs, was asked to choreograph some bits and pieces here and there, and then she stumbled across a need that she saw as a great opportunity. She began helping a lawyer, a friend of hers, who was in need of a housekeeper. She offered to take on the job and in addition to housekeeping she started running errands, doing the groceries, and, as she enjoyed cooking, she started preparing meals as well. Before she knew it she was acting as somewhat of a personal assistant to him and that's how she first began to reinvent herself.

From prima ballerina to housekeeper extraordinaire . . . not quite as glamorous you might think, but Rachel had a much bigger picture in mind. This discovery is what gave her the idea that she might like to start her own business. She quickly made up some business cards and fliers and in no time at all she had several doctors, lawyers, and even a pro ballplayer as clients. She imagined herself growing this business into a full in-home service company. It wasn't long after that Rachel's business card ended up in the hands of Brooke Hogan when she was looking for someone for her television show. Rachel began working for Brooke as her personal assistant and for two years she remained as her right-hand woman, both on the set and off the set. She wasn't missing dance so much at this point as she was having a blast working on the show, assisting in all areas, and travelling with Brooke. This had become her new life, an exciting one at that and it had taken over where ballet had left off. It wasn't until she started working out with Brooke and her personal trainer and sometimes her father Hulk Hogan that she truly found a passion to match the passion she'd had for ballet. As a ballerina she had never picked up a weight and knew absolutely nothing about fitness, other than dance. Now she was working out every day and she was quickly becoming obsessed with every aspect of working out. It didn't take Rachel long to realize that she had found her new passion and her new destiny.

Today at all of twenty-one Rachel has a whole new career that took her approximately three years to fully transition into. At present she is working as both a personal fitness trainer and group fitness instructor. Many of her personal fitness clients are people she met along her journey into her transition and the studio she teaches at today, Iron Flower Fitness in Miami Beach, was introduced to her by a personal fitness client. While studying to become a personal trainer she worked at a well known South Beach restaurant as a hostess. At this point Brooke had moved to Los Angeles and although she offered Rachel a job to continue working for her, Rachel did not want to make the move. And so she took on the job of hostess and began studying and planning for her newfound passion and career in fitness. Rachel despised working as a hostess, she really felt let down. She had gone from ballerina to model to personal assistant, all of them she thought to be "pretty cool jobs." She told me she went home depressed many nights and wondered why she was still there one year later, but even though she found this to be somewhat demeaning and the most difficult part of her transition, today she looks back on it as an excellent learning and growing opportunity. She said it helped her to come out of her shell and taught her about people skills, organizational skills, and how to handle crowds. And many of the regular customers she met during her time working as hostess are now personal clients.

Aside from her work as a personal trainer, Rachel teaches group fitness, Mat Pilates and is planning to become certified to teach Pilates Reformer as well. She also teaches a fantastic Ballet-Barre-Burn class which she has put her own special twist on. Still a young entrepreneur at heart, Rachel is now in the process of developing a new start-up company called Fitness Repetition where she is planning to incorporate her years of dance training and expertise along with her newfound passion for fitness and nutrition. Rachel's story has a happy ending and a lot of promise for a successful future and yet it wasn't without its trials and tribulations and hardships along the way. I hope that her story will serve as preempt for you in two ways; first to help you in your own future and career planning by understanding the need to plan ahead and be honest about what a career in dance can hold or not. And secondly, to always remain optimistic and be open and flexible knowing, that as difficult as things may seem and although we may not always be solely or one hundred percent in charge we truly can *take charge* of our own destinies.

JOE PERROTTA – BROADWAY PRESS AGENT AT BONEAU/BRYAN-BROWN, NEW YORK, NEW YORK

ON BROADWAY. Smack in the heart of it all in the city that never sleeps is where you can find Joe Perrotta on any given day of the week; that's if you're lucky enough to catch him at all! You might find him at the office on Broadway where he works for Boneau/Bryan-Brown Public Relations, writing press releases or planning the publicity campaign strategy for the next big Broadway hit. Boneau/Bryan-Brown is the leader and top Broadway press office whose client list is enviable, and includes such hits as *Mamma Mia!*, *The Book of*

Mormon, Anything Goes, Jersey Boys, Priscilla Queen of the Desert and *Stomp,* to name a few. Their collective list of Broadway and off-Broadway productions have won 144 Tony Awards, seven Pulitzer Prizes, 133 Drama Desk Awards, and ninety-seven Outer Critics Circle Awards.

Joe, originally from Rochester, New York, is forty-one years old and has been working as a press agent on Broadway for the past eleven years. I asked Joe what a typical day in his work life was like, to which he replied: "I spend my days working with both actors and most importantly the producers and the creative team (directors, choreographers, costume designers, set designers, etc.) to create buzz and fuel word of mouth about a show by generating print and online features, television and radio appearances, and driving social networking (Facebook, Twitter, and blogging)." He went on to describe the responsibility that falls on the shoulders of the public relations firm handling any given show. "A press agent pinpoints the strengths of a production or particular actor or designer and inspires the press to write about them or invite them into the television or radio studio. Press and publicity supports and augments the unique advertising and marketing campaign for a show that ideally will culminate in people buying tickets for that show, after they are made aware repeatedly and via different mediums, from reading a newspaper article, to hearing a radio spot to seeing a print ad in the newspaper or a banner ad on a website."

Joe and I are old friends. We go back some years and I first met him, you probably guessed, in the business when he was a dancer. Joe previously worked as a dancer and musical theatre performer. His exposure to dance was, as it is for many male dancers, a little bit later in life. Unlike most girls who start at three to five years of age, the men often tend to be exposed around their high school or college years. He was first introduced around the age of sixteen through a high school musical production of *Music Man* and then a production of *The Wiz* at a youth repertory theatre company in Rochester called RAPA. While he didn't study in a traditional dance school as a kid, his first introduction to musical theatre created quite an impact and an additional interest in studying dance. He then went on to take formal dance classes as a freshman at Niagara University in 1988 where he earned his bachelor of fine arts in theatre studies— which was also considered an English degree. "In addition to a full schedule of academic credits, theatre majors were required to take acting, voice, dance (jazz, ballet, and tap), stage combat, mime, and voice and speech classes—all that fell under the umbrella of a performance credit! And this was in addition to performing in shows and doing stage work, etc." As for dance, he loved jazz but he went on to excel at tap; when he speaks of himself as a dancer he says, "I was never strong in ballet and my technique was never my strongest suit, but I was more of an overall performer who could really sell a number." And that he certainly can do; Joe is a brilliant performer! We had the fun and true pleasure of getting to know each other over a few contracts when he worked with me as a dancer on *Costa* and featured performer in *An Evening at La Cage*, and have been great friends ever since.

College can often be a wonderful opportunity for dancers to find their place, and Joe certainly knew his was to perform. After college he went on to do several contracts for theme parks, cruise lines, and in Vegas-style revues. It was at the end of a run of *An Evening at La Cage* in Miami Beach and St. Maarten when he moved to New York and resumed classes. He quickly landed a job in the ensemble of *42nd Street* touring Germany—Munich, Mannheim, and Berlin. And, this is where he earned his first show jacket, he told me, "in 1995 doing the international tour of *42nd Street*." On his final contract doing a Mediterranean cruise Joe sustained an injury that unfortunately cut his contract short. When I asked him what it was in the end that caused him to stop dancing, he said: "The combination of two factors really, an injury on my last cruise ship contract on the Costa Riviera and a desire to settle down into a more routine and stable life following so many years of traveling in my early 20s. Although the travel was invaluable it left me wanting something more secure, something that I could build on and would allow me to stay in one place."

He went on to say: "I had started to think about this during my last cruise ship contract as I was approaching my late 20s and I was being realistic about what my prospects were in the entertainment industry. I knew I was a good performer, but not a leading man type who could tackle a life on the stage, and not a strong enough dancer who would pursue a career in a dance company. I was always able to do a little bit of everything, while not being the strong triple threat I knew you had to be to make a realistic go of it. I basically took an inventory of my talent and measured that against the amount of drive and ambition I also knew was mandatory and faced the reality that I wasn't hungry enough to chase the goal of performing. The old cliché of 'You have to want it more than anything else' is really true. I enjoyed performing and it took me around the world in a way I never would've been able to, but I was now ready to chase the next goal. I didn't exactly know what that was yet, so I was a professional waiter for the next couple of years while awaiting an epiphany."

I asked Joe to tell me about his career transition because it always seemed to me that one day he told me he wanted to pursue a career as a publicist, and

251

before I knew it, there he was doing it and not just anywhere, there he was on Broadway! Of course my memory left out the "getting there" details and so I asked him to remind me of how it all came about. He said, "I was a waiter (and exceptional at it, I will humbly say, due to the particular brand of energy I had in my late 20s, a bit of neuroticism and a lot of attention to detail!) And, people would always say to me, 'So what is it you're pursuing or you really want to do?' I honestly wouldn't know, until two different people told me I'd be a great theatre press agent as the necessary qualities for the job were a combination of everything I'd done from sales to performing on the stage. And it would also keep me in the entertainment business doing something I had a passion for. Just on a different side of the stage. While it wasn't something I immediately knew I wanted to do, a variety of these different influences and sequence of events led me to pursuing this career and once I knew that's what I wanted, I attacked it with a vengeance as I now had a goal." He also went on to tell me about how he greatly admired Liza Minnelli, and he knew that she was returning to Broadway with a new show. This gave him the fuel to go for it and as he said, "Through a series of connections I pursued and created, her personal assistant put me in touch with the press agent for the show. I met with him and completed a very brief internship before I was hired as an employee. I was twenty-nine and it was clear that this was a job I was serious about, I wasn't a young student doing an internship to explore a potential career path. I knew exactly what I wanted."

And that's how it all started. Today Joe enjoys an exciting career as a press agent surrounded by creative people in an area of the business that many aspire to yet only few ever make it in. He has the wonderful experience of working closely with some of the world's finest talent. I asked Joe to tell us a little about some of his favorite moments and shows that he has had the thrill of being in-volved with. "The revival of *Ragtime* was incredible," he said. "It was a beautiful, sweeping production that was completely re-imagined from the original by di-rector Marcia Milgrom Dodge, and it didn't have as long a life as it should have. The score is one of my favorites. And, I got to work with Terrence McNally (playwright), Stephen Flaherty (music composer) and Lynn Ahrens (lyricist), it was just incredible! The highlight for me was seeing my idea realized and bringing the creative team to Ellis Island, which was so relevant because the musical is an epic account of the immigrant experience and we did a big photo shoot for a *New York Times* feature, and that was incredible.

"The first show I ever worked on as a publicist was the enormous hit *The Producers* with Nathan Lane and Matthew Broderick and it was a huge, huge hit. I was one of the assistants on that show and that was really exciting. Another highlight was working on an original musical called the *The Drowsy Chaperone*, which won a Tony Award for its star Beth Leavel, who became a good friend of mine, and that was just a completely original musical and a great experience. I loved it! Also, the Broadway debut of the stage production of *Irving Berlin's White Christmas* because it was a huge tap musical and choreographed by Randy Skinner, a legendary tapper who was in the original Broadway company of my favorite musical, *42nd Street*. He staged these enormous MGM tap numbers that just kept building and building and would never end—you don't see staging like that on Broadway anymore. I also felt a real camaraderie with the company, almost like I was still a "gypsy" but just on the other side of the stage."

As you can tell this is obviously one of the things Joe loves most about his job, and when I asked him that question, he added: "Being a part of the creative process and being in the theatre business without actually having to be on stage and the fact that my job is always changing with each respective show—all the different types of people you meet and the collaborations you're a part of. That's probably the biggest draw. And having been a dancer and a performer I was able to use my skills and I always feel like I'm still on stage. I'm always performing and pitching and interacting with the cast so it's really not that different to being a performer except that I don't perform on the stage."

Knowing Joe as I do, I see him as someone who is extremely well focused, very intelligent, and far too sensible to ever play the starving artist role or to have sat around dwelling on the fact that he was no longer performing. Almost as though it was a business transaction or a simple decision that had to be made, he set aside the right brain and the left brain kicked in. When I asked him if this was accurate he said: "I don't really miss performing per se, but what's interesting is to know that you have the talent in you and you can tap and you can dance but you just don't use it, that's very interesting. But I don't regret it or miss it as much, like I said, because I'm still in the entertainment business. Maybe sometimes when I see a show like *Irving Berlin's White Christmas* or *42nd Street* or a big tap number it makes me want to do that again, but there's no regret and it doesn't make me miss it. I feel very fulfilled being around it." In that same vein we talked about how dancers can do themselves a huge service by taking advantage of their surroundings. As someone who is exposed to all facets of the business and seeing performers come and go and transform themselves as they age and take on new roles Joe suggests, "While you're in, while you're onstage, and while you're a performer, take advantage of learning and being curious about all the other roles and the entertainment industry around you. For example, for a time I thought that I might want to be a company manager when I was on the *42nd Street* tour. I thought, 'Oh, that's interesting what they do and all the things that they coordinate' or, if maybe somebody is interested in being a stage manager or on the technical staff. I would just use that insider backstage access that the performer has when they're in a show or on a tour or on a ship, to just ask questions and get to know exactly what those other careers are all about, because that way when they have to and they want to jump into that, they already have connections and they are already halfway there."

Press junkets by day and Broadway openings by night! Joe is very hard-working, he is extremely detail oriented, and will stop at nothing to get the job done. And as you've heard from him there are plenty of incredible moments and there's great reward in what he does. However, I will add that there are also extreme deadlines a lot of pressure and a never ending "to do" list; you need only try to reach him to find out. Public relations is an excellent and exciting career or career transition choice for anyone who is a real go-getter, a hard worker and who loves to be in the thick of it. There is certainly never a dull moment in the life of a press agent!

No two dancers' journey will ever be the same, we each make individual decisions and choices based on our capacity, understanding, beliefs, and desires. With aspirations in sight we head out into the world to set out on our journey, and it is with every step and new decision along the way that we create ourselves. And from all that we've discussed throughout the book and the varied examples and stories shared, you can see the importance of making concrete decisions. And although we don't possess hindsight we can certainly look ahead and use foresight to help us make the best decisions we can. Don't be afraid of unknown territory for often this is where we find wonder awaits us!

Dance till the stars come down from the rafters
Dance, Dance, Dance till you drop.
~ W. H. Auden

YOU ARE NOT ALONE – CAREER TRANSITIONS FOR DANCERS

I'd like to take this opportunity to introduce you to an incredible organization that has been instrumental in helping dancers to redefine themselves beyond their performing years. Career Transitions For Dancers has been changing the lives of dancers since 1985. They are dedicated to empowering dancers in all that they do and assisting them to pursue and continue living their full potential in secondary careers! They offer both online extensive resources and a physical presence in New York City, Los Angeles, Chicago, and a mobile national outreach project to help dancers around the country. This is a fabulous means available to you at all stages of your career and absolutely free of charge. The work they are doing is tremendous.

I had the pleasure of speaking with Lauren Gordon in reference to their organization and about my book and this chapter dedicated to career transitions. Ms. Gordon is the career counselor for Career Transitions For Dancers in New York City and holds an MSA (master's in social work) and LCSW (licensed clinical social worker). With all of her hands-on experience in dealing with so many various dancers that come through their doors regularly, I asked her if she would share some words of wisdom with us. And I quote her: "All our dancers will always be a dancer in their core identity and retain the qualities and the adaptable skills that make them so creative and special, throughout their many career transitions in dance and out. These include: presence, perseverance, attention to detail, quick study, teamwork, hard working, and poise. It is vital that dancers can manage feelings of loss and change, move through uncertainties, and be able to be offered the opportunities to continue to feel passionate and productive in whatever field they pursue for as long as they wish." As Ms. Gordon has just shared with us and as you've read throughout the book, dancers truly do possess some very special qualities, qualities that allow you to stand out above the crowd and make people take notice. Qualities that attract people to you. I want you to understand the value in all of this and learn how to best utilize it in all that you do.

Now, forewarning: Along with all of those wonderful and redeeming qualities there is at times—the biggest nemesis of all—that little voice I spoke of in the audition chapter, "the fan-club" or the "not-so-fan-club" to be more accurate. Often that little voice can cause some pretty big damage (if you allow it). It can cause us to lose self-confidence and to doubt ourselves. I reiterate this to reinforce in you all the power that you possess when you tap into all that you are and all that you have to offer, whether at the height of your career or when exiting the stage. Do not do yourself this injustice. Take inventory of all these magnificent qualities that you have and allow them to work for you as you begin your career and throughout your journey!

With a desire to educate you about Career Transitions For Dancers and all that they have to offer, the following information contained in this section has been directly reproduced from the Career Transition For Dancers' website with their approval.

Their mission—your future, their commitment—your potential, and as their website says, they believe in that potential and are committed to providing the

255

experience, insight, and resources that dancers need to define their career possibilities and develop rewarding post-performance careers. Dancers possess unique skills and unrivaled dedication. Their passion for discovery, innovation, and expression is an exceptional strength. In everything they do, they celebrate dancers' unique potential and empower them to continue to affect our world in positive ways.

Career Transition For Dancers first arose out of a partnership of several foundations and unions. Under the leadership of Agnes de Mille, this partnership led to the development and presentation of a conference in 1982 at Lincoln Center to discuss the need to assist dancers both during and at the end of their careers. Originally founded as an initiative of The Actors Fund in New York City, the program was also supported by Equity, AFTRA, AGMA, and SAG. And, although the original program was intended to provide career counseling and scholarship support for the members of these unions who were in the process of transition, in 1988 Career Transition For Dancers became a self-governing non-profit organization with a refocused mission to help all dancers, not just union members.

Career Transition For Dancers programs are developed and offered in an effort to help dancers find their individual paths. From pre-professional to mid-career and mature dancers, their programs help dancers in every stage of their career. Their programs can be grouped into three categories: Career counseling, financial assistance, and informational resources. All programs are provided free of charge.

- Career Counseling – Vital dialogue
  Providing both individual and group career counseling is at the heart of the organization's mission. They help dancers with the process of self-evaluation, guide their discovery of practical options, and motivate them to achieve their long-term goals.
- National and Local Outreach Projects – Beyond their offices
  Their outreach projects have taken their career counseling services on the road to reach dancers who are unable to travel to their New York City, Los Angeles, or Chicago offices.
- Scholarships and Grants – Financial assistance
  The various programs within their scholarship funds and grants offered provide assistance for dancers who are looking to earn undergraduate or graduate degrees, vocational certification, or the acquisition of new skills. The organization also provides seed money to entrepreneurial dancers to found new businesses, encouraging the community's vitality.

- Gallery –Slideshows and video
  Go behind the scenes of their programs and annual gala where you will be privy to conversations with dancers in transition, interviews with artists and patrons, and articles from influential individuals in the organization and dance community at large.
- Online Resources – Beyond counseling and scholarships
  Just as dancers depend on their knowledge of technique to develop their craft, they need the right information to successfully navigate their lifelong career moves.

Be sure to visit their website www.careertransition.org to fully appreciate and take advantage of the amazing wealth of information available to you. Browse the site to learn more about the various programs that you can take part in and all the online resources offered. Among them are a semi-annual newsletter titled "Moving On," various transition links, a national career network, and video career conversations covering everything from job search to starting your own business to career paths and training to financial planning and more. These invaluable online resources facilitate an ongoing exchange of information between their clients, experts, career counselors, and other professional mentors all thereby translating into a fantastic learning tool for you the dancer. In the New York and Los Angeles offices, they provide resource centers equipped with an online computer lab, printers, and a library filled with career development literature, university guides, and other relevant materials.

ONE LAST NOTE

I hope that by now I have imparted in you the need to look ahead and consider all that you might do beyond your years on stage. With the assistance of Career Transitions For Dancers and all of the dancers who have shared their stories, you now have plenty of food for thought. And if you take onboard the advice given throughout the book you will be in great shape! There are so many options available to you at all stages of your career, you need only be attentive, be flexible and open, and above all, be wise. The truth is that by simply looking at the potential for your "lifelong career" rather than just your time on stage, you will have a winning formula and a much better shot at a successful career doing what you love. Dance can be a part of your whole life, not just a period in time if that's what you so desire.

ENCORE:
You are not alone.

Take a bow. *La Cage*, Blue Angel, New York City

Chapter Sixteen
The Grand Finale—Summary

"Dance like no one is watching."
~ Mark Twain

As I look back over all the years that I have spent in the entertainment industry, I can honestly say that I wouldn't change any of it. Let me explain: Who I am today is a culmination of all that I have experienced and the many people who have touched my life along the way. Some moments, as you've already heard me say, have been incredible, while others were tough lessons, but, nonetheless, all worth it. Without them, I might be headed down a different road entirely; one that might or might not have included some of my favorite moments and favorite people. Sometimes, we merely cross paths with people—sometimes we tag along for a while, and then other times, we find those few gems that we collect along the way. The ones that we hold onto, never to lose touch with, they are the precious few with whom we may be blessed to share a lifetime.

My intention for writing this book was to fill a void that I have felt and seen time and time again. Through my work and many of the talented people who have worked with me, I am constantly reminded of how tough and often times discouraging, even overwhelming, this business can be. For someone first starting out, for someone a little less confident or shy, or for someone who simply may not have had the encouragement along the way, it can be so very intimidating, even downright scary.

And yes, it can be all of that, but the key is to expect it, accept it, and move through it. Just as Susan Jeffers says in *Feel the Fear and Do It Anyway*, (one of my all time favorite reads) "Pushing through fear is far less frightening than living with the underlying fear that comes from a feeling of helplessness."

I do know from my own experiences in the entertainment industry that the material in this book can be absolutely invaluable to you. These words of wisdom and knowledge that I share with you are lessons that I have learned along the way, some through personal experiences and others from my mentors. Many are the exact lessons that countless dancers and other artists repeatedly tell me they wish they had known before starting out. So I hope that you will refer to this book often. I hope that you will use this guide when you need to revisit a specific topic, such as preparing for your audition or signing a contract, and I hope that you will pick it up when you need a simple reminder. Most of all, though, I do hope that you will pick it up when you need a little encouragement.

I wanted more than anything for this book to be comprehensive and insightful, motivating and inspirational. I know that if you pay attention to the lessons in this book and put them into practice, you will be very well prepared for this sometimes scary, often crazy, but totally amazing business of show business.

Okay, let's recap:

BORN TO DANCE

Why do you want to dance? Remember the question? I asked this of you at the beginning of the book. I believe that within you is the key to your own success—the road map to your future—and knowing this is half the battle. The next step is simply tapping into it.

First, there's introspection, the art of becoming in touch and in tune with oneself. Next, focus: you must have peace with your conviction so that nothing can deter you. You must be in complete harmony with your big picture. You must visualize it, own it, breathe it, and live it! When you want something so badly and you know why, then you will be truly empowered! Your path will become undoubtedly clear.

> ENCORE:
> *I believe that within you is the key to your own success—the road map to your future—and knowing this is half the battle. The next step is simply tapping into it.*

GOALS, DREAMS, AND COMMITMENTS

Goals and dreams are the energy of life, and commitment is the outlet through which that electricity turns into reality. Our goals and dreams help fulfill us; they fuel us and drive us to great accomplishments. In other words, what moves you is what gets you there, and your passion is the fuel that propels and then keeps you going, headed straight toward your ultimate goal.

When you have passion, everything else falls into place. Everything that is required seamlessly comes together. They all go hand in hand. Hard work, dedication, and commitment all come effortlessly when you know where you are going. Nothing is too difficult when you want something badly enough. When you know what you want and why you want it, then there is only one thing left to do, and that is to just go for it!

So what is your ultimate destination? Be very clear about where you want to end up. Don't worry about how you are going to get there; just define what that final destination is, how it looks, and how it feels. The clearer your picture is, the more specific each goal can be along the way. Are you prepared to do everything you possibly can, and then some, to get to where you want to go? Are you willing to break down walls to get to where you want to be? If you have talent and the kind of passion and conviction that it takes to persist, even when rejection is staring you in the face, then you will succeed.

You must never lose sight of your ultimate goal and you can never compromise your integrity. The road may sometimes be hard and long, but stay the course. You'll get there and it will be so much more gratifying when you do.

Our journey in dance is no different than the dance of life itself, and if you treat life like the great opportunity that it is, you will find so many moments worth celebrating, even those once believed to be wrong turns. The truth is that often a "wrong turn" is the exact turn you needed to take at that moment to get to where you ultimately needed to be. You just didn't know it at the time.

Take every opportunity in life to build a solid foundation, because you are going to need it. When the going gets rough, as it can, you will want that foundation to be strong enough to hold you up. As we all know, things don't always happen perfectly or exactly as planned, so when you take a left turn and you think you should have taken a right, or if you are somehow slowed down along the way, just remember that there is a reason for it all. Take each one of those stumbling blocks and turn them into building blocks.

Imagine if you turned every little upset into a positive step toward your end result. Wouldn't the road naturally seem shorter? Wouldn't it be brighter? Wouldn't you enjoy your journey so much more? Always stand firm in your convictions, especially in those moments when you feel a bit discouraged. Try to remember the old Japanese proverb: "Fall down seven times; get up eight." The bottom line is, no matter how many times you fall down, the only way to make it is to get straight back up again—and again and again.

> ENCORE:
> *Imagine if you turned every little upset into a positive step toward your end result. Wouldn't the road naturally seem shorter?*

MENTORS AND INSPIRATIONS

Be grateful for those who touch and influence your life. Learn from others and their experiences. Be sure to recognize and acknowledge your mentors. Gratitude is food for your soul. When choosing a mentor, consider those qualities that you aspire to.

What do you admire in others? What do you want out of your career and life? Who in the business do you respect? What qualities of theirs do you most admire? Look for mentors with those similar characteristics—those that define who you want to be, and how you want to live your life. And most important, don't ever compromise your integrity.

> ENCORE:
> *Be sure to recognize and acknowledge your mentors.*

ATTITUDE SPELLED D.I.V.A.

Speaking of integrity, this would be a great time to remind you of that all-too-important attitude. It all comes down to this simple phrase—respect for yourself, respect for show business, and respect for the people within the business.

When you come from the right place, and by that I don't mean where you grew up; I mean when you come from a good place in your heart, when you have the right intention, and you go about your business with integrity and respect, you will find your way. A friend and business acquaintance, a very talented songwriter, has a great but simple saying: "You will find your people." They're not all going to be your people. Not everyone fits together and that's okay. Don't worry about it; just move on. You will find your people—those who just make sense in your world. They understand you and your needs and you understand them and theirs. When you find them, you will know.

Let's face it—all the right attitude in the world isn't a foolproof guarantee that you won't meet any real jerks along the way. But the right attitude will help you bounce back when you do. It will make you more resilient and, therefore, hurt a little bit less. And besides, if we never met any jerks, how could we be sure we'd recognize the good guys when they came along?

The truth is that the right attitude is a key ingredient in all that you do, not only in your career, but in life. Attitude is at the very core of all decisions; it is often responsible for how we do things, and how we view what is done to us. So often a simple shift in attitude is all we need to change the outcome of a less-favorable situation or at the very least our perception of it. Very important for you to remember is that a fabulous look and all the technique in the world is not going to guarantee you work if you have the wrong attitude. It may initially get you the gig, but if your attitude spells diva (and not the kind we often admire), then it's only a matter of time before you are found out, or you burn yourself. In the end, no one wants to work with a prima donna!

ENCORE:

Not everyone fits together and that's okay. Don't worry about it; just move on. You will find your people—those who just make sense in your world.

TRIPLE THREAT

Let's revisit training and the importance of being a triple threat. It goes without saying that technique is essential; however, versatility is such an important quality to possess—it is what often helps you seal the deal. The more versatile you are as a dancer and performer, the more you have to offer, the more work you will be suited for, and, therefore, the greater your chances for a full and well-rounded career. Proper training and technique will also help you to prevent injury and, thereby, ensure longevity in your career. Of course, accidents do happen, but a well-trained dancer will be in tune with his or her body and take all the necessary measures to ensure a healthy and able body.

On that note, I implore you to take your health seriously. Without your health, you cannot have longevity. If you don't take care of your health, it will come back to bite you, usually in the form of injury or illness. Proper nutrition for a healthy mind and body will help you to prevent such setbacks. A fine-tuned, healthy mind and body will also help you with early detection of any potential injuries or illness. When we are at our optimum health, we are much more in tune with what is going on inside our bodies and, therefore, we can feel the slightest of inconsistencies and/or ailments. Remember Dr. Baron's health pyramid. A solid understanding of our nutritional, physical, and mental health, and the intimacy they share, will save you a great deal of heartache down the road, not to mention other aches and pains.

> **ENCORE:**
> *The more versatile you are as a dancer and performer, the more you have to offer, and the more work you will be suited for, and, therefore, the greater your chances for a full and well-rounded career.*

MARKETS AND VENUES AND THE BUSINESS OF IT ALL

The dance world and the entertainment industry in general, cover a very large scope of possibilities, as I previously pointed out in "Chapter Six: Markets and Venues." One of my intentions in writing this book was to help educate talented people about the many possibilities available to them and to plant a seed about the importance of the business aspect of all that we do. As for the business side of our business, I will remind you simply of this: Treat your talent and what you do with that talent as a business, plain and simple. And if you use the business chapters in this book as a constant refresher for yourself, then I can guarantee you that you will save yourself a headache or two.

As we all know, the truth of the matter is that not everyone can be, or necessarily wants to be, the next Broadway sensation or film star. So if this is not in the "stars" for you, then what is? This is where once again you need to ask yourself a few key questions. If your dream is not ultimately to perform, yet you aspire to a career within the dance industry, there are many capacities in which you can work. You must first determine a few things. Here are some questions you might want to ponder: Are you a natural-born teacher or leader? If so, maybe teaching dance or producing is what you are looking for. Are you the innovative type? Do you have your finger on the pulse? Do you know what is happening and hip before the rest of the world has even clued in? Are you the next trendsetter? Trends come and go in dance as they do in everything else. Maybe you are extremely creative and have a natural-born talent for choreography. Maybe you envision yourself with your own dance company, or choreographing for stage and film. Do you have a great vision for the big picture? Do you see the story unfold in your mind's eye? As I asked earlier, do you prefer to be behind the scenes? The options are endless and it all comes right back down to tapping into your resources.

Who are you? What makes you who you are, what makes you tick, and what are your most important values? Now consider all that you aspire to in your career both on and off the stage. Does it align with who you are and most importantly, does it align with your values? Make your list! I believe that the key to living a good life and living it to the fullest all begins with that list of values. At the end of the day, will you truly be happy if your integrity is compromised or your values are not supported by all that you do?

> ENCORE:
> *"This is called show business, it's not called show playtime and if you don't take care of your show business you are going to be out of show business before you realize it!"*
> ~ David Bercuson, entertainment lawyer

AUDITION AND PERFORMANCE

My last recap is a favorite topic—audition and performance—very simply because performance is what it's all about! Why do you dance? You have got to love it, and so, if you love it, then you must always let your audience know. No matter who that audience is, whether at an audition, whether before a full house, or whether before two lonely ticket holders, they deserve your best performance and you should never cheat yourself or your audience of this. I say it again: Don't ever throw away a performance—not one single performance—ever.

Appreciation for the art of dance and the talent you've been given is a must. There is so much in life to be grateful for, and especially when, in life, you have been so privileged as to fulfill your dreams and have a career doing what you love. Always remember that to dance for a living is a privilege like no other. Despite the many ups and downs you may encounter in the business, it is a great business, full of exciting moments and people.

We all have heard many times that life is what we make it. As I look back, I feel very fortunate for the life I've led, bumps and all! And as I look ahead, I know that I do not want to, nor will I, leave one stone that interests me unturned.

As I have said repeatedly, this is your journey. How do you want it to unfold? Shoot for the moon and land on the stars. With a bit of faith, a bit of luck, a lot of passion, hard work and determination, you can create the life that you want. And with the right attitude and plenty of gratitude, you can truly enjoy the process. So as Mark Twain said, "Dance like no one is watching."

> ENCORE:
> *Shoot for the moon and land on the stars.*

My inspiration then and now: my mother.

Afterword

"Scratch the skin of any artist and you'll find a spiritual seeker; when artists resonate to that aspect of themselves, they do their best work."
~ **Shirley MacLaine**

When I first sat down to write this book, one of the very first things I wrote was a letter to my mother. I wanted to thank her, for without her sacrifices, hard work, and constant support I would never have known the life in dance that I have. I know that many of you reading this book have a mother or a father or both who have supported your every dream as did mine, or maybe you are the parent who's been that support to your own daughter or son. In either case I'm sure you will understand the sentiments, and I would like to close by sharing my letter with you.

Dear Mom,

For all that I have accomplished throughout my dance career, I owe you a huge debt of gratitude. Mom, you are the very reason for my career and, therefore, the reason I'm able to write this book and share my experiences with so many today. I have had an exciting and rewarding career as a dancer, choreographer/director, and producer. I have traveled extensively for my work and I've seen parts of the world that otherwise I might never have seen, all thanks to your love and devotion. Without all your hard work and determination, I certainly never would have gone to dance lessons, let alone fulfill my dreams. I have always known how fortunate I was to be given such a wonderful opportunity, and lucky for me, I have been able to share many of my experiences with you.

I'm sure that when I was nine years old, first starting out, you did not consider that dancing would be my career; you were simply a mother giving your daughter an opportunity to do something that she loved. What you did was encourage me every *step*—and I do mean literally—of the way, and when you saw the talent I had and how much I loved it all, you encouraged me more. You always taught me to do what I loved and to go for all that I wanted in life, truly supporting every dream and empowering me, whether you realized what you were doing or not.

It is said that there is nothing greater than a mother's love for her children—it is unsurpassed. Mothers are our "everyday heroes"; they go to amazing lengths for their children. They are incredible people, capable of great things all in the name of love. Mom, you have been the best role model of all, strong and kind, hardworking and honest, with great morals and virtues. You taught me to believe in myself and to go for what I wanted in life; you have always been a great source of inspiration in my life (in and out of dance) and I am eternally grateful. You are forever in my heart.

I love you, Armande

What I have shared with you throughout this book is who I am and what

I've learned and experienced along the way. In life we aspire to achieve certain things, certain people and events inspire us and affect us, and we win some and we lose some. If we remain open and flexible we learn and we grow, and our journey—all the more magnificent for it! My hope is that this book will inspire you and answer your questions and encourage you every step of the way as you start your career as a dancer.

Life is a journey and I hope that you will be inspired to dance your way through and to dance in all that you do!

Contact Information

May your journey be rich with opportunity and experience! Whether you dance your way through it, choreograph it, write it, design it, arrange it, or produce it, give it everything you've got, do it with integrity, and do it with style.

If you'd like to share your own experience or inspiration, or if you have any questions or comments, I'd love to hear from you.

Please visit my websites at:

www.mandedagenais.com
and
www.startingyourcareerasadancer.com

And feel free to contact me at: info@mandedagenais.com.

About the Author

MANDE DAGENAIS

Synonymous with style, Mande Dagenais' work as a Director/Choreographer and Producer has been appreciated by millions of people around the world. Her career has spanned over twenty-five years, seventy production shows and four continents. A seven-time award-winning author, Mande shares her passion for Dance and the Entertainment industry through her writing.

At age fifteen, she began working professionally as a teacher and choreographer. At nineteen years of age, she cofounded The Dance Academy in Northern Ontario, where she further demonstrated her love for teaching and nurturing talent. Mande's professional show credits include twelve years as resident Director/Choreographer of the world famous musical revue, *La Cage Aux Folles*, Los Angeles, and *An Evening at La Cage* productions worldwide. *The Tonight Show* starring Johnny Carson, *A Celebration of Legends* with Milton Berle and Tom Bosley, Caesar's Palace, The Fountainbleau Hilton, and three years as Choreographer for Deerhurst Resort in Canada are some of Mande's early career credits.

As the owner of Mande Dagenais Productions and ADC Entertainment Inc., Mande has produced corporate events for clients ranging from Amoco Corporation amd Umbro International to the Walt Disney Special Events Group and Ford Motor Company, to name a few. To industry talent and peers, Mande is also well known for her production shows on Celebrity Cruises and Costa Cruise Lines. The *Costa Victoria* was voted Best Production Shows & Entertainment in the Fielding's Book of European Cruises in her first year with the company. Mande lives in Miami Beach with her husband, Alex, and their two dogs, Sassy and Luigi. When not in production, Mande can be found writing in her library or at a local Starbucks, or designing jewelry in her home studio. She is a lot of right brain in perpetual motion, loving everything creative. Her passion runs deep and her compassion deeper; she loves to nurture and inspire talent, and to help others. She has created a line of jewelry called the "Forget Me Not Collection" as a tribute to her mother, and a way to help raise awareness for Alzheimer's.

Mande is currently developing a new dancewear and lifestyle line under her brand name Inspired to Dance® and she's very excited for its launch later this year. An honest and dedicated voice, a true teacher at heart, Mande tells it as it is, and hopes that her books will inspire young hopefuls everywhere to DANCE and pursue their dreams!

Special Contributors

Very special thanks to:

Dr. Spencer Baron for his enormous input to my fitness and health chapters: "Fit to Dance" and "Let's Get Physical." Without his participation and tremendous knowledge, I could never have brought such important information to you.

To Terry Fay for sharing his financial proficiency and knowledge in an interview with me that was the foundation for my chapter "Money Makes the World Go Round."

And, to Mr. David Bercuson, P.A., for giving so graciously of his time and expertise to assist me in bringing to you the "Contracts and Agreements" section of my "No More Starving Artist" chapter.

To the men and women, my very dear friends and business acquaintances, who shared their incredible real-life career transition stories with me, which were the basis for my "Life after the Stage" chapter. Your contributions are invaluable!

MARYANN DELANY – Entertainment director, Royal Caribbean Productions
STACEY ENYART – Founder and artistic director of Suncoast Dance Theatre
SUSAN SALGADO – Casting director/owner, Triple Threat Casting™
CHRISTOPHER DIETRICH – Partner/executive director of Actor's Connection
LILIANA MORALES – Classical Spanish and flamenco dancer
DEE FUJII – Rigger at *Cirque du Soleil's LOVE*
KIMBERLEY FUJII – Performer at *Le Rêve*

PAM KILLINGER – Former choreography specialist at Walt Disney World
RACHEL SPECK – Former Miami City Ballet dancer
JOE PERROTTA – Broadway press agent at Boneau/Bryan-Brown

Special thanks to Lauren Gordon and Alex Dubé from Career Transition For Dancers in New York for their assistance and for permission to reprint information from their website.

And to Actors' Equity Association; Canadian Actors' Equity Association; British Equity; the American Federation of Television and Radio Arts (AFTRA); American Guild of Musical Artists (AGMA); Screen Actors Guild (SAG); Stage Directors and Choreographers Society (SDC); Directors Guild of America (DGA); the National Writers Union (NWU); International Association of Theatrical Stage Employees (IATSE); and United Scenic Artists Local USA 829 for allowing us to reprint information from their websites.

References

CELEBRITY BIOGRAPHICAL INFORMATION
Bio: www.biography.com
Internet Movie Database: www.imdb.com
People: www.people.com
Tune, Tommy. *Footnotes: A Memoir.* (New York, NY: Simon & Schuster, 1997).

COLLEGE RESEARCH
Dance Magazine's College Guide 2006/07. (New York, NY: Macfadden Communications
  Group LLC, 2006).
Everett, Carole, J. *Peterson's College Guide for Performing Arts Majors 2009.* (Lawrenceville,
  NJ: Peterson's, 2008).
Everett, Carole, J. *The Performing Arts College Guide 3rd Edition.* (New York, NY:
  Macmillan, 1998).
FAFSA: www.studentaid.ed.gov

FINANCE INFORMATION
Morris, Kenneth, M. *The Wall Street Journal Guide to Planning Your Financial Future.*
  (New York, NY: Lightbulb Press, Inc. and Dow Jones & Co., Inc, 1998).

HEALTH, FITNESS, AND NUTRITION
British Journal of Sports Medicine, 40:700-705, 2006.
American Heart Association: www.americanheart.org
American Lung Association: www.lungusa.org
Ban Trans Fats: www.bantransfats.com
British Association of Sport and Exercise Medicine: www.basem.co.uk

Dr. Andrew Weil: www.drweil.com
The National Fragile X Foundation: www.fragilex.org
The Mayo Clinic: www.mayoclinic.com
The Rader Eating Disorder Program: www.raderprograms.com

MISCELLANEOUS

Career Transition For Dancers: www.careertransition.org
World Casino Directory: www.worldcasinodirectory.com
World Intellectual Property Organization: www.wipo.int
Internet World Stats: www.internetworldstats.com
U.S. Copyright Office: www.copyright.gov

NEW YORK

Gordon, A. L., "To Live & Give In L.A.: NY vs. LA: Exploring the Differences," *The New York Sun*, Page 11 January 15, 2007.
Internet Broadway Database: www.ibdb.com
The Broadway League: www.broadwayleague.com and www.livebroadway.com

THEME PARKS

Cedar Fair Entertainment Company: www.cedarfair.com
Six Flags Inc: www.sixflags.com
Valhouli, Christina, "The World's Best Amusement Parks," Forbes.com

UNIONS

Actors' Equity Association: www.actorsequity.org
American Guild of Musical Artists: www.musicalartists.org
British Equity: www.equity.org.uk
Canadian Actors' Equity Association: www.caea.com
Directors Guild of America: www.dga.org
IATSE: www.iatse-intl.org
Screen Actors Guild: www.sag.org
The American Federation of Television and Radio Artists: www.aftra.org
The National Writers Union: www.nwu.org
United Scenic Artists Local USA 829: www.usa829.org

278

Index

Books from Allworth Press

Allworth Press is an imprint of Skyhorse Publishing, Inc. Selected titles are listed below.

The Profitable Artist: A Handbook for All Artists in the Performing, Literary, and Visual Arts
by Artspire (6 x 9, 256 pages, paperback, $24.95)

The Health & Safety Guide for Film, TV & Theater
by Jim Piper (6 x 9, 256 pages, softcover, $24.95)

Acting the Song: Performance Skills for the Musical Theater
by Tracey Moore and Allison Bergman (6 x 9, 304 pages, paperback, $24.95)

The Lucid Body: A Guide for the Physical Actor
by Fay Simpson (6 x 9, 224 pages, paperback, $15.95)

Actor Training the Laban Way: An Integrated Approach to Voice, Speech, and Movement
by Barbara Adrian (7 ⅜ x 9 ¼, 208 pages, paperback, $24.95)

Movement for Actors
by Nicole Potter (6 x 9, 288 pages, paperback, $19.95)

Making It on Broadway: Actor's Tales of Climbing to the Top
by David Wienir and Jodie Langel (6 x 9, 288 pages, paperback, $19.95)

Great Producers: Visionaries of the American Theater
by Iris Dorbian (6 x 9, 212 pages, paperback, $19.95)

Stage Combat: Fisticuffs, Stunts, and Swordplay for Theater and Film
by Jenn Zuko Boughn (7 ¾ x 9 ⅜, 240 pages, paperback, $19.95)

Building the Successful Theater Company
by Lisa Mulcahy (6 x 9, 240 pages, paperback, $19.95)

To request a free catalog or order books by credit card, call 1-800-491-2808. To see our complete catalog on the World Wide Web, or to order online, please visit www.allworth.com.